You know this path.

It's yours.

A journey you have taken so many times. Up hill and down dale.

Struggled up mountains, slithered down scree. Stumbled and slid on your backside a few times! Every tussock, every hillock, every stride measured again and again.

You know this business.

It's yours.

Or do you?

I thought I knew mine. Building your confidence in public speaking.

Based on decades of commercial experience, twinned with speaking competitions, MCing, radio broadcasting, singing, even Sunday school teaching. I knew my business.

And yet...

Joined on my path by Martyn and Richard, whether in step or pausing to review, the landscape took on a different hue. Gently emerging in dappled sunshine, dramatically revealed in flashes of inspirational lightning... A palette of colour and content with hitherto unnoticed clarity: my unique story, theme, IP.

What I have learned can never be unlearned.

My business will never be the same again.

Will yours?

Ges Ray, author of *Speak Performance*

STORYSELLING

give your business a happily ever after

martyn pentecost

mPowr

First Published in Great Britain 2019 by mPowr (Publishing) Limited

www.mpowrpublishing.com
www.immersivepublishing.com

A catalogue record for this book is available from the British Library
ISBN – 978-1-907282-59-1

Cover Design and Illustrations by Martyn Pentecost
mPowr Publishing 'Clumpy™' Logo by e-nimation.com
Clumpy™ and the Clumpy™ Logo are trademarks of mPowr Limited

The mPowr Legacy

Every moment of your life has the potential to be more than every moment of your life. As you invest each day into something greater than yourself—lasting longer than your lifetime, influencing those yet to be born—you create a legacy. A legacy that serves others beyond the minutes, hours and years you will ever spend on Earth. The mPowr Publishing mission is to inspire your legacy—to help you create it through the books and media you develop. Every title we publish is more than the sum of its parts, with deeper impact, broader transformation and, at its heart, a legacy that is yours in this moment, right now.

To access the accompanying digital content for Storyselling you will need:

A smartphone or tablet with a camera and a QR code reader app, which must be able to read colour QR codes. (We recommend *i-nigma* which is available from your app store.)

Contents

This is Storyselling

This is Storyselling.

Harnessing the power of stories to build and enthral your audience of potential clients. Growing your business and expanding your range of products and services through digital content, books and other media.

Before I share the secrets of storyselling with you, so you can best use it in your business, there is something important you need to know...

Think about how **successful** and profitable your company could be...

Imagine the **impact** it can have on your clients...

How it could **transform** their lives, offer immense **value** and be the catalyst for change they will **always** remember?

Ponder how you can **drive** your business to become so successful for you and your **clients** that it exceeds all expectations, both yours and theirs.

Reflect upon the **potential** and **power** you and your clients can discover when your business **achieves** its maximum potential.

What is the **symbol** of this success?

What company **brand** would sum up everything you can attain?

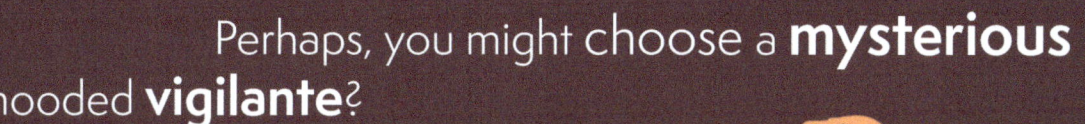

Perhaps, you might choose a **mysterious** hooded **vigilante**?

One that fends off the
gang of **villains** your **client** faces,
such as **loss**, **pain** and **fear**...

Or a **benevolent** and **wise** alien intelligence, who possesses **revolutionary expertise?**

THIS!

Meet Clumpy.

He is the brand logo for mPowr Publishing—
that merry band of misfits turned publishers
who brought you this book.

Most people who see Clumpy think something
along the lines of...

"Aw! He's sweet!"
"My five-year-old daughter would love that!"
"WTF are these guys on?"
#WTFAreTheseGuysOn

However, for us, and those who appreciate what Clumpy stands for, he is the spokespuppy of everything we can achieve for our clients.

He reminds us that we do not offer information...

we offer transformation.

He tells us to strive, every moment, every day for the best we can give... To create and publish that one title that will make the most powerful, lasting change for its reader. To be the thing our clients have been searching for for so long—the answer to how they achieve success.

Yet, more than this, Clumpy represents all that our audience or readers, clients and advocates can achieve for themselves. Once you know what Clumpy is asking you to remember, you will always think about your highest goals and achievements, whenever you catch a glimpse of him.

Over the years, Clumpy has taken on a life of his own, often wandering around the pages of books,

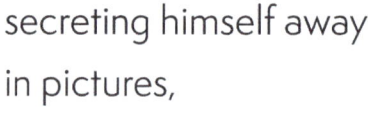

secreting himself away in pictures,

disguising himself or generally messing around!

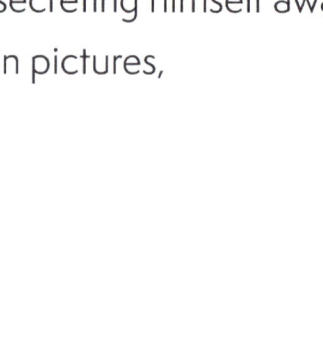

Sometimes he pops up in places of significance and on other occasions he gets a little clumsy and makes a mess.

We have come to learn that when things go wrong, we achieve something even better because of it. And Clumpy is there to nudge us in the right direction, should we forget it.

Clumpy to us is more than a logo or brand. He is a guiding force that says...

Don't just make books...

...Make a difference!

And to make a difference, we must do things differently.

Therefore, there is **one very,**

very

important thing you need to know about this book, before we dive in.

And that is...

Storyselling

Strange

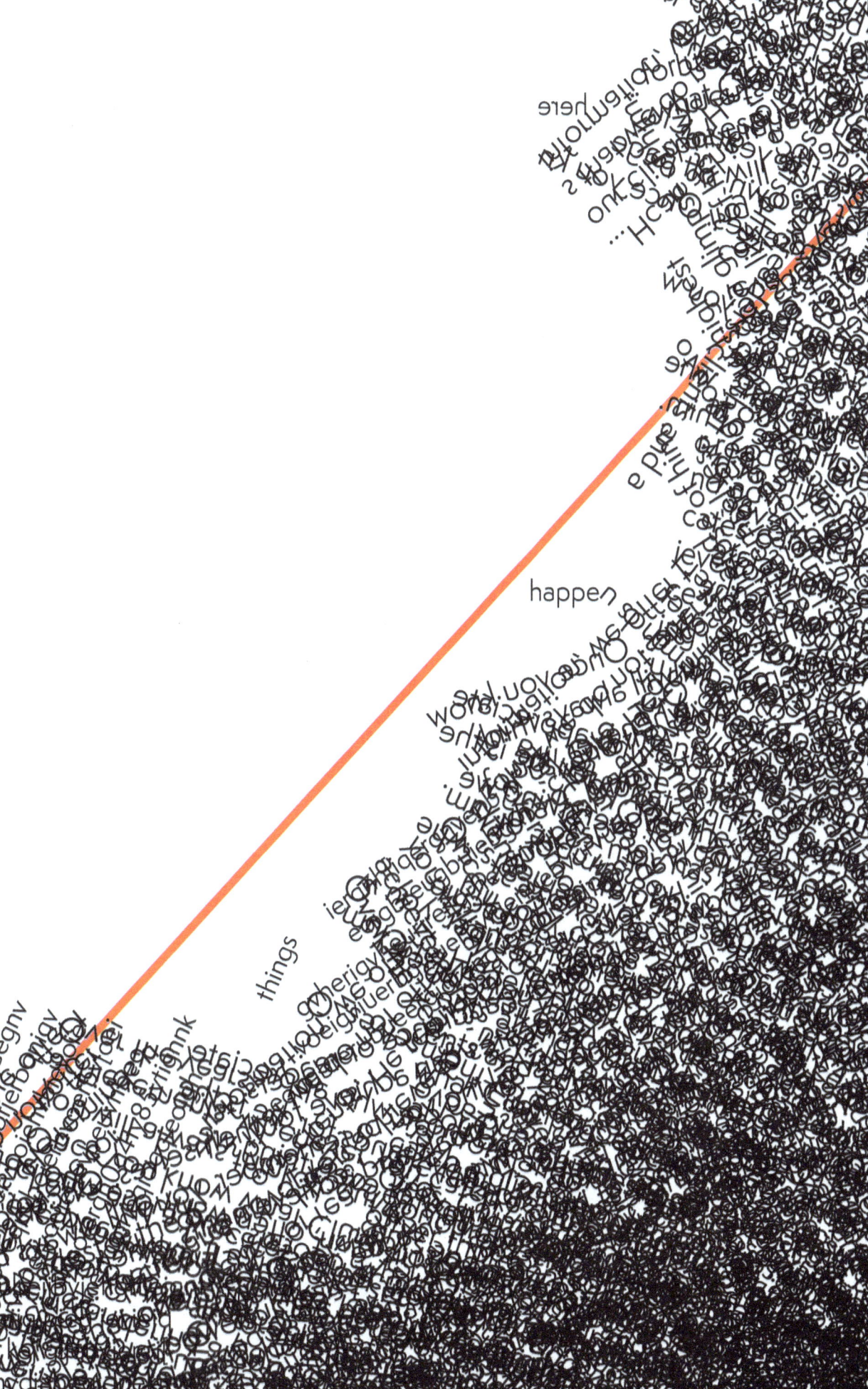

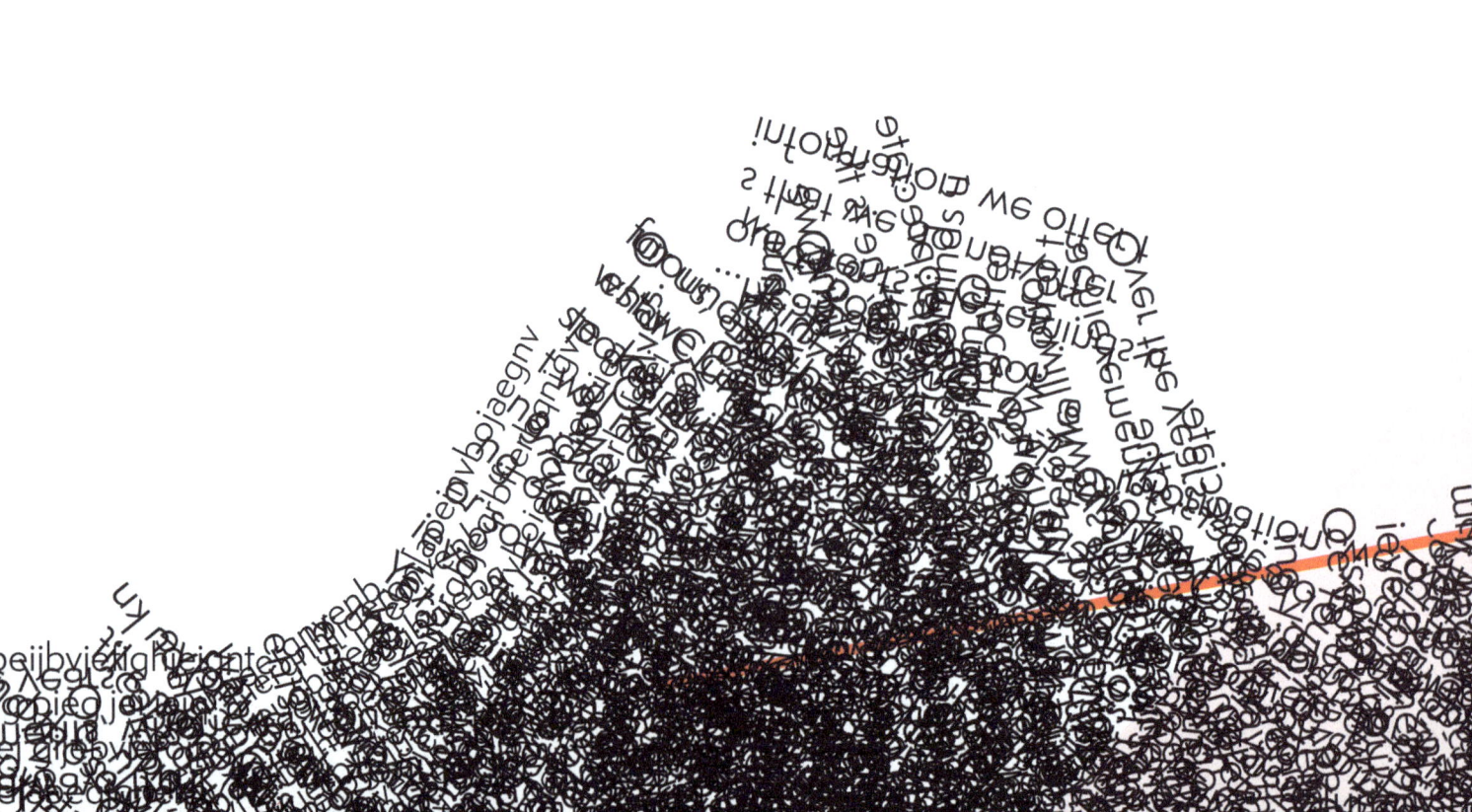

Section One

Once Upon a Time

One

Inflatable Forest

Out of the Darkness...

It came...

To our ancestors, words were more powerful than we can ever imagine. They feared words with greater depth than we can ever comprehend. For words had the ability to summon unimaginable terrors from the darkness. To use a word aloud caused it to be real. Words were the precursor to reality.

One did not speak of those who lurked in otherworldly places—to say their names, was to get their attention. And if there was one thing you really did not want to do, it was to make them aware of you.

Only those fearless enough and knowledgeable enough would tell stories by the fireside of those creatures that hid beyond the security of the light—and even then, they narrated their tales with reverence and respect.

For storytelling was not something one did for mere entertainment. It was a crucial part of life: instilling within the younger members of the clan the rules of life. How to survive in a hard and horrifying world. Stories helped people to make sense of the world—to understand what came next.

Each allegory evoked the imagery and symbolism of a path; one that would keep you safe, away from the clutches of those you could not see until it was too late.

For even knowing about those monsters would put you in harm's way. But knowing about them was also the only way a community could arm itself against the avarice of their inhuman intentions.

But I have said too much.

For we may be in a world where words seem to have lost their potency, however, it is not the words that have been diluted; it is how we use them...

Summoning Demons

For some of us, stories seem unimportant—they are just stories, after all! However, the power of story is more integral to our very survival than we could possibly comprehend. Whilst many still believe in demons of the old world, for most, these elusive creatures are merely the stuff of fiction; fodder for the suggestible mind.

However, in an enlightened world, our true demons are no longer foul horrors, secreted away in the dark forest or desolate wilderness, but rather a more nuanced strain of sophisticated monsters. They wait, hidden away at the back of drawers, in unopened emails and lurking, ready to ambush, in the next bank statement.

Poverty, failure, loneliness are just some of the words that conjure up deep-rooted fears within. These may not have faces or corporeal form for us, but their presence exists in a myriad of experiences.

These situations and circumstance have taught us what it feels like to find ourselves lost and straying from the metaphorical path our ancestors valued with such sacred fervour.

For every person,

the horrors that haunt us—

just on the verge of consciousness—

are different.

They evoke contrasting emotions and unleash a unique set of memories. These may not be the demons our ancestors feared, but they do summon the same strain of feelings, to the same degree of intensity.

Yet, the words that invite anxiety, fear and terror into our hearts and minds all do one very important thing...

Before we seek out that one thing, there is something I have not mentioned. Just as words can be used to lift the veil on those troublesome demons, giving them free rein over our emotions and thoughts, words can also exorcise their hold over us.

When thought, spoken or written in a specific and necessary way, words can free us from the darkness and guide us back to life, happy and fulfilled.

That one thing words must do to usher in the darkness or the light is so simple that it seems somehow out of place amidst the complication and complexity of our digital world. And whilst the context may have changed, we are essentially those same tribal humans, seeking a way forward that brings happiness and security.

Words, amalgamated into a compelling story—one that raises the heartrate, just a fraction—can summon all manner of experiences. The particular events of each story will decide what the reader feels and thinks, but it is that simple speeding up of the heartbeat that causes a whole slew of neurophysiological behaviours.

Electrical impulses cascade into chemical interactions. Using just the power of words you can inspire an audience to achieve great things or plague their waking thoughts with how much they need your solutions to their problems.

This is the potential of storytelling. A way of using words to rip a person from the trancelike monotony of daily life and place something awe-inspiring directly in their path.

The master storyteller can blend narrative devices with the perfect words as an apothecary would blend medicines—both create drugs; one chemical and the other linguistic. Whilst stories may seem more subtle, a tale that interrupts patterns of behaviour and magnetises its reader into another way of thinking has longer-lasting effects than any pharmaceutical!

The idea of words having a potent, definable effect on an audience—both physiologically and psychologically—has been leveraged in many different instances. To cause the mass outpouring of emotion, to rouse people to war or to get millions of people to purchase goods and services.

These are all forms of Storyselling. Using story to sell products, ideas, ideals or yourself. By taking whatever you are offering, associating it with a range of real benefits and presenting these through the mechanisms of story, you will convert a hungry audience into ravenous customers and brand advocates.

The pursuit of storyselling is at the very of core of this book. As a business owner, entrepreneur or motivated professional, you can use storytelling techniques to increase your audience of potential clients, create sales of your goods and services and develop a buying culture within your brand; one that continues to grow over time.

Storyselling is now more meaningful and urgent to successful business than ever before. Whether your story exhilarates, challenges or comforts, by leveraging the emotional needs of your audience, you will engage—encouraging them to start a relationship with you.

Beware though—how we sell through storytelling has drastically changed. Tactics that were once ultra-popular are now actively damaging to your brand and business. Audiences are now so sensitive to being sold at, they can sense sales tactics before you have even thought of them.

The common (mis)conception surrounding storyselling is that you simply tack on a story to your sales pitch. Tell an anecdote that is emotional, then when you have your audience all teary-eyed, smack them about a bit with your latest service offering.

The ultra-savvy, marketing-proof breed of audience cannot be fooled by this clumsy approach to storytelling. They know exactly what you are doing and simply ignore you. For most people are so marketed-out, they do not even get as far as acknowledging your message. They completely filter it out before wasting an iota of conscious attention!

Increasingly, the only way to establish an ongoing and successful relationship with potential clients is to build the relationship first and then nurture that relationship until they want to be sold to.

This profound, internal shift in your audience transitions them from hostile passers-by to drooling groupies who want a piece of you and what you are selling! This degree of artistry takes us to the point where storyselling effectively becomes a craft that needs mastering.

While sharing an anecdote detailing how your company has helped others or producing a lengthy sales email will now bounce off the attention filters of most audience members, clumsy storyselling can be worse than either of these.

To sell using story, you need to match your writing expertise with the level of professional experience you possess in your chosen field. Failing to do so will position your skills at the level of your writing—turning a university education and two decades of professional knowledge into the mouth-mashing of a six-week-proficient charlatan.

Business owners are becoming increasingly aware of how essential story is to their brand—and not a quick and inconsequential story, but master storyselling at its most effective.

With this understanding, the growing of authoring and storytelling skills will not take years to master and match to your expertise. You simply need to understand what you are striving towards and why this is so vital.

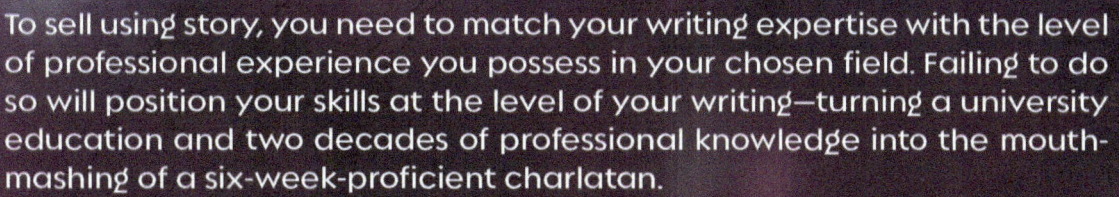

And this begins by focusing on your business and yourself. For story is not simply required to sell your brand; the story needs to be your brand...

Are You Sitting Comfortably...?
Then Let's Begin with the
Story of Storyselling

We have all experienced those faded, monochrome scenes of silent movies. Pioneering ventures into the cinematic world; where shadow hands oozed up gloomy staircases and the gleaming metal costume of a robotic woman birthed a quintessential archetype, one that has inspired an indelible experience of wonderment for generations.

To millennial consumers these seem primitive, with their makeshift effects and simple stories—mostly imagery and performance, cut with an occasional interstitial of text.

Without a soundtrack, these stories were told solely through the visual experience... one that calls for inventive use of the effects available to catapult audiences through degrees of emotion, from wonderment and enlightenment to downright panic.

Yet, these movies have leeched into the psyche, becoming something viscerally primal with the audiences who first gazed in awe at the gleaming, silver screen. Their stories inspired audiences to fall in love with the film industry; boosting it to become one of the most profitable of our age.

We've experienced killer dinosaurs, hungry for human flesh, and axe-wielding maniacs, time-travelling cars and enchanted, beast-infested castles.

From *Psycho* to *Alien;*
Brief Encounter to *Moulin Rouge,*
we turned our eyes to that light in the darkness
and we still gaze,
with transfixed wonder, upon screens large and small,
at the more refined stories we are experiencing today.

Our thirst for story is so intrinsic to life that it is preceded only by air, water, food, shelter and companionship. We are so ravenous in our hunger to consume stories that almost every part of our lives is storycentric.

This integral, emotional desire for story and the effect that story has upon us is something exploited by salespeople for decades. From brand knowledge to improving finances, the effectiveness of story to sell has also been refined exponentially.

Just as storytelling evolved through stage, books, radio, cinema, television, mobile devices, VR and now experiential augmented reality, storyselling has evolved. The level of sophistication required to develop stories that truly inspire people to buy products and services is staggering.

From the hit of pleasure, jolt of pain or slow, brooding terror provoked by an advertisement, to the intimate desire for an alluring consumable or phobic reaction to a competitor, implanted through the artistry of subliminal product placement—storyselling has transitioned from silent and simple to complex and cunning.

The degree of finesse that is critical for storyselling in our information age is astounding. Now, we must develop a long-term, trusting relationship with our potential advocates; their degree of discernment is so extreme and their affection so fragile that the slightest mistake or error in judgement could lose us their loyalty and compel them towards the terrible traps laid down by a competitor.

More than all this, the core focus of storyselling has shifted. Rather than seeking to shout at your audience, instructing them to be loyal companions, you now need to spark interaction—narratively wine and dine them with all the authenticity and heartfelt conversation of a first date.

So, what specifically is storyselling? Why is storyselling so important in developing a community of potential clients? And how will storyselling convert an indifferent stranger into a treasured, loyal advocate?

On the surface, storyselling is the use of stories to sell a product, a way of life or anything else you care to think of. Stories are so effective at nurturing an emotional response from prospective clients that businesses, politicians and orators have always used this method for genuine results.

Rather than just telling people about the benefits, stories go deeper, have a broader scope and longer-lasting effect on the audience. A story can be so profound to the audience they will march to their death, debt or damnation for the message contained within.

Due to very specific factors within evocative narrative and how we process it, authoring stories in different ways will have varying results. If you get these wrong, you risk a potential client just disengaging and moving on to the next thing. Conversely, when you present a story that works, you will genuinely rocket your sales and profits through the roof.

The challenge, besides getting the story right in the first place, is this... the instant one company makes a killing through using storyselling, a hundred other companies divert their marketing strategies to mimic the story. The hope that they too can recreate the results has the effect of diluting the power of the storyselling style very quickly.

The law of diminishing returns applies to storyselling techniques, so when organisations, *en masse*, begin using a particular style of storyselling, the audience becomes fatigued within a matter of months or weeks.

As if that were not enough, when a particular style of storyselling works, various entrepreneurs will pull it apart, analyse the inner workings of the story and then make these into acronym-laden training programmes for others to study and implement for themselves.

Even online, storyselling has become the stable form of marketing for SMEs and giant corporations alike. So, whilst it is the most effective form of selling, storyselling comes with a vast amount of audience fatigue. To overcome this, businesses need to stay ahead of the majority, using pioneering and visionary storyselling styles to lead from the front.

To appreciate the true nature of innovative storyselling and how to keep riding that wave, we must first explore the voyage from primitive types of anecdotal and commercial storyselling, to the complex strategies of cutting-edge, contemporary storyselling—from silent movie to IMAX blockbuster, in movie terms.

Storyselling has always been the artistry of telling stories to capture the attention of potential clients and call them to action. Many different forms of storyselling have been invented over time, such as direct mailing, commercials and sponsorship.

Direct mail often involved long sales letters that presented an anecdote, detailing the joys of a buying a product or the pitfalls of a person not using a particular service.

These were intended to elicit the sign-up to a mailing list or even an instinctive purchase in response to the pleasure of what a person could achieve or the pain of losing out to somebody else.

Direct mailing is still present, with organisations attempting to broaden their brand consciousness, however, we often characterise this as junk mail.

The strategy of casting a wide net to catch one or two new clients does not stop with snail mail—email is also used to send sales letters to subscribers or, at times, anybody who has entered their email address somewhere online! This is often blasted as spam and deeply frowned upon.

Storyselling commercials would tell short stories to their audience or present an ongoing arc over many commercials. These brief moments of time compelled the viewer by interweaving their feelings with a product or service.

To achieve this, a company would hone in on relationships, emotional attachments or even shock tactics. These became embedded at deeper and deeper levels of consciousness with every viewing.

The **horrific** public service announcements that appeared on **British television** in the 1970's were examples of how **people were shocked into modifying their behaviour.** From **drowned infants** to **bodies mangled in car wrecks,** these **visceral** and **unrelenting narratives** demonstrated the **perils of everyday life** and were so **haunting** they **affected people** when **encountering similar situations** to those depicted.

On a lighter theme in the early eighties, the *Oxo* brand of stock cubes used a quirky, humorous family to tell fun, self-contained stories in a series of vignettes. These associated the comfort of home, family and good food with their product. The campaign ran for a staggering sixteen years, such was its popularity with viewers.

From 1987 to 1993, *Nescafé Gold Blend* ran a series of adverts involving two people in various, will-they-won't-they, romantic interludes. These gripped the British public and became an integral part of pop culture of the time. Unlike the Oxo adverts, these had a story arc, rather like a soap opera (that sold soap) or tv serial, which had people and the media guessing as to what would transpire next.

Sponsorship was a means of associating one's business with other people's stories. Through the funding of soap operas and other television shows, companies leveraged the storytelling of popular shows to sell their products and services. This tactic also included product placement; where a product or brand name would appear in a scene.

Thousands of companies still sponsor television shows and billions of dollars are invested each year in movies as a way of pushing products in front of audiences. From *Under Armour* in the *Marvel Cinematic Universe* (MCU), to *Coca Cola* in just about everything else.

There is a whole barrage of reality shows, such as *Project Runway* and *RuPaul's Drag Race*, that are sculpted around a sponsorship format. With regular on-screen appearances of various brands, and contestants interacting with those brands as a part of the show, the episodes are funded and prizes are supplied for the winners of each season.

However, one of the most audacious examples of storyselling concerns an episode of the US TV show, *Modern Family*, in which the whole plot centred around the three protagonist families using Apple products to *FaceTime*, track each other's iPhones and demonstrate the usability of Apple products.

The critical challenge with all the modes of storyselling is they have been leveraged to death! Consumers are so hyperaware of being sold to, there is a disconnect at the very millisecond they become aware of the slightest manipulation. Even the most inventive, peculiar and avant-garde promo materials now seem tired and obsolete.

We have witnessed the internet explode into our daily lives, both personally and professionally. Ushering in the information age, our ability to explore and process information online is not only changing the way we think and feel, but is also impacting society in major ways.

At first, most businesses denied what was happening; procrastinating to the point of paralysis before the cold trickle of reality became too profound to ignore. This provoked a mad scrabbling around, as companies tried to catch up with the all-encompassing changes taking place.

Just as the business world was beginning to appreciate the nature of the paradigm transformation, we shifted again from home-based computing to mobile devices. This had further ramifications for us, psychologically, socially and professionally.

As those with pioneering, tech-savvy minds shifted from purely digital delivery of content to experiential and augmented reality content, further changes started to take place. However, as the digital domination appeared to be all-encompassing, a radical demonetisation of platforms, such as *YouTube*, produced a renaissance in physical media products.

With a cursory glance at this shift in culture, we might assume that digital or physical products can be used to grow sales of big-ticket services and so on. However, for an organisation or entrepreneur to truly grow their sales success, whilst navigating this completely unfamiliar terrain, they need a change of strategy.

When a business is focused on the relationship between their brand and the audience (rather than selling a single product or service) they transition from the old, obsolete methodology and towards a landscape of untapped potential.

A Christmas Tale

An example of relationship advertising versus one-off product sales can be seen in the advertising approach of two major British retailers. One Christmas season saw the campaigns of *Marks & Spencer* and *Iceland* both involve Mrs Claus, Santa's wife.

M&S depicted Mrs Claus as a sophisticated, helicopter-flying businesswoman and philanthropist. She jets around the world helping children find redemption for past mistakes, as well as performing other acts of compassion.

The Mrs Claus of Iceland's brand was a housewife whose sole focus seems to be cooking food for her Yorkshire-pudding-obsessed husband.

Now both companies are targeting their own, specific audience and in these advertisements there are visual clues as to who their particular client is. One has a polished appearance, a knowing smile and is imbued with a sense of mystery; the other is metaphorically apron-clad, gurns like a thoughtless automaton and is positioned in a home that looks exactly as it would have done circa 1972.

Yet, the storyselling takes place beyond what we see or hear. It is in the underlying message of the campaigns that we realise what is being sold to us.

The Iceland approach is to show us inexpensive products and tell us what great value these are. It then explains how this woman's greatest achievement will be to prove her womanly intelligence and wisdom by keeping her husband well fed without emptying his wallet.

M&S is not focused on the one item it presents, but the ongoing relationship with their client. The woman who is independent, makes a real difference in the world and does not need to take away from anybody else to feel good about herself.

However, there is a third level of storytelling occurring in these ads—a layer that instructs and leads the audience, rather than simply selling a product. M&S sculpted this layer by design, whilst Iceland let it happen by default.

The power of this layer is not in the parade of wares—the hope of getting a few sales; it is demonstrating to each targeted audience member the person they aspire to become. That archetype also *happens* to be an M&S brand advocate!

These advertising campaigns are a pointed social commentary about the ongoing evolution of women's equality in the world. One looks back to an age when a woman's only joy was to pleasure her husband (by spending a little to give a lot).

The other shows a woman who loves her husband, but is not defined by him—she is fulfilled in herself and her independent spirit (she is also wealthy and likes to spend money on others as well as herself).

The questions asked with this third degree of story are: who do these companies want people to be? How should they act and behave? What are their priorities, personal values and who do they aspire to be?

When you ask yourself these questions about your audience, you will have a

clearer idea of what your brand needs to relate to your audience, through storyselling. For storyselling is not, "Buy this product." It is not even, "This is our customer." Storyselling is "This is our world and when you enter the world we have created for you, you will be validated as a successful human being."

Large corporates in their sometimes painfully slow lumbering way make changes to their approach which trickle rather than flood the sales and marketing arena. Thus we can look to large organisations for clues, but often, it is with SMEs that tomorrow is witnessed today.

For whilst large companies like M&S and Iceland present their very different views in advertising, modern storysellers are not interested in this outdated and old-fashioned form of marketing.

Whilst we can explore contemporary advertisements to gauge where marketing is currently positioned, we need to remember that advertising is essentially obsolete when it comes to direct selling. That old method of beating

people over the head with a "Buy Me!" message does more harm than good with modern audiences.

Studies conducted by Google suggest a large majority of audience members will automatically leave websites or unsubscribe from mailing lists where disruptive advertising is used. Various reports from organisations as *Forbes* and *The American Press Institute* confirm that the millennial audience do not respond to ads. And when you encounter one of those very obvious and very long, long, long sales-letter-websites, are you more likely to purchase the item on sale or just navigate away?

Master storysellers seek to build their world with the understanding that once a client is inside the world, they will keep purchasing, keep spreading the world and help grow the business in many other ways. The client will transition from purchaser of the product to advocate of the brand. And this relationship is worth more to an organisation than any advertising, sponsorship or product placement can ever achieve.

Storytelling 101

Storyselling uses the narrative devices of storytelling to develop a trusting (and trusted) relationship between your business and your audience. This will, over time, sell your products and services, while also developing your brand.

The world-building, storytelling businesses of our digital age are not focused on storyselling as a way of making one-off sales that cost the business more than the retail price. They view sales as symptomatic of a healthy, ongoing relationship with their audience. Their message is not, "Buy me! Buy me!" It is, "Buy into my world!"

Expert storysellers focus on relationship rather than product. They seek to build an ecosystem of media content that immerses an audience (rather than poking them in the eye to make them cry). The goal being to get the audience into the world where the selling takes care of itself.

Using the storyselling approach refines your company's brand, making it more relatable, sophisticated and trusted. It engages your audience of potential clients in very compelling ways, whilst developing a trusting, ongoing relationship between you and your clients. Creating a story-based world also leverages new markets and audiences, by harnessing viral media, social media and other online channels.

Sophisticated audiences will instantly know if they are being sold to, manipulated or persuaded in some way. The challenge for businesses is

to present their brand in such a way that these audiences do not mind being sold to—indeed they welcome it!

Traditional marketing is to sales what VHS is to home entertainment. If you were to show a group of friends a VHS recording of a movie, they would know instantly. Old styles of advertising have the same effect on modern audiences; and they are better at switching attention towards something completely different, usually another form of storyselling.

Whilst storyselling is the presentation mechanism, it is also the product itself; creating a seamless interaction between promotional item and valued product or service.

When the story is woven through your products, services, brand, audience and sales journey, it places your clients in a position where they recognise the need for the sale and buy into the act of buying, before they buy into what you are selling.

However, in this brave new world of storycentric marketing, many brush off storyselling as a fad or gimmick. Nevertheless, storyselling is closely linked with the channels and platforms that deliver it, therefore it is bound up with technology. Storyselling will continue to evolve and be relevant, for as long as technology does.

So, how does a small to medium-sized business, an entrepreneur, a self-employed person or motivated professional storysell without the resources of large corporate businesses?

This was a question that became very important to me in the noughties. For over a decade I had worked in one of the most disturbing, traumatic and vicious industries known to humankind—the field of complementary therapies.

As a pioneer in the realms of therapy and personal development, I had originated several modalities or *paradigms*, which were used across the world. I had written thousands of pages of course materials and resources, including the foundations for several book titles.

Nevertheless, the challenges, presented to me on a daily basis, propelled me on a nerve-shredding learning curve, steep enough to give the most intrepid mountaineer palpitations! From the quick to judge and name-call, to the dogmatic ravings of people who became rabid, teeth-clackers at the slightest suggestion of anything that conflicted with their own worldview!

Whilst this was mainly dogma and pseudoscience from sceptics and therapists alike, my experiences escalated into everything from intellectual property theft to death threats. And these provided me with a choice.

To give into the hatred and loss—to let competitors make money off the back of many years of my own hard work. Or to get back onto my feet and to claim my territory—my legacy—in a demonstration of defiance.

With over ten years of digital product out in the world under the name of my competitors, I knew I had to develop a way of presenting media that prevented many of the common issues businesspeople face.

Media that deterred piracy—and if it was stolen, it would be easily traceable back to me. Media that transcended all the trivial minutiae of industry politics (the low-level rhetoric of spectators who knew very little and vocalised a lot) and the general misinformation woo-woo that saturates so many business areas. Media that was unlike anything my audience had ever known before.

Beyond this, however, I could not just remove the problems and patch over the gaping wound with a plaster. This was going to take a very different approach to how I developed, presented and curated media products.

Plus, I had lost everything at that point. I had nothing other than my own skillset and sheer determination. The newly formed *mPowr Publishing* was to be the brand through which these new media products

were produced and distributed. Yet, both Richard (co-founder of mPowr) and I knew it could go awry very suddenly.

Yet, on a budget of next to nothing we have published a huge ecosystem of transmedia products and we used storyselling to completely shift the audience expectation of what home-study training can be.

Taking my existing material and transforming this into a very different media creature; the journey of how one, £10 book can turn into £10,000s worth of product ecosystem, is another story.

Storyselling—at its core—is the story of you. Your story presented as an ecosystem of products and services. It is how your story relates to the stories of your audience that develops the relationship between you and brings them into your world.

Your story can be presented through a variety of platforms and in many different forms of media—multimedia. However, master storyselling is when you present your story by strategically leveraging media in a sculpted or modular way—*Transmedia*.

Each media *chunk* has value as a product or service to your audience; so you may sell some of these or offer them in some other form of transaction: sign up to a mailing list, share on social media, review on Amazon and so on. Whatever the specifics of the transaction, your modular ecosystem of content is designed to exude value at every point, for your audience and for your business.

The first step of this process for the forward-thinking businessperson is to identify your audience—avoid demographics in favour of really knowing the person beyond the labels. Get inside their heart and head, know what motivates them, how they feel and who they aspire to become (with your help).

Next, author a series of content chunks with the purpose of starting a relationship with your chosen audience. Many YouTube sensations have attained millionaire status by creating their channel as a hobby. Once the relationship with their audience gained trust and traction, the businesses were founded and physical products developed.

Ponder the journey your audience member will take through your stories. Starting with engagement through compelling narrative. Think relationship before sales,

yet ensure the relationship is aimed towards an audience who need your products and services.

Know what problems they think they have and how these affect their thoughts and emotions. You also need to identify what the problems *really* are—what your professional expertise tells you is truly at stake for your audience members.

Know what their problem is, why it is such a big problem and how you, your products and services can best help them (without giving away the *how*). Then ask yourself what your audience needs to know before they can even comprehend the gravity of the problem you know is so perilous.

You could create a series of emails, videos or a pocket book that collates your knowledge into a quick-reference guide that focuses your audience on the problems they have. Then uncover the problems they did not even know were there and explain (in profound depth and with great impact) why these problems will blindside your readers/viewers, if they do not heed your warnings.

Looking forward, you can demonstrate your expertise through an authority book, supplemented with workbooks, training manuals and other forms of media, such as online training and resources.

With a series of framework products, you can fill in knowledge gaps, deepen the experience and create long-term relationships through ongoing media efforts on social platforms, through articles, blogs and media platforms, such as YouTube.

This, of course, is the broader view of your ecosystem. To begin, you will need to focus solely on your very first title. And this is where our journey truly begins.

Downton Abbey became a success in a very short space of time and not just in its native UK. The British television series became staple viewing for people all over the world and has infiltrated popular culture in remarkable ways; something that is rather unusual for a gentle period drama.

It has launched the careers of many new actors, who now have prolific Hollywood roles to add to their resumés, whilst making many established actors recognisable to a new generation of viewers. Over the span of its six short seasons, it captured the hearts and minds of millions, with its blend of mild scandal, intrigue and cutting humour (usually delivered by Dame Maggie Smith).

Yet, the reason behind this surprise hit seems unfathomable at first glance. Why would a drama set in England at the turn of the twentieth century be so addictive to its audience, when so many others have failed to ignite such popularity?

TITANIC DEAD

The answer is because Downton Abbey had a secret. The secret of master storytelling. Very few television series, movies or books use storytelling to achieve this degree of success. But when a story is told by a master, it can captivate and enslave *en masse*.

The art of storytelling is woven throughout Downton Abbey, even from the very beginning. At the opening of the first episode we see a member of the household staff carrying a newspaper—the headline announces the sinking of the Titanic.

This is one of the fundamental tools of storytelling; a powerful opening. Often, an author will drop their reader immediately into the action and then leave them hanging for a time, whilst they introduce characters, describe the setting in greater detail or go back to the beginning to return to the action later.

However, what happens when to be gripped by the action you have to know the characters, setting or story so far? The way skilful authors hook an audience quickly and long enough to get their ongoing attention is to use a situation that fascinates a great number of people.

The sinking of the Titanic evokes an oddly sinister, slightly nostalgic, rather romantic experience that intrigues us and then thrills us as we go deeper down the rabbit hole. As an actual event, the loss of life and unbelievable miscalculations in judgement are both startling and tragic. Yet, it is a very clear and indicative insight into the Edwardian mindset.

Using everything we know about the Titanic from films, television, books or even just hearsay, Downton plugged into all of those experiences the moment we saw the headline and were told that a relative of this family was a passenger.

This character actually had no bearing on the main story arcs, but was there simply as a means of engaging the audience; to give the writer a little breathing space to play with. And, whether it is the Titanic, Jack the Ripper, sharks, extraterrestrials or zombies, when

storytellers use a compelling context to indirectly introduce their stories, it is known as a McGuffin.

This is all well and good in fictional writing, but what about educational materials, personal and professional development content or business books? Introducing a flesh-eating, reanimated corpse at the beginning of your book on coping with bereavement might not be the most appropriate approach to engage your audience!

Authors and speakers may have a dramatic, powerful or inspirational anecdote to open their narrative with; those who do not can use a connection, however tenuous, to associate their content with a compelling event in the common psyche.

Some business people, trainers, coaches and consultants do actually use this technique directly, to engage their audience and embed a call to action. I have heard an entrepreneur begin a speech with the words, "I was due to attend a meeting at the World Trade Centre in New York on September 11, 2001..."

One might even use two or more experiences to open a book, for instance, beginning with a terrible maritime accident, then a globally successful television show, followed by evocative images of characters from history and popular fiction and then mentioning the most horrific and poignant event in living memory.

Yet, there are other ways of using storytelling to create a successful and transformative book (or other content-related titles). These techniques are not directly transferable in content, but they do use the art of narrative to turn the presentation of content into a conversation with a gripped reader.

Increasingly, business people are turning to storyselling to create a brand and business. This can be done through a media platform, such as a YouTube channel, a series of *freemium* products or authoring a book as a way of promoting their business.

They pour information out, sharing their expertise and years of experience with a potential audience. They may even illustrate and support this information with memories and anecdotal evidence. Conversely, what they achieve for their readers is information overload. They create disengagement of their audience and boredom—rather than promoting their business, they tarnish it.

Developing a storyselling strategy that builds relationships through a content ecosystem is not promoting your business—it IS your business. And as your business, you need to get serious about it.

Very often, a successful book or media product is not successful until it is positioned in a product range. A media product, from video training to marketing media, a mobile app to a book, needs to engage its readers before it does anything else.

The purpose of your storyselling is not to give information—*Google* does that perfectly well, thank you very much! It is to create transformation for your readers through the information at its core. Thus, how you present the information across your media ecosystem is all important.

The deeper the value you offer by expressing yourself, particularly in written form, the deeper you will impact your audience—and the more successful you will be in terms of new clients and business growth.

Taking information and expressing it in a way that truly moves your reader for the better (changing their perspective and their life overall) is the art of the storyteller. In our information age, the need to overcome sales fatigue and an increasing ability to completely filter out marketing has never been more relevant.

Caitlin Doughty is a YouTube personality and mortician. Two *undertakings* you would not expect to hear in the same sentence! Through her business she is seeking to revolutionise the Western funeral industry, while in her media content she strives to change our relationship with death.

She appreciates how so many of us fear death and the prospect of our own demise. In her web series, *Ask a Mortician,* and her books, Caitlin uses her quirky sense of humour, gentle demeanour and deep sense of wisdom and compassion to advocate an acceptance of death as part of the human experience.

Through storyselling, she nurtures a relationship with her audience that impacts them deeply—she transforms beliefs, sometimes in less than ten minutes, through a simple shift in perspective. This does not take place because of those ten minutes alone; it is the pre-existing trust her audience has which enables a transformation within the framework of a short video story.

Storyselling, used over time and constantly evolving, is a powerful method for combating audience overwhelm and piquing their interest in a product or service. Here, marketing is creatively wrapped in a story; a sales pitch hidden within a compelling narrative.

Stemming out of the product placement ideal of showing a product within a movie or television show, the use of story to sell has become a far more nuanced and sophisticated creature.

In the context of product, such as a book, storyselling is so much more than *product over here* and *story over there*. You are not only looking to associate your product with a set of emotions or experiences, you want those emotions and experiences to underpin the relationship you have with your audience.

In most storyselling examples, the audience is engaged and compelled to take some form of action—and this is where the story ends. Business owners leverage a *hard sell* with anecdotes tacked on. These are included to provoke an emotional response, which places the audience in a customer position.

After the act, however, many in that audience feel manipulated and used. Their associations with you and your business are those of being taken advantage of! This is not a good look, nor does this approach create a lasting relationship. More importantly, it damages your business in a market crammed full of savvy, sales-sensitive people who will filter out everything you present.

When you write a book or develop a range of content-related products, you are not looking at initiating a simple call to action, a quick win. You are seeking to forge an ongoing, long-lasting relationship with your clients. Essentially you are using your expertise to offer real quality, quantifiable value and tangible benefits—to create measurable transformation for the reader and therefore lay the foundations for an ongoing conversation.

By deeply transforming the lives of your readers, offering them lasting results and having a broad impact upon their way of thinking, they will proactively want to use your business and spread the word to their associates. These are the members of your audience that are called *advocates*.

A fascinating trend in broadcast platforms is how video content producers are now turning to printed books as a way of developing ongoing sales. The printed book and other physical *merch* have shown longevity in the market as a valued and preferred product over the digital resource that floats within a wide ocean of digital resources!

When most are paying lip service to storyselling—underestimating its power and gravely misunderstanding what it is—those with the competitive advantage are the businesspeople who know the secrets of storyselling. Not cursory add-ons, but the discreet narrative devices that storytellers have used for millennia to engage their audience and compel them to make specific choices.

As you decipher how to engage your audience through story across different platforms, you will increase the value of your relationship and intensify the impact you have upon them. When you also employ a transmedia approach to develop various products you will easily take a client from first purchase to big-ticket items, such as live events or training, as well as subscription-based continuity products.

As you demonstrate your value and prove why you are the authority in your professional/business area, your audience will grow to love you. They will reward you with their loyalty and custom in ways that multiply your time and financial investment.

More than all of this, you will glean a greater understanding of yourself, your values and qualities, your business and your legacy. Because to understand how to transform the lives of others, you first need to start by realising one fundamental truth...

What you believe your business to be is not your business...

No Matter What Your Business Book—
Your Book IS Your Business

Your first product does not need to be a printed book; eBooks, iBooks or other forms of digital media are also excellent choices. However, a printed book or series of books give gravitas and authority to your brand.

This is particularly relevant when considering PR opportunities in the media. Editors and TV producers are inundated with businesspeople attempting to promote their business or latest product. It is important to remember that in this tsunami of clamouring pitches, it all rests on what the editor or TV producer needs for their magazine or programme.

When you have a printed book, you switch from desperate businessperson to expert in your field. You become an authority. You have written a book on a specific subject, you must know what you are talking about. Print wields gravitas—it is a tangible, physical thing in an information-overloaded world.

Printed books also achieve another goal that many, in their haste to create electronic products, fail to recognise. Any titles that offer value via an electronic device are associated with the device. A printed book will forever be associated with you and your brand.

Those of us who read printed books as children will remember the rush of joy we feel when seeing a book cover twenty, thirty or fifty years later. When you look at an *iPad*, no one book comes to mind—just all the amazing things you can do on an iPad!

Since the printing press was created, we have developed a profound relationship with books; for entertainment, for information and for the sheer joy of reading. As the first generation in modern history to have little contact with physical media, millennials are so desperate for a slice of reality they have triggered a renaissance in physical product.

The resurgence in vinyl records and other physical media is mostly in the 18-24 age range, according to Forbes. Yet, there is a vital and distinguishing factor in the buying patterns. People stream digital as a casual listener/viewer and buy physical copies when they love the content.

Do you want your message to be rented or do you want to be loved?

Again, the most successful YouTubers met the demonetisation of the platform with physical product. From clothing and fashion, branded sundry items to printed books that collate their content into something a person can hold in their hand, feel, be a part of.

Therefore, whilst you may choose to begin with and enhance your storyselling relationships in some other form of media, let us focus upon the printed book as an entry point into a wider, deeper and longer-lasting ecosystem of products.

Not only is this a valuable starting point, it will also offer context to the power of storyselling your business.

Your book is not simply a promotional product for your business—it *is* your business. And you need to invest in your book as you would any core aspect of your business. If money is the fuel of your business, your story is the engine!

The modern world is an environment that is becoming increasingly intangible. The need to demonstrate your knowledge, wisdom and expertise in a very real way is crucial to your ongoing success.

The greater the frequency of virtual encounters, the more we drown in an ocean of data and information. This brings opportunities and challenges that most cannot fathom, especially from a professional, business perspective.

Large social media companies are growing exponentially from the monetised content that billions of us develop for them every day. From our thoughts and photos to videos and various other media memes, we have become a global workforce who share ourselves for pleasure and create profits for corporate enterprise.

As we create content, we also consume it with ever-increasing voracity. With such a need for content to consume, we are hanging out virtually more and more. Which also means that we are a receptive audience for other businesses who want to advertise to us. This advertising generates revenue for the social media companies who are thriving as a result.

The challenge for small- and medium-sized businesses is therefore, how do we compete in this vast conglomeration of information? How do we get noticed? How do we maintain relationships with clients?

With the average attention span shortening as a result of easily digestible chunks of content.

As audiences become savvy at filtering out advertising from their viewing choices.

When every piece of content you create is associated with the platform, rather than your brand.

And the amount of available data swamps anything and everything you put out there.

How do you make a difference? Impact the lives of your clients? Forge success for yourself and your business?

We are navigating the digital realms for the first time in history and this throws up unexpected and unknown issues. It is progressive publishers of media content that leverage the best of old and new platforms to stop presenting people with more information and to start offering them transformation.

We process information—and then we may or may not have an emotional reaction to it. As we are given the opportunity for transformation it affects us psychologically, emotionally and physically, as well as having an enormous effect on the way we live our lives. It changes us and modifies our behaviour.

When you change a person's life, they will never forget it, or you.

Many approach their book as they would a business card (and spend about as much time in authoring the book as they would designing a business card). Indeed, the *business-card book* is a very real phenomenon in the entrepreneurial world.

Business cards are disposable—taken, squirrelled away and eventually tossed in the bin. Business-card books have the same effect after a cursory glance. With a well-crafted book, you can engage your reader in the story, as they take a quick glance at page one! From there you author a narrative that leaves an indelible mark upon them.

Over the past decade, it has become increasingly apparent that SME owners and entrepreneurs need to change the way they seek out and communicate with their clients. Handing people business cards and paying for blanket advertising is just more information—and not valuable information at that.

These attempts to attract clients simply bounce off into the ether, completely unnoticed or worse still, they proactively damage your brand.

Audiences across the globe, with interests in anything you can name, all have one thing in common: they demand instantaneous value. Time is extremely precious and whilst a person can while away an afternoon browsing, the decision to browse is based on the value of the content. This initial choice about value is made in microseconds.

When you present them with a valuable experience—one that changes them in some way—they will develop brand loyalty that gets stronger with repeat encounters.

Traditional forms of advertising and networking do not offer much value in a world that is full-on information. It is all just too insignificant in the greater scheme of data overwhelm.

Many entrepreneurs and business owners have therefore taken to giving value through introductory seminars, online resources or even books! Live seminars can be compelling, especially if snake oil sales techniques are used. However, prospective clients are rather more sensitive to this approach, especially if they have been stung before.

Online resources may create a chink in the armour of content desensitisation, but invariably result in information overwhelm or as something bookmarked, but never visited again. And even books will often be put on a shelf, never read, because again they are information—information about this businessperson, who owns a business, doing business at you. Where is the value?

To create a book that truly builds your business, you need to engage your clients, compel them to read your book, haunt them emotionally and obsess them through transformation. The obsession will form a habit that has them coming back time and time again for your knowledge and expertise.

This is only the beginning. A single book will produce a single purchase and, in some cases, multiple purchases if the book is bought for associates, colleagues and friends. When people love you, they ask one question, "What's next?"

Remember, the purpose of storyselling is not to create a destination involving one or two sales, but to result in a relationship with your audience where purchases are the essential by-product.

To grow an ongoing relationship, you will need to develop a range of products that take your client on a narrative journey. This journey starts with their first purchase and continues towards big-ticket and continuity products.

There is also another aspect of this evolving market you need to be aware of. With giant tech companies building devices that deliver content in more contextual ways, you need to appreciate how this affects the way an audience will interact with your products.

Currently, a reader may experience your book at home or in the office, on public transport or in their car, they may be in a quiet room or a buzzing coffee shop, inside or out.

In the very near future, however, an even greater factor will come into being. Content in its many media forms is already beginning to overlay our world. The augmentation of our everyday lives with content, will ensure that only authors and content creators who understand how to enhance their audience's lives in tangible ways will get their attention.

Here, both digital and physical products (media) will play a part. We need digital content (and the technology that delivers it) to create an augmented reality—however, digital is just not tangible enough to make it real at the depth physical products can.

Yes, we have book smell and feel and this is an important point to make—books are not just about words that you read on a page, but also the sensation of holding reality in your hand. Yet, as we move beyond books to explore the other media products of the future, will we be drinking out of our mobile phones? Will we walk through the streets naked, allowing our *neural laces* to *fill in* the clothing perceptually?

No, until we are living in pods, mere batteries for our Artificial Intelligence overlords, we shall need physical products, which are the foundations for navigating our world, tangibly and digitally.

Google Glass failed because it did not enhance the audience's experience of their real world—it divorced them from it. This, combined with various legal, privacy and intellectual property issues, caused the product to be abandoned.

Conversely, *Pokémon Go* was the first widespread example of an augmented reality success story (one which spawned a series of other products, such as *Jurassic World Alive*). Here the story is simple—collect digital characters augmented onto the physical world—yet this paves the way for more sophisticated storytelling.

If you can engage, compel, haunt and obsess, whilst overlaying your reader's environment with an experience of your creation, you will not only transform their life you will transform them from a client into an advocate for you and your business.

To truly grasp what this means, let us take the example of *Facebook*. This social media giant currently encourages users to create content for delivery through the site. This content is used to piggyback advertising and other forms of monetised marketing. In some case the content itself is actually the sales pitch, cleverly disguised as a viral video.

Users have to visit to the site via a desktop computer, mobile device or other form of appropriate technology. This is how we consume social media at the moment and it enables Facebook to learn about the users' habits and deliver to them based on those habits. The challenge is that it is virtual and essentially isolating.

As social media evolves it becomes about a person's physical environment: where content is delivered as an augmentation to their physical environment, social context and other factors, such as mood, time of day and so on.

With greater sophistication in technology, we hunger for something more than going online. We expect specific, tailored and transformative content to come to us wherever and whenever we are. This is augmented reality. And it is created by using transmedia.

Transmedia delivers media in a very specific and tailored way to augment a person's life with content: not information, but transformation. Early adopters are already clambering towards avant-garde strategies of delivering transmedia augmented realities to their audience/clients.

To truly make a difference by impacting the lives of your potential clients, you need to be planning your business strategy for developing a product range of transmedia products.

Transmedia is very different to a multimedia or crossmedia approach, however. Here, we are not simply creating or duplicating content across different forms of media. Transmedia requires a very specific and strategic approach—a world-building ethos where every piece of content, across each platform, is placed to achieve an augmented purpose.

The traditional, multimedia form of information-giving would involve a piece of online text, accompanied by a video, an audio track with a slide show and a downloadable PDF, a printed advert or leaflet with a QR Code and some form of digital content.

To develop transmedia, you need a fundamentally different approach, which is more about a change in perspective than the core information and the forms of media you employ to present it.

The mPowr range of transmedia Home Experiences are training programmes that begin with printed books. These act as gateways to online, digital realms, which are viewed as worlds with their own characters, timelines and regions.

The student explores these realms, as they would a real environment, looking for audio, video and textual experiences. Yet, this is not only a question of where they go, but also when they visit a realm.

The settings change from day to night: bright sunshine at midday and candle-lit streets at midnight. Certain characters will be found at one location in the morning and another at night. Mid-afternoon opens up a cobbled street with pertinent resources to explore, whilst bedtime has a whole other area, with very different resources!

Students are not only learning chunks of data, they are venturing through an environment, engaged, compelled, haunted and obsessed by the path they walk. This is storyselling at its most addictive and profound.

Traditional advertising has historically offered companies a means of broadcasting their message to an attentive audience for between thirty seconds and several minutes. This has now reduced to a few seconds (or even microseconds, depending on the medium) to a distracted and sceptical audience.

To reclaim this space and even extend it to several hours, businesses are now developing a range of content, such as books and video, to capture and hold the attention of their audience.

If a reader spends seven hours reading your book, they are learning to trust you, to respect you and to partake in whatever products or services you offer.

When you expand your book into a product range that transforms their life in some way, be it minute or massive, those hours become days, weeks, months, years or even decades.

These are your advocates and their loyalty goes way beyond buying your products and services. An advocate will recommend you to others, go out of their way to act on behalf of your company and will be the greatest defender of your brand, even in the face of adversity.

According to the *Journal of Social and Personal Relationships*, it takes an average of fifty hours to develop a sense of friendship and trust between people. The more you broaden this time frame, the more trust, respect and loyalty will form between you, your clients and your business.

A typical journey for your audience is to progress from an unknown person who encounters you in some way, to a loyal and dedicated evangelist of your brand. There are usually four steps to this process: Prospects, Customers, Clients and eventually, Advocates.

- Prospects follow you, read your articles, know of you in some way
- Customers have made a single purchase (your book, etc.)
- Clients are repeat purchasers of your products and may also recommend you to others
- Advocates buy continually (including unrelated or lateral products), they recommend you to others and will take action to proactively help you reach a wider audience

To truly create a book, product range and ongoing experience for your audience and advocates, you will need the basics of writing your book, how you can use anecdote to illustrate your information and storytelling to engage, compel, haunt and obsess.

When you know these aspects of authoring, you will be able to expand a single book into an entire ecosystem of products and eventually understand how your transmedia product range will augment the reality of your burgeoning audience in remarkable ways.

Before the Story Begins...

So, let me be very honest. When you strip away the story, *Disney World* is a shopping mall, *Netflix* is a subscription service, and most of the world's most successful businesses sell you products with less physical matter than air.

If you have ever experienced *Expedition Everest*, binge-watched *Orange is the New Black* or enjoyed using the internet, you will know that the experience is very different to the reality. This is purely down to the stories we are being told.

When you go on a ride at Disney World, you proactively suspend disbelief by making a conscious decision to enter into the world of Disney's creation. When you watch a movie or series on Netflix, you know you have paid the subscription fee, but disconnect that purchase from the story you are watching unfold before you.

When you use an app or software, the story comes with such subtlety and is so integrally tied into the complex tangle of other stories we base our lives upon that you will probably be completely unaware of how much storytelling is going on.

A rather cynical view of modern media is how content creators use a methodology, identified by eminent psychological behaviourist, B.F. Skinner. In 1948 Skinner defined *Operant Conditioning*, glimpses of which form the basis for systemic thinking.

Here, a series of reinforcers and punishments are presented in a precise way to cause addictive behaviour. Starting with greatest frequency and lowest effort, positive reinforcement engages and compels the audience.

Over increasingly lengthy periods of time, the positive reinforcements lessen and negative reinforcements/punishments increase, along

with a need for more and more audience effort. This leads to haunting and obsessing.

Positive reinforcers are often tied into an abundance of the basic needs for living, whilst negative reinforcers are a lessening of these and punishments are a complete (if temporary) removal of these factors.

We need air to breathe, water to drink, food to eat, shelter/health to keep us safe and companionship to give life meaning. The best stories are rooted in these necessities and Skinner presented us with a rather mechanistic way of using them to achieve a result.

Yet, beyond these foundations that enable us to survive, everything—absolutely everything—is story. Story is more important to us than religion, government, society, business, technology and just about anything else that is not air, water, food, shelter, health or relationship-based.

Money is a story. As are religious and political views, mathematics, science and technology. Stories take the fundamentals of survival and show us something that transforms survival into living. So, we can boil everything down to the essential elements for survival and the stories that turn living into more than simply surviving.

Every story is based on information that helps us survive. If the story is not about survival, there are very few perceived rewards and punishments, hence it is not important enough for us to pay attention. Any information you wish to present to your audience needs to be directly or indirectly related to their survival (and drip-fed as pleasurable reinforcement and painful punishments).

Savvy marketeers take products that are not essential to survival and they associate them with something that is strongly linked to survival of oneself or one's family. The most commonplace example is when sexual imagery is employed to sell unremarkable products or services.

When we are doing something that enhances our chances of survival we feel pleasure. If we are on a path to not surviving, we feel pain. These pleasure and pain responses create an emotional spectrum which exists at the heart of story, storytelling and storyselling, and always has.

Several tropes in horror movies aim directly to punish the audience with a removal of the essentials to living. Suffocation, ingestion of toxic substances, home invasion and loss of a loved one are just a few examples.

The information, upon which our stories revolve, must tap into these emotional experiences and be enhanced by the context of the story. It is also vital to look beyond simple manipulation of your audience—this is hollow; it does not build trust and while you may get a sale, that sale will be at the expense of a lasting advocacy.

To truly elevate storyselling to its most powerful and valuable effect, you need an altruistic destination: a desire to give real and lasting transformation to your readers. You need to focus on legacy—theirs and yours.

The Author-Reader Paradox

Many new authors begin their book with the romantic idea of it being all about them. For most, authoring a book is an ego massage, rather than genuine caring about the reader. In fiction terms, we can get away with this much of the time, but in the context of business and educational books...

It may be your book, but it is not about you!

It is about the person who is investing their time to be with you and listen to what you have to say. There is absolutely no reason why they should do this, other than to benefit themselves.

The time they give to you is precious. If just fifty people read your book, you will never match the time your audience gives to you, hour for hour, in the authoring of your book.

Indeed, if your book is successful to the readership of 100,000 copies, your audience will invest more time reading your book than you have in your whole lifetime! This is a gift to you, so cherish it, value and respect it.

Many authors approach writing their book as a simple exercise in presenting information. This information could be data-driven, centred around their own story or even fictional. However, they all make one crippling mistake.

The author will work feverishly thinking about what they want to say and how to say it. They will get lost in their story or stick firmly to a brainstormed list—all the while making choices about what they think the reader needs to know.

There are thousands of examples of books which were written to please the author. These range from those who pay lip service to the reader—attempting to give some value and have a certain degree of impact upon them—to those that are tantamount to an exercise in pleasuring one's self.

Whilst most authors, especially in the self-publishing arena, are focused on what they want to say, the secret to writing a successful book is to only think about the reader's journey from first word to final page.

Rather than approaching your text with an attitude of "What do I want to tell my readers?" or even "What do my readers need to know?" begin with a very different question.

What is my reader's behaviour at every point of the book?

When you appreciate how your book is affecting the way your reader engages with your book, you are able to pre-empt their behaviour. This is almost mathematical in its application, because the physical act of reading a book is linear.

That line of words on a page is like a steel girder in the imagination of your reader. The girders form a framework you build for your reader and this becomes what they will fill with your world, once you have given them a compelling reason to do so.

They will make it a fluid, breathing, living place where they meander from moment to moment. They will feel compelled to take another step and develop a genuine, emotional relationship with you: the author and creator of this world.

This relationship will cause them to remember your book long after they have finished reading the very last sentence. It will also bring them back for more.

And while they flesh out a corporeal, visceral world using your words, the book remains a framework for that process. A nuts and bolts and metal rod frame that is put together with artistry and finesse.

Not a box or collection of boxes, but a sophisticated, beautifully-crafted sculpture that guides your reader, keeping them immersed, intrigued and interested in every moment—provided you have given them a powerful enough *why*.

And what are the mathematics of this framework?

Typically, you have only the first page of a book to get their attention. If they are not intrigued enough before the first turn of a page, you are likely to lose them. Once you have that initial turn of page, you have a further two pages to get them actively interested in your narrative.

If they turn the page a second time, you have six events to immerse them in the narrative. If by the seventh event you have them creating a world around themselves, using your textual cues, you will be stirring their emotions and be at the start of an intimate, hopefully long-lasting, relationship with them.

Beyond that, it is a case of three contrasting features to your narrative framework: repetition, undulation and expansion.

Reiterate your reader's engagement at the beginning of every chapter or section, without the need to turn a page. Use the following two pages to compel them onwards and use the seven-step strategy to strengthen the emotional attachments they feel.

You will also need to undulate your narrative in mood, pace and texture. Use contrasting dramatic tension, humour and specific points of resolution to develop a landscape for your narrative. One that takes the reader soaring to great heights and plummets them into the abyss.

You will also need to maintain a steadily increasing expansion of scope, depth and longevity that keeps growing until the very end of your book. Over time, as you introduce a new subject, character or piece of information, you will need to increase the emotional connection with your reader and impact them in a transformative way.

If you simply add new information, without depth of feeling and long-lasting value, you will confuse, bore and eventually lose your reader. This three-dimensional approach (scope, emotion, value) can also be improved through time and within a specific context: the fourth and fifth dimensions of authoring.

Another vital aspect of writing, when it comes to the undulation and expansion of your narrative is to change things up at least once, preferably twice in your book. This creates acts, usually two or three.

When you are working with two acts, you will pinpoint a juncture in your book—usually around midway—where you turn everything on its head. In a three-act work, you will have three distinct aspects of your narrative.

Act one grabs attention and utterly immerses your reader. Act two turns everything on its head and makes everything even more powerful. And act three creates a quick-fire resolution to everything presented in the first two acts.

An amateur mistake most people make is giving away too much *how* in the first two acts. The most compelling read begins with a problem. In act one you define this problem and if it is different to the problem your reader *believes* they have, you clarify this.

Virtually everybody in your audience will know they have a problem and don't know how to fix it. They will ask questions in forums, contact your competitors and search Google to find answers.

With these activities it will not be long before they get conflicting advice, inferior service and a huge data dump of information. When your book (and other media) uses storyselling to transform your reader, as opposed to simply *inform* them, they will realise the problem they thought they had is not the real problem!

By the time they reach you and your book, they will have the information they thought they needed. It did not help them! So, rather than giving them more of the same, use your expertise—your authority—to shatter the tired old marketing speak everybody is using and demonstrate in very specific, real-world terms why your audience needs you.

In the second act you invest the majority of the book explaining to the reader why this is such a big problem. Layer the depth and complexity of the issue, using emotions to truly encapsulate why this will be your reader's undoing.

Finally, the shortest and most concise act offers the how and resolves the issues for the most motivated of readers. Those who still need help, can come to you, your business and your products for further support.

Developing a solid framework for your book, before you write a single word, will be an invaluable blueprint when writing. You will have a landscape to navigate that is not simply about the information and anecdotes you want to include. You will detail a storytelling map that will enable you to do exactly what needs to be done, when it needs to be done, to affect your reader in exactly the way they need to be affected.

Mapping out your narrative with a view to understanding what needs to happen in every paragraph to keep your readers reading, relating to and relishing your book is a far more effective approach than pondering what information you

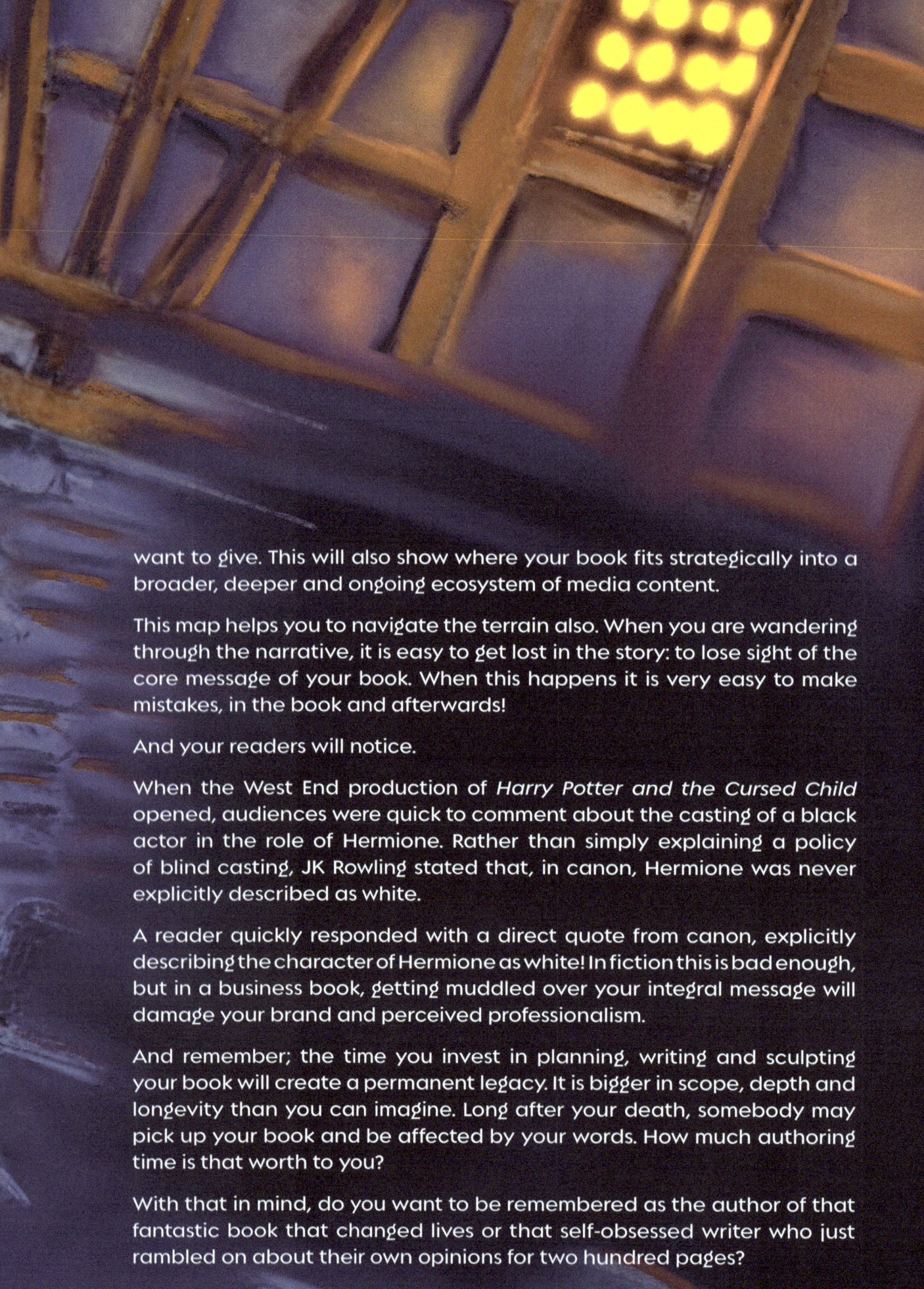

want to give. This will also show where your book fits strategically into a broader, deeper and ongoing ecosystem of media content.

This map helps you to navigate the terrain also. When you are wandering through the narrative, it is easy to get lost in the story: to lose sight of the core message of your book. When this happens it is very easy to make mistakes, in the book and afterwards!

And your readers will notice.

When the West End production of *Harry Potter and the Cursed Child* opened, audiences were quick to comment about the casting of a black actor in the role of Hermione. Rather than simply explaining a policy of blind casting, JK Rowling stated that, in canon, Hermione was never explicitly described as white.

A reader quickly responded with a direct quote from canon, explicitly describing the character of Hermione as white! In fiction this is bad enough, but in a business book, getting muddled over your integral message will damage your brand and perceived professionalism.

And remember; the time you invest in planning, writing and sculpting your book will create a permanent legacy. It is bigger in scope, depth and longevity than you can imagine. Long after your death, somebody may pick up your book and be affected by your words. How much authoring time is that worth to you?

With that in mind, do you want to be remembered as the author of that fantastic book that changed lives or that self-obsessed writer who just rambled on about their own opinions for two hundred pages?

Once Again...
This Time with Feeling

If grabbing the attention of your reader is paramount, the very next purpose of your storyselling—and the most vital aspect of writing for the long-term impact of your book—is to gain a powerful degree of emotional engagement with your reader.

When there is an emotional connection between you and your reader, you will develop a trusting relationship. This trust is essential if your readers are going to believe what you have to say. Whilst having an audience that likes you is really helpful, liking you is not as important as trusting you!

Once you have their trust, they will make more effort to implement your methodology into their lives. Creating emotional engagement at the relationship-building level, where your reader feels emotions even when they are not reading your book, is not as straightforward as we might believe.

When a reader is reading your book, they must feel a compulsion not to put it down, but if they have to do that for some reason, they must feel an emotional pang that drives them to pick your book back up again at the first available opportunity.

When you think about emotional connection with your readers, chances are you are thinking about emotional connection with empaths or sympaths. These are people who feel their world strongly—they are emotional by nature and will react to stimuli in a profoundly emotional way. Often kinaesthetic in their experience of the world, these readers will respond very easily to any narrative that stirs their feelings.

Your audience is also equally as likely to be driven cerebrally—not responding emotionally to all the usual triggers. They may know they should be responding with emotion, but they are simply not wired that way. Others may be so cerebral they will find the usual emotional cues to be too twee or even trite.

These readers will often notice very quickly when you are attempting to pull on their heartstrings. If you author your book without considering these readers, you will turn them off very quickly. In business, a large proportion of your readers will be cerebrally focused.

Forming emotional connectivity with the unemotional reader needs to be an important consideration when you author your book. Achieved with a different approach to the empathic and sympathetic style, you need to focus on what does create an emotional response to the unemotional reader.

This could read as a paradox, but even people with serious personality disorders have emotional responses—just to different triggers. These triggers are focused more upon survival—health, money and desires. Regardless of where we sit on the emotional scale, when it comes to physical survival, we are wired to react when it is threatened.

For instance, when writing for an emotionally-driven reader, an anecdote that pokes around in areas such as injustice, relationships, painful events and so on, will grab their engagement.

When appealing to the logical or calculating intellect, use your language to push buttons and keep it in the realms of survival. Think in terms of threats (poverty, injury and mortality) or pleasures (material gain, physical gratifications and winning).

Bold words and powerful statements work well with the intellectual reader—just keep these connected to their survival (or detriment to their survival), rather than emotional or relationship needs.

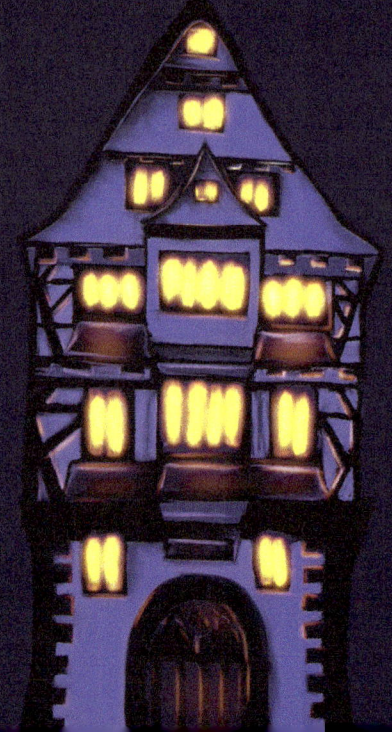

Using language such as necrotic, tumour, risk and so on, or exploring a lack of control in unknown circumstances, humiliation and loss, can really communicate with those who deem emotion to be too touchy-feely. Of course, you will need to strike a balance between the different emotional orientations—from empath to megalomaniac!

Those on the more emotional end of the scale will also respond to the pressure points you leverage for the intellectual readers. Though you will need to check in with them regularly, presenting feeling-based narrative.

As an author, you could think about your audience in terms of givers and takers—who are focused on themselves and who look to the needs of others? If you present personal gain to the more altruistic readers, they will view it all as rather cutthroat and ruthless. Conversely, caring for others can be construed as weakness and time-wasting to egocentric readers.

And this is an important aspect of authoring a trusting relationship. The relationship between emotions and intellect is a spectrum, not just between each other, but also in intensity and context.

Another consideration when creating emotional connection with your audience is the type of emotion you seek to provoke.

Avoid overusing the paralysis or inertia-inducing emotions, such as frustration, worry or jealousy. Strive for the emotions that spawn movement—anger, fear, grief, joy and so on.

When a reader feels frustration they will go around in circles, without noticing the exit signs which offer release. If they worry, they will just wallow in it as if stuck in quicksand. Trepidation has them bouncing between one direction and another. You want your reader's emotions to inspire movement towards an outcome or away from some trauma.

You will also want to steer clear of situations where the strong emotions negate each other, such as joy and grief. These will cause the paralysing experience of ambivalence. Complementary emotions such as anger and passion are marvellous, but avoid polarity emotions at all costs.

The Creative Breakdown

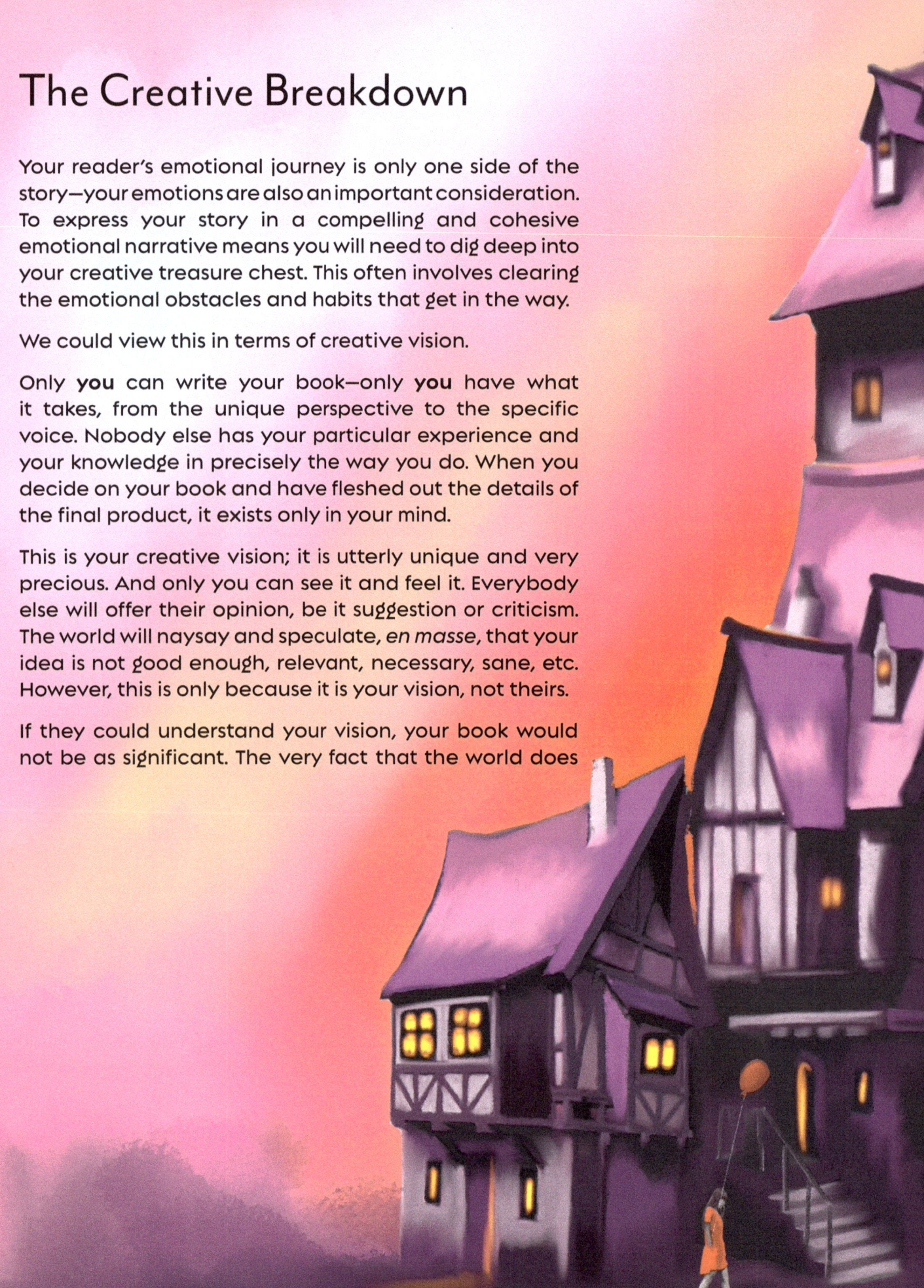

Your reader's emotional journey is only one side of the story—your emotions are also an important consideration. To express your story in a compelling and cohesive emotional narrative means you will need to dig deep into your creative treasure chest. This often involves clearing the emotional obstacles and habits that get in the way.

We could view this in terms of creative vision.

Only **you** can write your book—only **you** have what it takes, from the unique perspective to the specific voice. Nobody else has your particular experience and your knowledge in precisely the way you do. When you decide on your book and have fleshed out the details of the final product, it exists only in your mind.

This is your creative vision; it is utterly unique and very precious. And only you can see it and feel it. Everybody else will offer their opinion, be it suggestion or criticism. The world will naysay and speculate, *en masse*, that your idea is not good enough, relevant, necessary, sane, etc. However, this is only because it is your vision, not theirs.

If they could understand your vision, your book would not be as significant. The very fact that the world does

not yet appreciate your message is what makes your book a landmark in your field and you the authority that creates it.

Your book is your opportunity to explain why your audience needs to pay attention—by highlighting the problems they did not even realise they had and how you can help them to solve those issues.

Holding the creative vision when the reality around you is so different is difficult. You have to change the vision of the world around you, which will seem impossible at times. It is far easier to change your vision to fit the reality of the world, changing or diluting your message—even worse, losing momentum and second-guessing yourself into not completing your book.

So as you hold your vision for the duration of your writing period, you will need to manoeuvre the obstacles that present themselves to you in the world around you, whilst coping with the emotions these obstacles stir within you. All creative people go through this journey, confronting their own self-doubts.

This may manifest as mild frustrations or concerns, possibly even meltdowns. Do not become distracted by these; they are a very natural part of holding a creative vision until it is made real. Simply experience those moments, let them have their say, then let them go and move on.

This will make your finished book more potent; for as you move beyond each hiccup, you will discover new ways of influencing each reader towards the results your vision has in store for them. You will unlock new ways to impact different members of your audience and create transformation in an indelible, uncompromising way.

This is the difference between writing THE book that revolutionises your industry or a bland, generic book that gets lost in a crowded market. Your readers will overcome their own knowledge gaps because they trust you to guide them forward.

All seasoned innovators and creatives know the dichotomy between the real world and their imagination. The only certainty is one must change to match the other. The question is, will you change your book to suit the world or will you change the world with your book?

Do not allow the good intentions of others to distract you from your vision. Most of the time, it is a question of people thinking they can do a better job (without actually doing anything other than attempting to distract you from manifesting your creative vision). You are not walking their path, living their life or writing their book—it is your vision of a better life for your audience!

If you can use their words as a way of addressing challenges to the content of your book you will satisfy many more readers. By learning how to change minds in the creation, you will change minds in the reading. By overcoming your own doubts, fears and blind spots, you will develop from being another expert in a saturated market of experts to being a leader in your field.

All leaders have heard the haters, the sceptics and those who have yet to think outside their own quagmire of problems. The only difference between the pioneers and the followers is that leaders change the world to their vision and do not allow the world to distract them.

Is your book going to demonstrate your leadership or simply be another person rambling on about how good they are?

The answer to this question will demonstrate if you are writing to truly make a difference or are just self-pleasuring your ego. The writing of your book needs to be almost totally transformational for you before it transforms the lives of your readers. If you are not willing to step up to that particular challenge, then you are more focused on your own needs than offering any value to your audience.

This is a tough challenge, but a fitting one! Striking out with a pioneering original spirit is a true mark of the person you (and only you) are. If you are not prepared to be a leader in your field; to be an authority who speaks with a voice that goes against the grain, then do not write a book!

The world has too many books that begin with *I* and talk incessantly about *me*. Make your creative vision your own, by focusing on how it helps others; how it changes the life of your readers.

Know that you cannot achieve real, profound change for them if you match your vision to the world as it is in this moment. They know the world that already exists—you need to demonstrate to them, in a way they appreciate, what the world can be for them.

This is all very well for writers with big imaginations, however, some of us have a greater sense of the world as it is now, rather than the reality of tomorrow. The vision of what *can be* is great, but it is, by its very nature, disconnected from what is real in the here and now.

If you live your life through what you can hold in your hand, instead of what you can hold in your mind's eye, do not despair! Your book will rely on using your imagination to impact the lives of others and focus greatly on how your professional and life learnings can create change for your audience.

In summary, only you have the ability and the right to write your book, but to do so, you will need to hold the creative reality of a world where your book has made the difference. If you change to suit others you will negate any need for your book to exist. It will become a drab and absolutely worthless collection of bland words.

The journey of writing the book is yours. But the book is not about you and your experiences. It is about how your journey, knowledge and distinct viewpoint translates into helping your readers. It is important to write by this mantra, because the way you usually do business is contextual. Your book will need to help others in a variety of ways, based in many different circumstances.

When you are seeking to walk a path to help your reader, spewing everything you know onto the page will confuse and baffle. Have a strategic system that you share with your audience. One they can learn and then apply to their problems for themselves—that is the key to balancing your experience with their needs.

The First Steps to Writing Your Book (And Developing a Product Range)

Disney World, Netflix, internet and software-based companies in general are all rooted in story. However, the businesses behind these brands are not focused on the creativity of their stories. It is the business purpose driving the stories that is important.

When you listen to a piece of music, what you hear is the creative work—the story. The electricity powering the device that plays the music is equivalent to the business purpose. Directly or indirectly, business is behind all lasting creative works.

The business purpose for Disney *imagineers* is to get people into the parks (where guests can buy things) and to put them into queues where they wait their turn to buy things (that they do not realise they are going to want to need yet).

Netflix is not concerned with developing creative television as much as it is getting people to subscribe and keeping existing subscribers. As such, they have turned the process of creating binge-watch telly into an art form. Such is the finesse of their strategy now, Netflix know exactly how to engage their audience and at exactly what point they will become addicted.

Obviously, the internet and software companies are so numerous we cannot explore them all here, except to say that the most successful tech businesses also have a way of wrapping story around their core missions—turning retail, subscription, advertising, commission, franchise businesses, and so on, into stories that completely enthral their audiences.

The difference with all these companies is not the audience being unaware of the intent to sell. It is that the story is so pleasurable (or painful) they do not care that they are being sold to. They want to buy and buy again

To achieve this degree of rapport, the companies that are best at storyselling use story at its most complex to wrap the audience up in the narrative, over and over. It is not simply a matter of bolting-on a story to the information.

"Come, come to our theme park and buy stuff you don't need! Oh, there's some rides and people in costumes too!"

No. The business has an aim to sell, to be self-sufficient and profitable—the audience has physiological, emotional, cerebral or spiritual needs to fulfil. It is the story that connects these contrasting needs and develops a potent relationship between company and client.

So, how does this help you turn your business needs and expertise into a powerful storyselling ecosystem?

The very first aspect of writing a story is to decide what your business is. You may already have a clear vision about the base model, however, most businesspeople start with the story, failing to see the underlying business process.

Your company may employ several models, however, it is important to identify what the foundations are. For example, you may be a consultant, who sells your consultancy packages (retail), offers training to others through weekly online webinars (subscription) and accredits qualifying consultants to practise (franchise).

An extremely important fact to remember is that you can create success through storyselling your business models in a pre-existing modality (*NLP, Myers-Briggs, The Atkins Diet,* for example) or you can pioneer your own system and storysell that instead. The advantage here is you are the originator—nobody else now or in the future can tell that specific story!

Now, this is not an acronym or five-point plan (although these can be individual elements of a much greater system). You want to create a framework that adapts from person to person, reader to reader—one they can apply to their own life and that adapts to their needs.

Once you have identified what type of business you have and the modality system unique to you, you will have a clearer insight into what information, expertise and wisdom you want to share with your audience.

So, the next step is to decide upon the information your story needs to convey. To achieve this, you will need to get the information out of your head and recorded in some form.

By having a record of what you want your reader to know, you can then adapt the raw data into emotional experiences that affect your audience and finally into a story that captivates, enthrals and utterly transforms your readers.

In this context, you are seeking to write a book that presents your professional expertise and storysells it into something utterly essential for your potential clients. However, this is not just A book. It is YOUR book and, most of all, it is THE book.

THE book will give your reader what nobody else has managed to offer. It will make a difference by impacting them and their lives in extraordinary ways and it will create transformation in some form for them.

There is an eight-point paradigm that will help you know how you achieve this in the most natural way for you, personally. This system approaches storyselling as a method of ensuring different aspects of the story match with the contrasting perspectives of your audience members. Of knowing who you are, how you experience the world and how your individual readers can relate to you.

The system will help you identify how you speak to your audience, how they interact and what you will achieve for them and your business, through this relationship. Furthermore, this paradigm will help you view your story strategically, developmentally, creatively and professionally.

And whilst this may appear to be an oversimplification of writing a book, as you visit and revisit each step of this process, you will realise how powerful this tool is in developing more than THE book!

The eight steps of this system are:

Create
Brand
Audience
Proposition
Transaction
Analysis
Strategise
Refine

You could view these steps as part of a storyselling process, a book-writing process, or a business process. These eight steps are actually intrinsic to all three.

For example, you Create a story, tell the story (Brand) to your Audience, who want the results of the story (Proposition) and experience these on an ongoing basis (Transaction). You then gauge this response (Analysis), decide how to achieve greater results from the story (Strategise) and finally Refine the story in the retelling.

You will naturally be better at some of these tasks than other aspects of the overall strategy and will enjoy certain steps more than others. Initially, you will need to complete every step, but eventually you can focus on the elements you enjoy, whilst outsourcing the stages that inspire less enthusiasm!

In the writing of your book alone, you will progress through this cycle many times—developing an initial plan, creating a foundation document, rough draft, first full draft, editorial draft, etc.

Once you have written and published your first book, the strategy will assist you again and again as you expand your range and develop your business. An initial authority book can lead to a workbook, reference book, quick-tip guide or detailed series of guides, educational programme, professional development programme and so on.

Now, this process may at first glance appear to be time-consuming, but there is a very important point to bear in mind. The more you complete the cycle, the more you will immerse your audience in the narrative and the more intense the relationship will become. Additionally, you will add greater value to your business by multiplying your time.

What does this mean?

A consultant will spend an hour meeting with a client. That hour results in an hour of pay. Now, the consultant may increase the price from time to time, as their popularity increases and their availability decreases, however it remains an hour of pay for an hour of time.

When you create a book or other content-related product, based upon your expertise, you are multiplying your time. An hour of time invested in strategy, writing, marketing and selling your work is potentially worth many hundreds or thousands of hours. As you leverage your products into up-sells and widgetise them into side-sells, you multiply your time further.

So, the more you develop an ironclad strategy at this early stage (continuing to adapt and refine that strategy as you monitor strengths and weaknesses in your product ecosystem) the greater the multiplication of your time will be at a later date.

The information contained in your book is essential in offering value to your readers; it is the lifeblood and value of what you offer. When you present an original, self-originated system that works, your advocates will recommend that system to others. Apart from the original work and your marketing efforts, you will not need to lift a finger for this to happen!

The storyselling of your media ecosystem is implemented to attract their attention and to place you in a position of leadership. Developing your voice or brand will increase the impact and sales of your book.

Identifying your audience will improve purchases even more. Offering a unique and valuable proposition will push sales beyond anything you will achieve without these additional areas of planning.

The very first objective when authoring your first book is to develop a foundation manuscript. This is the basis for your finished title, but it is more focused on the information you want to give, rather than the stories you want to tell—to sell.

Therefore, you need to work through this eight-step strategy to develop your foundation manuscript, creating the main body of information, deciding on your brand, audience and how your information will hook into their basic survival needs.

From then, you will expand this into your first proper draft by analysing your foundation, strategically developing a plan for your storyselling and refining the manuscript into a first draft. At this point, we shall begin to create that first draft, weaving in the storyselling techniques presented in this book.

The Basics of Storytelling and Selling

We all know that feeling of listening to somebody in a meeting, at a bar, on the phone... they launch into an anecdote and we just want them to get on with it already! As they drone on and on, retrospectively filling in gaps and generally running away on tangents, we retreat inside and begin listening to our own thoughts instead.

Most of us also appreciate what it is like being on the other side of the situation. Wanting to tell somebody a story and trying our hardest to relate it as quickly as possible.

Unsure of how to explain and missing key points that are vital to knowing what happens next and then becoming distracted by those other very interesting pieces of information until, finally, it's all a hot mess and, oh crap, their eyes have glazed over... now what do I do now?

This very common set of circumstances leads many new authors to make an absolutely fatal mistake—to jump to the end of the story without taking the time to tell the story. Here, we discover on the very first page that he was dead all along, it was only in his head or those things all happen to her in the future, not in the past!

Yet, without the story and the context of that story, those endings are completely meaningless. They lose all sense of impact or emotion. They fail to haunt us or bring us back for more. However, the fear of losing audience members to reader fatigue is so overpowering many fall back on simply giving information, rather than weaving a gripping story.

We are so used to writing for quick and concise, the most important aspect of storytelling gets lost—we need to tell the story, step by step, word by word, event by event. This is known as breadcrumbing.

The way around reader fatigue is to ensure that every breadcrumb is placed in a way that grips the audience, holding their attention and compelling them to seek out the next breadcrumb. This introduces us to the rhythm of the story, which is another vital aspect of storytelling. Then we need to shift the tone and alter the melody of the rhythm to create surprise and wonder for our readers. You get the theme here?

Without understanding the multifaceted craft of storytelling, the wisdom and expertise you have to share will literally become dumbed-down to the level of your narrative skills.

Lazy storytelling, where authors make things happen just for the sake of a sale or bolt on stories just to pay lip service to the latest trend, will actually damage your brand. If you have ever witnessed an Uwe Boll movie, you will know what I mean!

You have worked hard to achieve everything you have professionally and personally. The magnitude of your wisdom is not only what you know, but who you are as a person. Why devalue your knowledge, your life or yourself by not presenting your expertise as a storyteller?

Ask yourself how much an hour of your time is worth?

Is it just the spending of a particular hour with a client? Does this include all the hours you have invested in learning, gaining professional experience, making mistakes and rectifying them (or not)? Have you accounted for the successes and the failures, the pains and expenses, the breakthroughs and the unique perspective only you have?

Is an hour of your time worth just an hour? Or is every hour of your life valued at the sum of all your life?

Many extremely experienced professionals take a lifetime to know what they know. They invest years into being the best in their field, the go-to authority. Then they devalue their expertise by making excuses when it comes to writing the book.

They moan about not having the time or not caring if the book is actually read. Some even naysay about the value of writing a book in a way that echoes businesspeople of the nineties who, when asked about their online presence would reply, "The inter-what? No, that'll never take off!"

For, when you match your level of polish in professional leadership with authoring mastery, you can match the time and effort you have already invested with the quality and transformational impact of the telling.

Here we shall explore how information provides the scope, anecdotes cause emotion and the storyteller's craft presents a journey. This journey meanders through the building of a lasting relationship between you and your reader.

There are three elements of writing a book: information, anecdote, story. If we use the analogy of a meal, the information would be the meat; the vegetables, the anecdote; and the story would be the preparation, seasoning, presentation, as well as the actual experience of eating the meal.

Before working in depth with this section, you will need a foundation manuscript for your book—one that focuses on the information and anecdote. This is a living document that you will sculpt, expand and refine over time.

When it comes to storyselling, you want to develop your ability to write narrative at ever-increasing levels of length and scale, as well as depth of emotion.

You are not only writing more, but also bringing together a wider collection of themes. Integrating them with a greater level of cohesion and understandability, whilst impacting the reader with real feeling.

Storyselling is about organic growth in every aspect, developing a narrative, increasing the value of the information contained within and enhancing your own skills as an author.

As you complete your foundation manuscript, you will have created a document that is now ready to be used as the basis for your finished book—a magnetic and rich source that will connect you back into ideas and inspire you to wondrous heights of expression.

Your foundation manuscript could be based upon a previous attempt at writing a book, a compilation of notes and brainstorming or you may have worked through a strategic process to achieve your completed foundation.

The foundation manuscript needs to achieve a significant number of contrasting aims, so the better this foundation, the stronger and longer-lasting your finished title will be. What you require is a foundation document that:

- Presents an overview of the results you intend your readers to obtain and the paradigm you have originated to achieve this
- Is a complete working document of everything you wish to include, when considering information and supporting anecdotal evidence/illustrations
- Divides into coherent, relevant and self-contained chapters, which progress naturally from one to the next
- Contains anecdotes that are thrilling, dramatic or humorous— or connected to powerful events in history
- Discusses initial thoughts around your author voice and brand, as well as focuses upon your specific audience (avoid demographics and focus on the needs of the individual or psychographics)
- Identifies how the book sits within a wider media content ecosystem and what this ecosystem will be, how it is experienced/delivered, etc.

Once you have your foundation manuscript completed, it is time to begin work on the storytelling and selling of your document, into a fully-realised book. Stripped back to the basic framework, this process consists of seven steps...

- Devise an overall story arc
- Plot the basic framework
- Refine your voice and how your audience will best respond to this voice
- Clarify the audience proposition at every stage of your book

- Write and revisit your first chapter several times
- Write your rough draft
- Refine/Plus your draft into a first complete draft

Adventuring further through the narrative landscape to come, you will have the opportunity to explore these seven steps in much more detail. You will also discover how master storysellers approach these different aspects of creating narrative and how they ensure the production of the most compelling and profitable media content.

For now, however, let us take an overview approach to the first few steps of turning your foundation manuscript into a completed editorial manuscript. Having a rudimentary idea of how you intend to progress the overall writing of your book will help build momentum, whilst creating valuable authoring habits.

Devising the overall story arc of your book will give you a rough idea of how the narrative will unfold from the beginning of your piece to the end. This could be a time frame and characterisation or more in-depth breakdown of the events that take place within the story.

As part of this exercise, identify the most gripping, funny or profound anecdotes from your foundation manuscript and mark these as important to use near the beginning of your book.

From your cursory notes, you will then be able to plot the framework of your story, linking specific events to the chapters you have developed in your foundation manuscript. Here, you can connect particular circumstance and situations to the anecdotes and information you want to present to your audience.

You will need to decide upon a two- or three-act format for your book (there are other ways of dividing narrative, but these work best). A two-act story will contain a turning point halfway through the story. This is when you turn everything on its head so that all that has come before is somehow different or new.

A three-act piece could contain a trio of sections, each building on the last. This could focus on why, what and how, or beginning, intermediate and advanced, etc. Somewhere between the middle and end of the second act you will also include a turning point that changes everything, ramping up the tension.

With regards to tension (or humour in some cases), you will need to continually undulate the emotional experience for your audience. Building tension, then releasing the tension, to form peaks and troughs. As the book progresses, the peaks must become higher than the last, the troughs deeper.

The next step revolves around your narrative voice. Which voice will be most authentic to you and how will your readers resonate with that voice? Much of this process is related to the context and content of your book, however, knowing whether you need to be authoritative, friendly or argumentative, etc. will help you determine the voice you need.

An important distinction, when considering your voice, is to remain authentic to yourself, without getting stuck in being totally accurate about past details. There are three people involved in every book: the author, the character they play in the book and who they *really are* in their daily lives. The latter does not exist in the narrative world; only the narrator and the narrative.

Many authors are so focused on getting every detail *exactly as it was*, they lose the engagement of the reader. Never sacrifice your audience experience for the sake of somebody who is not involved in the telling. The role of a good author is to keep reader engagement at any cost; even if it means skipping details or tweaking certain anecdotal events.

It is important to fact-check and to ensure that you remain truthful to the essence of a story. However, keep a distinct and uncrossable line between that person who washes dishes and goes to the supermarket, and the narrator.

To help you hone your authoring voice, we shall explore a little later, various narrative archetypes that will help you choose the right voice for your particular story. In order to decide upon the best voice, you will need to know who your audience is, what they respond to, what their needs are and how to excite them into engaging with your narrative.

When it comes to your first chapter, you will need a powerful and engaging opening that raises the reader's heart rate. This will lead into an emotional reaction that you can tailor, depending on your story. The most important thing is an increase in the heartbeat per minute. This will immerse them quickly into your narrative.

The first chapter must also contain *The Magnet*. This is the emotional stimulation or magnetic pull that will get your reader to the end of the book—the reasons for reading the book. This is usually expressed through emotional benefits, pleasures and pains. The greater your explanation of the value in your book, the more compulsion the reader will feel to turn the page.

In the first chapter and in relation to your overall arc, you need to decide whether you are going to top and tail the information in the book with anecdote and story, weave it throughout, or use some other form of integration between the three layers of narrative.

It is also important to breadcrumb your narrative. Many new or inexperienced authors want to get the story out as quickly as they can. They rush to give all the details and every grain of wisdom.

Yet, the most gripping narrative is drip-fed to the audience, weaving and meandering as it goes. When the reader understands they are in for the long haul, they not only relax into the story, they begin to trust you as the storyteller.

Upon completion of your first chapter, go back and reread it several times. Add new information and hone the text until you are absolutely enthralled with the work you have produced. Only at this point should you progress to the rest of your manuscript, because knowing how to achieve your best work will assist you in writing your best work first time!

When you have completed your first draft, go back and revisit each chapter, refining and polishing it until completely satisfied. Remember to be really strict with yourself over proofing and editorial correctness. Your publisher will insist upon a professional quality manuscript!

Also, invest time in getting to know the intermediate and advanced techniques from this journey until they are second nature. Then introduce them into your manuscript as you revise and sculpt it.

This very basic overview of the process will give you a taste of what you need to do. With this in mind, let us delve deeper into the craft of writing a book and how to make it the best you possibly can.

Creating Your World

Many influential commentators and experts in modern entrepreneurial and business approaches discuss the value and often, essential need for writing a book to grow your business. Often presented as the tech-age business card, your book introduces you to prospective clients and the world in general.

The similarity ends here however, because a book not only claims your niche and enables you to micro-niche your way to a successful business, it encourages a relationship between you and your audience.

The disposable book or business-card-book mentality, advocated by some book coaches, often leads business owners to view their book as something that will never be read and does not matter beyond the appearance of authority it provides them!

This ethos will saturate the writing of the book and those who tread that path will never achieve greatness, never pioneer original thought and never be a true authority in their field. They are not authors. They are data-input, corner-cutting charlatans who do not believe you—or any client—is worth the effort.

They can waste three weeks on writing a book that acts as a business card, but would you honestly give your money to a businessperson who wastes three weeks on designing a business card, so they can fleece you into thinking they are an expert?

Your book is a benchmark for the quality and professionalism of your business—it demonstrates not only what you do, but why you do it and how you do it. More importantly, your book nurtures a trusting relationship with your audience.

Your book is a measure of your values: of how determined you are to achieve the best results for your audience. Your book will outlast the moments it took to write it—an indelible inscription in time that will never go away. It is the standard you will be judged by, not only by your contemporaries, but also those yet to come.

Your book is your epitaph. You can give your audience statistics and clichés or you can, through the impact you have upon their lives, demonstrate the values by which you lived.

Business cards are introductions—relationship initiators not relationship builders—and most people hold onto the business cards they collect until they get around to filing them in the bin! If they cannot be bothered to act upon your business cards, why would they read your book?

Throwing together a book with the same effort as it takes to design a quality business card will overwhelm your audience with information, disengage them and essentially unsell any potential deal you may have had with them. No, a book has the opportunity to be so much more in their lives.

Knowing that you need at least fifty hours of media interaction with each audience member (preferably 200 hours), you seek to create media content that fills this time with active engagement.

By investing time in reading your book, engaging with it and putting it into practice, your readers will have this length of time and more in your company. They will get to know you and believe in your ability to help them. In short, you will have an impact on them and in their lives that will stay with them, long after they have turned the final page.

Whilst most will tell you that business cards are virtually obsolete (just another whisper in a world full of content noise) and that your book is the starting point for building your business, they do not mention that writing your book is merely the beginning of an exciting and very powerful journey for your clients.

When you position your book in an expanded world or ecosystem of products, you not only grow your business, you are actually creating a completely new, time-multiplication business. This expands out of your existing business, but is a discrete business in its own right.

Writing one book can seem like an immense challenge when you have yet to place a single word on the page; developing a whole range of titles may seem impossible. Nevertheless, constructing an ecosystem is actually easier than you may think—and by carefully considering your entire product range at the planning stage you can actually negate the need for endless duplication of effort later.

Through leveraging one set of content into various products and widgetising one product into a series, you can develop a vast range of titles in a short period of time. Thus, applying an initial investment of time and effort into building your world can result in an ever-growing and diversifying business.

You now have in your hands a living organism—your foundation manuscript—for your first book and the ecosystem of products to follow. It is a

powerful framework for the creation of an entire business empire of content-related products. What you choose to do with that document now is the difference that separates you from other business owners.

With a little polishing and expansion on the topics, most would now be ready to publish their basic document. What you have created to this point is what most businesspeople-turned-authors believe to be the book that will transform their company.

Yet this is little more value than a quick search online. This modern business card is nothing more than a basic marketing tool that tells the reader this author does not have much to say and is rather boring in the presentation.

Even when anecdotes are added to illustrate a context for the information to perch on, these are written as more information.

So, there's this person and they read online that cheap slats were just as good as brand names, but their friend, who was an architect, said that would never work, because the slats were too wonky. So, the first person ended up going to their local supermarket and had a real shock when they realised how much non-wonky slats cost!

Your book is a foundation to an entire world of media content. This world is not built with slats (wonky or otherwise) and it is not built upon information, because that is the domain of Google. Your ecosystem is constructed of products that offer real-world, definable value. Every single piece of content you create is a product and must be treated as such.

To construct an entire product range that becomes a business in its own right, there are several improvements your document now needs to go through. This begins with clarification, enhancement and testing of your system.

You may have conducted business in your field for twenty years and in that time you will have formed connections, identified patterns and established a seemingly intuitive ability to navigate your profession. The moment you convert all of that wisdom into your own unique system, the need for extensive research and testing arrives.

As with any system, the basic components act in a specific way (or series of ways). But how does adding another component or altering the relationship between components affect the whole system?

You work with clients using an established methodology and know from years of experience they are likely to react in specific ways. However, when you begin using your unique system that is based upon your knowledge, your expertise and your story—well who can say what will happen!?

This testing process may seem like a lot of work, but here is the incredible side effect of this testing process: by creating a new system, you have a new product and your established audience will be hungry for it. So, run a pilot programme and fund the creation of your product range!

When I personally create a new methodology and want to develop a year-long transmedia training programme to deliver accredited qualification in that system, I run pilot and pre-launch programmes aimed exclusively at my existing audience members.

Through experience, I know building content ecosystems can take months of resource-intensive work. However, by funding the process with these one-off and never-to-be-repeated programmes, I not only pay for my time, but I also cover the initial setup costs for printed material, etc.

This also enables me to conduct further research on my new system and test how both the methodology and training are received. This feedback offers me a whole other level of refinement and polishing, before the book ever hits Amazon.

Once you have the blueprint for your unique, branded system, you are ready to present this methodology through your foundation manuscript in a clear, concise way. This will take your document from a random and vast collection of brainstormed data into a cohesive, quick-reference guide or roadmap.

To be a credible authority in your field, you will need those infamous anecdotes to underpin and explore each piece of information you present to your audience. These are not only the experiences from your life and career, but also (if you are delivering a pilot programme) the case studies, feedback and quirky little stories from your test audience.

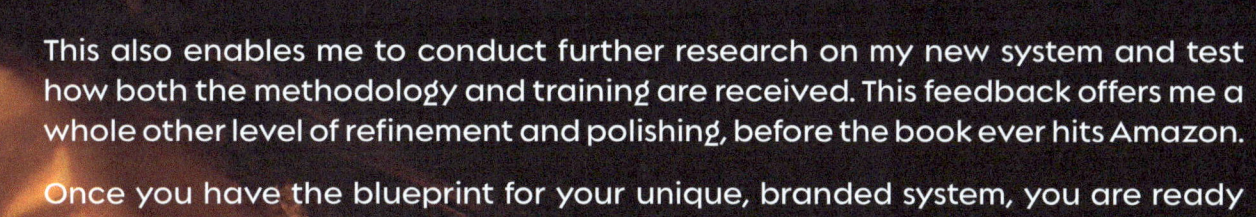

With the inclusion of illustrative anecdotes, it is time to sculpt your living document into a full ecosystem of content, which includes the complete marketing and social media strategy, live events, big-ticket products and continuity products. Each aspect of the ecosystem needs to be grown organically and exquisitely designed.

Simply bolting each section onto the next, will not create a seamless journey for your audience, so you must extrapolate detail to leverage further content and summarise content to form promotional products. You will also require the development of themes that can be changed and adapted to widgetise your products.

Each of these regions of the development process is vast and requires you to push yourself further into the creative process than you have been before. Not just because it involves the creation of titles, but also because you need to master every aspect of the eight-step *Compass* system.

Only when you sculpt each aspect of the system will you be designing, with volition and foresight, products that truly possess quality, value and magnetism for your audience. Building an ecosystem involves a blended process—creating a cohesive world of content.

So, with this in mind, you need to revisit your document on Brand, Audience and Proposition. Reflect on who you are and what it is that you want to share with your audience.

Think about how you are going to present this to them and how you want them to perceive you. Get inside that communication and attain a deep appreciation for how the person you are can develop the voice that will best speak to those people.

Explore the depth of the relationship you want to form with them, how you want to affect their mood and behaviour. Be honest about your needs and how you can fulfil your own goals, by offering value to your audience. Then expand that into the journey they will take with you, product by product, learning curve by learning curve.

With this in mind, start to write the anecdotes from your own experiences which most powerfully illustrate the information in your living document. You may have memories and incidences that you can recount or maybe a piece of information needs some other form of anecdote, such as a hypothetical description, an image, graphic or even a fictional account that brings the information to life.

It is possible to start and end each chapter with anecdotal elements or story theming, although avoid at all costs the emotion-by-association approach many advocate. Triggering an emotion to sell an unconnected or tenuously-linked product creates distrust. And will not have the same power as layers of anecdote and story that weave throughout each chapter.

By integrating relevant and intriguing stories within every chapter and enveloping each nugget of wisdom you want to share, you build relationship through your message, your values and your vision. Whether it be textual narrative, imagery and design elements or even transmedia threads, you seek to take the audience into your broader ecosystem of media products through compelling story, not emotional extortion.

An Attractive Voice

A way of pinpointing the most effective and fitting anecdotes comes with a more complex appreciation for the attractive voice (and how audiences respond to this).

There is a series of attractive voice archetypes that will offer guidelines for you to follow. Getting a sense of which voice you resonate with and how you can employ this voice will help you filter your anecdotal narrative.

The attractive voice archetypes are:

- The Secretive Hag
- The Powerful Master
- The Reluctant Hero
- The Beautiful Chalice
- The Benevolent Donor
- The Provocative Villain/Antihero
- The Wise Oracle
- The Plucky Adventurer

Before we explore each of these voices in greater detail, there is a question that must be asked about anecdotes and the voice we use to relate them to our readers. This question is about authenticity and whether we are being disingenuous when using an attractive voice.

Many businesspeople function on being absolutely transparent about themselves and their professional ethos. When they come to writing their book, they will frequently get so bogged down in the detail of *telling the truth,* they overwhelm or disengage the audience.

So how do you use an attractive voice to communicate your experiences, whilst maintaining a clear, genuine presentation of who you are?

Whenever you are authoring a book, YouTube channel, digital ecosystem, blog or other title that involves your life experiences, be it in a business or professional context, educational materials and so on, you are actually three different people.

Firstly, you are you. The person that you are by yourself, with loved one, friends and work colleagues, etc. Then you are the author. The one doing the writing and who facilitates a two-way communication with your readers. Finally, you are the character that is the subject of your reminiscence or anecdote.

This third person is not who you are or ever were; it never can be.

Your book, content or media ecosystem is about presentation, not imitation—you are not attempting to mimic the person you were, but demonstrate how your wisdom can impact your reader now.

Focusing on the accuracy of every event, foible and detail from a past anecdote is not telling the truth! Firstly, it is lying to yourself about how your memories are not distorted in the making and secondly, those events in those circumstances are contextual.

Let us imagine that you are writing about a life-changing experience from your past... attempting to write as the person you were *before that event* will always be impossible. You now write from the perspective of the person you became—that's why it is called *life-changing*!

Plus, at that time you acted in relation to that situation—not in the way of somebody being observed by an audience of thousands of people! No more than you are behaving that way right now whilst reading this book... if you were being watched by thousands of people would you be doing what you are doing?

Well, as soon as there is any acknowledgement of them, you would not, because you'd be acknowledging your audience, not reading a book!

Each memory and anecdote is present in the writing to act as a receptacle for the information given: revealing to your reader how they can get the best from what you have to say, to help them avoid making the same mistakes as you, and to deeply affect your audience in a profound, inspiring, sometimes devastating way.

Who you truly are is who you are. Who you present to the world is a character that communicates a message to those listening. The author is the one who orchestrates the effectiveness of that message and filters actual events in such a way that they are of the most value to your audience.

A person may have thirty years of experience in their field, that is a fact. However, they may choose to present that as an authority—I have thirty years of experience so you need to listen to me and do what I tell you! Or they could be a fellow adventurer—as I share my experiences, I cannot wait to see what benefits you get from them.

Your delivery through the voice you write (or present in) will affect your storyselling in immeasurable ways. A fantastic tip is to begin with a dramatic moment and then jump back to the information.

The habit of everyday communication is to be linear:

"I was going to the supermarket. I needed to pick up a few non-wonky slats. it was a miserable day. It was raining, and the roads were wet. Then this car mounts the pavement..."

The storyselling method would use a voice that presents in a different way:

"I felt my arm crunch against the bonnet of the car and I thought to myself, this cannot be it! I can't die here, in the rain whilst doing the weekly shop! How boring is that for my epitaph?"

The fact is you were never in danger of dying. The car just bumped your arm as it bounced off the kerb and back into the road. But you want to engage your reader, so you bring in a thought that somebody might really think in that situation.

The attractive voice is not about distorting the truth. It is about acknowledging how your audience will get the most value and then expressing your anecdotes in that voice. The voice you choose will greatly change the way you write, but the most essential aspect of your writing is the message you want to convey:

"It took 1.7 seconds from the moment the car left the tarmac to the point it ricocheted back into the road. It was just 1.7 seconds—that is all it took. Those 1.7 seconds changed my life..."

Was the author really using a stopwatch? No, of course not! Yet, the number 1.7 could be important, as a foreshadowing of the brevity of time, as a sticky meme or as an actual number of significance the reader needs to remember.

This voice is more analytic; it presents through numbers. However, the voice is using a mundane number to describe something very powerful. There is a vast array of voices you could use, although we could group these into eight *archetype* voices.

Each of these voices were identified by Vladimir Propp, who based his hypothesis on the common voices used in folklore and fairy tales. Whilst each archetype has a generalised perspective from which the narrative plays out, there are many nuances and complexities within each overall type of voice.

The Secretive Hag

The Secretive Hag is the voice that is wise and knowing, but will often disguise what makes the author powerful behind another persona. This could be humour, a humble or self-deprecating nature or some other diversionary tactic.

The hag demonstrates their wisdom through action or incident, rather than making it an explicit statement at any point in the writing. They use the setting, circumstance or interactions to reveal the power, rather than ego.

This is an excellent voice if you feel shy about detailing your accomplishments and want a gentler way of describing what you have achieved or if you are in a field where mentioning your success could be viewed as egotism or self-gratification. The value will still permeate your finished narrative, but in a really unassuming way.

The challenge here is that many readers may completely miss the power of your experience and voice. They are unable or unwilling to see beyond the veneer, to the depth and profundity of your knowledge.

Often the hag is not recognised or respected—readers may form the belief that they know better, especially if they are very strong-willed. The confident corporate reader or highly egocentric audience are unlikely to respond well to the hag. Think about *Beauty and the Beast*—the prince did not see the hag who begged for his help and paid the price!

The hag is the most powerful of all narrative voices, but you absolutely need to know your audience and their ability to recognise what exists beyond the surface.

The Powerful Master

The Powerful Master is the best voice to use when you want to demonstrate authority in your field. If it is important that your readers appreciate your standing in your particular profession the Powerful Master voice is the best choice.

This is particularly important if your industry is regulated or if there is a reason why your qualification/expertise is needed to train others. Maybe you are writing products that have accreditation and it is important that people do not go out and practise what they have learnt from only reading your book or until they have achieved some form of certification.

And so on.

This voice exudes authority and knowledge, whilst being forthright about what to do and what not to do. Here, you will write in a direct and directive form, without the option of reader choice.

You will stress things, not as opinion or feeling, but as it is. You are the one with the knowledge and this is your arena. Those who visit here will only respect you if you command them with skill and true leadership. We are so familiar with *ifs, what ifs, maybes* or *could bes*, we regularly dilute our voice of mastery—so be forthright, because it is not a question of *if*, but *when*; there is no *could be* about it... only *is*!

The challenge for the Powerful Master is that of arrogance—you will be seen by many as self-centred, narcissistic and authoritarian, but there are many audiences who need this and will respond well to the master approach. The Powerful Master is akin to Merlin in Arthurian Legend. Benevolent, powerful and wise—yet with flaws in the eyes of some.

The Reluctant Hero

The Reluctant Hero never wanted to be on this journey, but now they have found themselves upon this particular path, they embrace it and want to share it with their audience.

The most frequent reason for using this voice is to present a person who, in the past, has been through some form of trauma. This could be an illness of some form, a challenging life situation or something that people in similar circumstances are affected by for the rest of their lives.

You did not choose to experience what you did; it was painful and damaging, but something within you got you through it and, now you have come to the other side, you want to support others on their journey.

The reluctance always stems from what has occurred previously and not from current activities—they are driven by the past and how it sculpted them into the person they are now. This approach needs to be presented with great enthusiasm and passion or your audience will focus on the dirge and not the inspiring message which came after.

This provides the greatest challenge with the reluctant hero—their fallibility can make them seem weak in the eyes of a less empathic or sympathetic reader. If your audience are more cerebral or intellectual, avoid this voice. The more emotional, passionate and altruistic your audience, the better they will respond to triumph over adversity.

In terms of pop culture, a wonderful example of the reluctant hero voice is that of Dorothy in *The Wizard of Oz*—she just wants to go home, but ends up transforming a world and saving the lives of her newfound friends.

The Beautiful Chalice

The Beautiful Chalice is the rewarding voice; one that is constantly reminding the reader of benefits and what they can achieve. To this extent, the voice is not necessarily associated with you as a person, but is more symbolic or even ethereal in nature. So, this is not *I will reward you*, but *You will be rewarded if you....*

The Chalice offers great riches, health and well-being, love or some other desired thing; while all authors need to offer benefits or magnets to their audience, the Chalice voice only speaks in this way.

Whilst the Powerful Master will educate in their authority and the benefits that come with listening to them, the Chalice voice only explores the benefits of a subject, rather than focusing on why you are the person to write about it.

So, maybe your product ecosystem concentrates on an area that is not regulated or on fairly common information and you simply want to spread the word, etc. If you do not have many years under your belt, are promoting somebody else's system or want to keep the focus on benefits, this is a great voice.

The challenge with this voice is the promises will appear to many as hollow, unsubstantiated or too good to be true! As many authors overuse this voice, the fatigue it carries as baggage is often best avoided completely... just spare a moment to think about the Golden Goose and what eventuality befell that poor creature!

The Benevolent Donor

The Benevolent Donor also speaks in rewards, however, in this situation, the voice initiates a journey, rather than focusing on the end destination. The most common form of Donor is the author who explains, "If you do this for me, I will do this for you..." In exchange for the audience's time, money or effort, they will be given something in return.

The ideal voice for a franchise or pyramid-based company owner or a service provider who does the job for their audience. A very powerful way of employing this voice is when the author explains what they do and why it needs to be done.

They then use a description of how it is done to overwhelm the reader; placing them in a position where they are more likely to want somebody else to do the *how* for them! Of course, the key word here is *benevolent*—you are not seeking to exploit your audience, but to genuinely help them achieve the best results for them.

This voice can be challenging as it attracts people who do not want to do the work. They seek magic wands and kind benefactors who take the pain away by magic. If you need a successful client to actually do something to achieve results, this can be a tricky voice for a proactive audience.

The Lord of the Rings trilogy involves a quest to save the world, where Frodo Baggins must take the fabled *One Ring to Rule them All* to Mount Doom and destroy it. In this instance, it is Gandalf the Grey who act as the Benevolent Donor voice: the one who sets the quest and spells out both the challenges and the rewards.

The Provocative Villain/Antihero

The Provocative Villain or Antihero will present the opposite of what is actually happening or provoke unwanted experiences in their audience. Here you will expose, go against the grain, rebel and generally do the unexpected thing—say what people do not want to hear.

This may seem counterintuitive at first, but there are audiences that respond better to this approach, rather than to an author that constantly acquiesces to what is *right*. Some of us are simply wired to go against the grain—this can seem contrary in nature, but is how we actually achieve *different*.

If the audience you identified has extreme views, is highly (or better still, absolutely) sceptical or contains a high percentage of teenagers, then this may be the best voice for you to use.

However, be utterly sure that your readers will resonate with the Villain/Antihero before plumping for this voice. If you misjudge their receptivity, it could be a disaster for your brand or attract the audience you really do not want!

The pragmatism of this approach can be off-putting for all, except the most pessimistic audiences. Those who get the most from the Antihero are often fixed upon how bad things are or how everything turns to crap in the end. Anybody who is not of this mindset will find this voice rather distasteful.

The Riddick movies possess the quintessential antihero; a serial-murderer and escaped felon who is somewhat psychotic. Yet he is the voice of reason and eventual hero in a universe that makes him seem positively delightful!

The Wise Oracle

This gentle voice is soft and nurturing, it engages the reader through enduring messages that spark little emotional hits of feeling good. Woven through each passage is a guiding, benevolent, comforting voice that assures and reassures with the depth and scope of knowledge the author has.

Like the Chalice, this voice is almost disembodied or universal in nature—in other words, the author's only distinct feature is the wisdom they present and that wisdom speaks louder than the author as a person.

The Wise Oracle offers answers and solutions at every turn, but more than this, it is a voice that speaks so in tune with the reader that it is as if the author knows the reader better than they know themselves.

The Oracle whispers truths so profound that they become an authority on the subject without ever justifying themselves. Rather than telling the audience that the author knows his or her stuff, the wisdom demonstrates this by itself.

A major challenge with this voice is it can appear disembodied or divorced from the reality of your book and the world. This creates disconnect for the reader—yes, that is all very good in theory, but in practice...

This disconnect between the reality and proposed results is a mistake almost all business authors make. They rectify this for those with a similar perspective or outlook to their own, but when it comes to readers with a contrasting approach, they fail to make the connection.

Cohesion between what you promise and what the readers feel they can achieve with your guidance is imperative to your writing success! Just as the three witches in Macbeth foretold: a magnificent future awaits thee, but with the clicking of our thumbs we three shalt not sayeth the best road by which to travel there!

The Plucky Adventurer

This cheery personality is a very popular voice, as it evokes the sense that the author is journeying with the reader, experiencing the narrative as it happens. It is a sharing voice, rather than an authoritative voice—here, the author is an equal to their audience.

As the journey unfolds, the adventurer will express their joy and wonder, their fear and anxiety, as the reader feels those same emotions. The learning and transformation comes with the friendship and rapport that is built between these two travellers, you and I.

In the appropriate circumstances this approach can yield wonderful results and a long-lasting relationship between an author and their readers. It will feel like a relationship, rather than simply reading a book.

Beware, however, as this voice can in some contexts diminish the value of your authority, knowledge and experience. Your audience may interpret the *we* as a sign that you are in the same situation as they are and why would they want to listen to that?

Conversely, some authors find when using this voice that readers become too familiar and value the relationship more than the content contained within the products. When you are a peer, a colleague and friend, your readers may stop getting value from your message as an authority and start haemorrhaging that value by putting you onto a pedestal (and not necessarily in an appropriate way!).

When used with a fitting audience, however, the adventurer will create some of the most rewarding advocacies we could hope for. Who did not shed a tear for David, the naïve robot in the movie *A.I. Artificial Intelligence*?

As we travelled with him through being forced to love a person who could never love him back, facing rejection and then being thrown into a dark, abusive and dangerous journey in the hope of finding his reality, we were reminded of our own lives and journey.

When you have decided upon an attractive voice for your book, think about compelling anecdotes from your life. Are these funny, dramatic or profound in some way? The greater the engagement your anecdotes create, the better!

How do your anecdotes illustrate the information in your foundation manuscript? Are there similarities between an anecdote and the learning you want to present to your reader? Perhaps you learnt a valuable lesson in that situation, one you wish to share? Or perhaps the anecdote is a metaphor for the information you are offering?

Adapt previously noted anecdotes if you need to, as well as adding new memories that support the information in your document. Write these down using the attractive voice of your choosing. If you are still unsure of which voice to use, try each voice that you share an affinity with and discover which one comes most naturally to you.

After you have written at least one, though ideally two or three for each chapter, begin to rewrite a summary of each chapter, using your anecdotes to communicate the relevant information that you want to present.

As you are writing, you may find new anecdotes come to mind and if so, make a note of these for inclusion in your living document. Remember to stay focused, however, as this stage of the writing can lead you down many a tangent!

Your document will now be well-formed and contain an enormous repository of information. As you sculpt and refine the content of each chapter even further it will become the roadmap which helps you navigate during the storyselling aspect of the development process.

Imagine you are journeying into the unknown. Without points of reference it is very easy to get lost! This region is uncharted, so there are no maps, other than the map you create for yourself. As a pioneer in your own field, professional methodology and media content ecosystem, your foundation manuscript will keep you on the path, as you tell a wild, imaginative and audience-addicting story!

This is also a great juncture to start forging the beginnings of your foundation marketing content—a YouTube channel, a blog and even put out the word you are available for podcast interviews, etc.

You will need to develop a comprehensive strategy around this, but even at this early stage, you can be creating an excited buzz with your existing clients, whilst attracting new potential advocates to your ecosystem.

It is very important to remember that your ecosystem is not merely about a range of individual products. There are many other aspects that need to be a part of the creation process, which include your content marketing strategy, blogs, articles and so on.

These are not separate from your books, courses, events—they flow into each other so that you may reiterate and reemphasise the core information you are sharing.

Depending on how many chapters you have, identify twenty-one sections from your living document. These could be a whole chapter summary or a portion of a chapter (if you have more than twenty-one chapters, combine the content from two or more chapters).

Once you have chosen which content you are going to use, write a self-contained blog post for each content piece (twenty-one separate blogs in total). In these blogs, you are aiming to summarise the information through anecdote or supportive narrative, whilst adding greater depth and scope to the piece.

You may choose to write a blog a day for twenty-one days or to create several over a few days. But at the end of three weeks, if not sooner, you will have your cornerstone of content.

As you write your blogs, why not try different voices to discover the ease of writing for each?

It's Not a Book—It's YOUR World!
(and more than this,
it's THE Game-changer for Your Audience)

Understanding that a baseline relationship takes fifty hours to curate, you are seeking to create at least this timeframe of interaction with each audience member. Taking the relationship to a deeper level of trust involves 90 hours—and lasting advocacy is at least 200 hours of regular interaction between your audience member and your media.

From bestselling book series to blockbuster movie franchises and even the most subscribed YouTube channels, the ethos is the same. Each are formed from individual pieces of media content (a book, movie or video upload). Yet, it is the world-building that differentiates temporary interest from lasting (ever-growing) success.

Transforming a stand-alone chunk of media into a fully-realised, cohesive and nuanced world of media products is the art twenty-first century businesses strive towards. Yet, this *world* will still be an impossible distance away from achieving its goal unless a third factor is present.

The media ecosystem must also be a game-changer for each audience member—interrupting their current patterns of behaviour, making them take note and then changing their perspective with irrevocable consequences. And these consequences must be of real value to the audience member.

All the juggernaut franchises began with a single book, comic or movie. Every multi-million-dollar channel on video streaming services was born from the first upload. The media product was merely the first step, which at some point became a regular feature in the lives of those taking the journey.

Each audience member was invited into and immersed within the world: the books, movies, videos and other media became something that made a real difference to the reader or viewer. This *difference* is the measure of the relationship between a content developer and their audience.

So, next time you hear businesspeople mentioning their creating a book-as-a-business-card or Vimeo-channel-as-a-marketing-tool, remember they are expecting to embark on a round-the-world journey by taking a single step!

One of video streaming's greatest success stories is that of Shane Dawson, an American YouTuber who started out making content on conspiracy theories. Over the years, Shane adapted his media content into world-building by developing multiple themes of content. These changed with the needs and wants of his audience, whilst bringing them into his arena and life-brand.

When Shane came out as bisexual to his audience, his popularity grew sharply and now, with frequent collaborations and regular uploads, Shane has a channel that explores everything from urban legends and supernatural investigations to self-referential *I cloned myself, adopted a baby, sold my underwear on eBay* videos.

The *Shane* channel on YouTube continues to get more and more meta with commentaries on the YouTuber phenomena and self-parodying content that continually reinvents Shane to the tune of tens of millions of subscribers.

Shane's ethos of constant evolution and reinvention worked initially to sell ideals. It then grew into selling a personal brand and now is a thriving business in its own right—A one-person (that is not just one person) broadcasting and merch company that is the benchmark for any aspiring YouTuber.

When it comes to media-ecosystems or world-building, understanding and delivering your ethos is essential. Knowing your audience, what they think their needs are, what their real needs are and how to fulfil these is vital.

Many organisations struggle with their ethos, relying on an outdated or obsolete perspective. However, there are several major brands (undisputed leaders in their industries) who have cracked a storyselling approach very successfully.

These companies use storyselling and their own, unique methodology to create ecosystems: product ranges that span different forms of media and exist in a world of their company's creation.

Adobe's Transmedia Ethos

Adobe are best known in the field of design and media for products such as Photoshop. Their approach to content is somewhat meta, because it focuses on the customer's need to fulfil their own client's needs.

They achieve this through immersion—immersing an audience within a multi-channel ecosystem. From the perspective of storyselling, the power of Adobe's ethos exists in the way they approach content and content creation.

In a multifaceted experience of media, where every piece is discrete and yet, integrated with every other piece, the Adobe platform enables us to make media of different forms in a seamless range of apps and software packages.

Adobe's mission is to enable you, as a content creator and business owner, to build a journey for your audience which attracts them, engages them with your content in some way, then inspires and helps them to the point where they trust you.

According to Adobe, you do this by aiming for the highest available life values for your clients. Rather than offering simple changes or *life-hacks*, your strategy needs to be one of transformation. Put simply, to enable-engage-transform.

The story, according to Adobe, connects a basic visceral reaction to a piece of content and then inspires the audience to be the best they can be. This is important, for when an audience member takes this journey for themselves, their relationship with you will forever be associated with the changes they make.

By making your clients into winners, they become your champions. And by ensuring customer satisfaction, you will achieve loyalty and eventually advocacy from your audience. As you facilitate their success more and more, the deeper the relationship between you will become and the longer it will last.

As with any modern business, we do seek the one-off purchase or hard-earned sale. We also aim to develop a lasting relationship, where sales are the frequent, regular and easy-to-obtain by-product of the partnership.

Here, the demarcation blurs between your business and your clients as you create an augmented reality where your products blend experience, action, shopping, platforms, everyday occurrences, perception, inspiration and so on.

As you manage experiences across a complex transmedia ecosystem, you are not only looking to deliver across various channels and devices, such as mobile, social and immersive *environmental* platforms, you are also focused on surveying and gathering data from your clients.

This outside-in approach enables you to appreciate what your clients experience and how best to match their needs. Using Key Performance Indicators, you can produce marketing innovations, such as: being nimble and quick to respond, knowing your clients better, forging intimate consumer-brand relationships and so on.

All this comes with the need to avoid the silo effect—a development of clusters or pockets of advocates that work against each other and ultimately expend energy on contracting your business, rather than expanding it.

The *Star Wars* fan base—who are absolutely passionate supporters of the franchise—became so fervent and vitriolic about the Disney-produced films, they started to damage the brand for audiences in general.

When the critically-acclaimed *The Last Jedi* was released, it was not what the fans were expecting or wanting from their beloved movie series. They were proactive in publicly vilifying the film—such as a misogynist re-editing of the film appearing online, with all the female protagonists edited out of the cut. The backlash became so nasty in tone it endangered production of planned Star Wars films.

Avoiding this requires an understanding of transmedia—the sculpting of an ecosystem from a whole, overarching vision. The habit for many is to lump together a conglomeration of chunks that piece together a construct. Here video, audio, imagery, audience interaction and so on are created in isolation and then placed in a group.

Adobe's platform is designed to see all media through a filter of interrelation. Here, a world is built around the audience and every expression of the world in media form is essentially connected to every other.

Apple's Cohesive Ethos

Apple is a rather divisive corporation that polarises people into two positions. On one side, people get frustrated with Apple products, finding them inflexible and controlling. They are often rather vocal with their disdain, which is voiced at every available opportunity.

On the other side, brand advocates pore over every keynote, spend hours in the Apple Store and cherish their iPhones, MacBooks and iMacs like one might love a pet or child!

An aspect of the Apple ethos, which exists at the centre of this polarisation is the organisation's knowledge of ecosystem. No large company, with the exception of Disney, appreciates the concept of ecosystem quite like Apple does.

Many other corporate enterprises attempt to emulate the Apple ethos, but they have a tendency to focus on the outward results or *symptoms* of ecosystem, rather than achieving the core philosophy.

It is this failure to truly appreciate the ethos that causes onlookers on the outside to be so vehemently opposed, whilst those immersed in the ecosystem enjoy not having to put up with all that pesky *other stuff*. The *stuff* Apple exclude from their walled-garden.

Whether or not you advocate Apple's products and services, once you apply the Apple ethos to the creation of your content, you will discover something very powerful. This is not simply how ecosystem envelops the client experience, it is how the polarisation of people's attitudes in very definite ways gives strength to your brand.

Their walled-garden ecosystem divides the world into inside or outside depending on whether they have made a purchase or not. With the philosophy that by building great products, people will buy them at a premium price, Apple strive to make something that people will love.

They also want to limit the experience of using the device you have purchased to a controlled environment. Inside that environment you will have a very specific range of very useful interaction with the device, but attempt to do something that is not in that environment and you will simply not be able to.

For those who have previously used a non-Apple product, such as an Android phone or a Windows PC, they find this lack of cooperation absolutely infuriating. However, those who want to use the product, without needing to know anything about the technical stuff behind the scenes, cherish the ease and simplicity of being inside the ecosystem.

From the ease of syncing between devices to the security of tested apps, even the software and services of Apple contribute to the ecosystem in a carefully thought-out strategy. Yet, these are all symptoms of ecosystem, not the root ethos that is so important.

Commentators that analyse the Apple ecosystem tend to focus on the iTunes and App stores, along with iCloud in more recent years. Nonetheless, the Apple idea of ecosystem goes way beyond the services and virtual experience: it is a seamless transition between hardware, software, user and their environment.

Here, the ecosystem bends around a user's thumb so that a device can be completely controlled with a single digit. Then it aesthetically flows and shifts to match the smoothness of the sleek design. It presents every piece of music, each book you read, every tool you create with, and it converts some of the satisfaction, joy and love you have for that piece of media to itself.

The gradient of each curve on an iPhone or iMac, matches precisely the gradient of columns and handrails in an Apple Store—the macro and micro combine to give a sense of familiarity. Each product box is designed to open slowly, so the new advocate feels a sense of magical awe with the reveal of their shiny new piece of tech.

A child that is entranced by a paperback book, will always associate that book, its cover and pages with the author and the experience of that book. A child reading the same book on an iPad,

will surrogate the device as the originator of that experience and love the device more, rather than the book itself.

Hence, developing a piece of tech that plays music is one thing, creating a music service where you can store, sort and buy music creates an intrinsic link between device, service and content.

Every song that is stored within the service, sorted onto a playlist and played onto the device will create a greater attachment to the device, or even more accurately the company that constructed the device.

There comes a point where service/app, hardware/tech and third-party content creators all meld into one single, cohesive ecosystem that is the Apple brand. When people become enamoured with one Apple product, no matter how inexpensive or insignificant it seems, they become accustomed to purchasing from that brand and they are more likely to trust it. After just seven hours of playing somebody else's music!

An iPod, leads to an iPhone, to an iPad, to an iMac and so on. Each product expands the ecosystem and is held together by a software wrapper—a wrapper that delivers content created by other people.

It is easy to mistake this approach as a sales funnel, where bigger-ticket items create a step-by-step selling voyage for a client. The ecosystem ethos is different—it focuses on the sales. Apple focuses on the relationship—and the advocacy that comes with that relationship.

If you create products that are delightful and enchanting, products that offer real value to customers, those products will sell.

Furthermore, when you view Apple's evolving policies of employer brand and their activities in equity for employees on a global basis, you see the extent of their ecosystem. It is not distinct between products/services, business operations and clients. They are all part of the same universe.

Apple knows it is not perfect, but it strives to be better with an ethos that says, "This is what an Apple advocate believes, feels and cares about." If you buy Apple, then you buy into the ideals that are inherent in the ecosystem.

Elon Musk's Big Vision Ethos

The colonisation of Mars may seem the main arc of a science fiction movie, but it is the grand vision of Elon Musk, CEO of *Tesla* and *SpaceX*. Like other businesses with storyselling at their core, both Tesla and SpaceX present their grand design, not as the immediate reality, but as slow burn, breadcrumbed narratives.

From solar panels to cars, Hyperloop to space travel, the visionary attitude of Musk's enterprises demonstrate how businesses can monetise their story of products before they are even created.

Tesla created billions of dollars in pre-sales for its Model 3 car, whilst the vehicle was still in the final design stages. The ability to self-fund the design and creation process is a key benefit of the storyselling approach. The idea of something, the potential of it, can be so profound in the narrative that people will buy into the dream before it becomes a reality.

The Tesla story is not simply about cars, however. The company is revolutionising both the automotive and energy industries. Through solar panels and revolutionary batteries, Tesla presents a brand that is intent on changing the world.

Behind every magnificent story is a bigger picture, a higher purpose or game-changing vision. This is the uncharted territory that nobody else has ventured through and that only you can weave into reality. The grander the design and the greater the impact it has on your audience the more successful it will be.

Tesla sought to change the world and with each model of car, improved battery design or solar panel with increased efficiency, they did change the world in tangible ways. This was not simply a question of improved metrics. All car manufacturers can demonstrate how their cars were better than any other brand.

No, Tesla was led by a person whose sights were fixed on an overwhelming, overarching vision. And although many sniggered at Elon Musk's apparent hubris when it came to his extraterrestrial plans, the story became ever more possible with the development of SpaceX.

The numbers about a car's performance may be tempting, but the narrative of owning a car that is associated with the colonisation of another planet? That transports our minds further than the car itself could ever take us, perhaps.

For storyselling to transform your business and the hearts and minds of your audience, the vision must have both scope of imagination and real-world achievability. If the plan lacks originality or a strategy that produces quantifiable results, it will never be as effective as it could be for you and your business.

The high-speed transport system, Hyperloop, is Musk's SpaceX project to revolutionise travelling over long distances. The speeds presented and the travel times suggested are startling; again, the realms of science fiction. When added to the mental imagery of tunnels and pod-trains, the concept conjures up the vision of a better future.

As the tests are documented and minor victories catalogued, we the audience start to believe the story—that Hyperloop could be an actual, functioning reality. This same approach to the SpaceX programme also fires our imaginations for what is possible for humankind.

Through every launch, every successful landing, we see the flight of fancy become the flight of a game-changing rocket system. Even the failures, the crashes, explosions and general mayhem feed our imaginations, because we see the determination; the tenacious will that never gives up and continues to drive the programme.

Yet, the story revealed its first masterstroke with the launch of *Starman*—a mannequin driving a *Tesla Roadster* into space. Launched within the Heavy Falcon mission towards Mars, suddenly the many story themes were tied together. The rockets, the cars and the single step closer towards living on another planet—all the narrative arcs, subplots and characters came together to give us video of a little plastic man in a car, rocketing through the darkness of space.

Each time the massive blue orb of our Earth was reflected in the paintwork of the Tesla Roadster we could not look away. As the darkness of space was suddenly snatched away by the awe-inspiring sight of our home, acting as backdrop—the secondary player—to the star of the show, the power of storytelling was revealed in ways that no marketing letter, sales pitch or brand metrics could ever hope to offer.

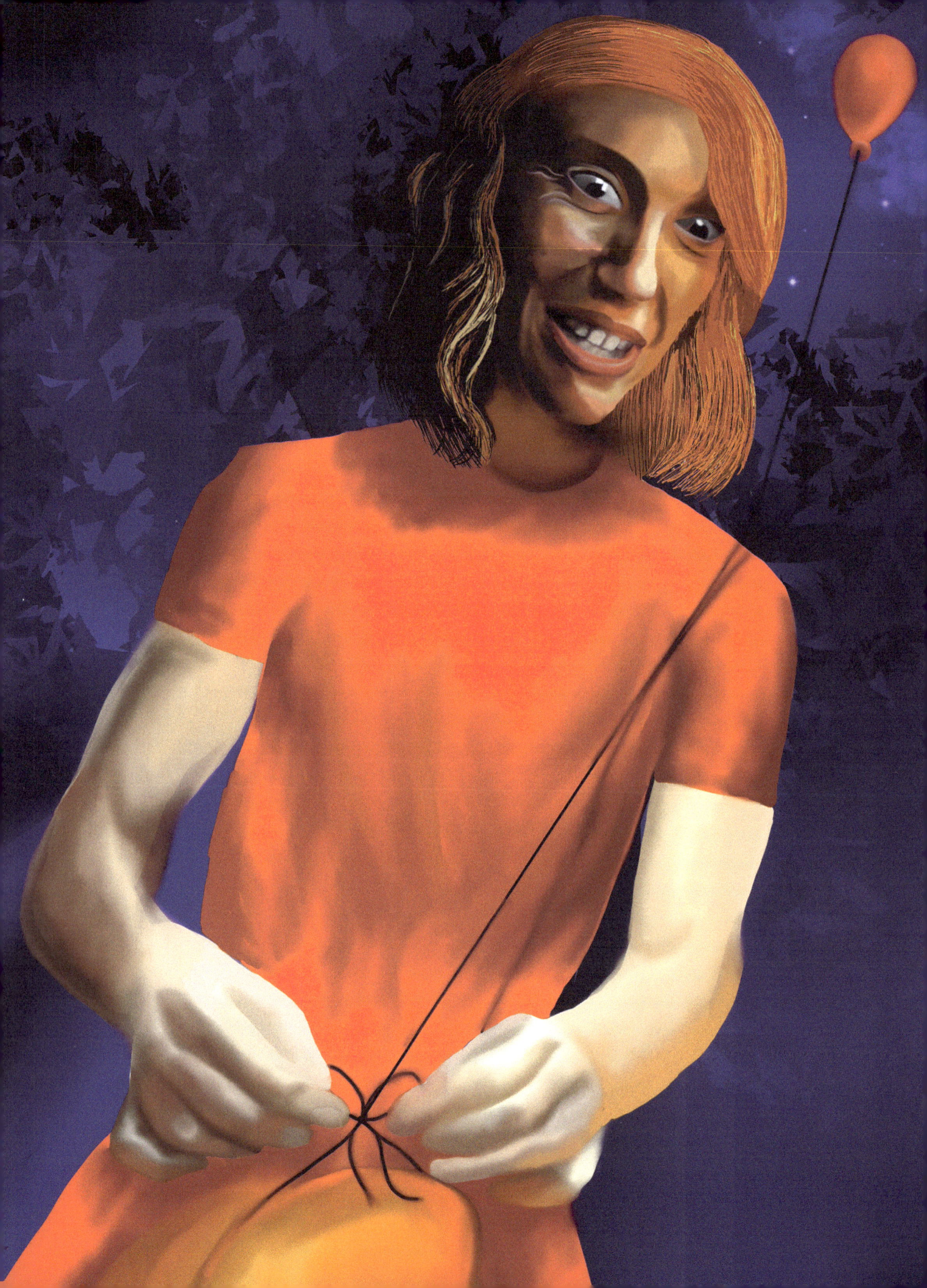

Netflix's Redefining Ethos

The approach of Netflix towards storytelling and storyselling transformed the media world from the old broadcast approach which attracted a mainstream audience, to a specific, tailored platform that redefined the mainstream audience.

With narratives that many would see as minority or agenda focused, Netflix not only did something different in their storyselling; they refused to even acknowledge the old way of entertaining people. They are so effective at creating engaging and addictive shows, they have developed algorithms that hook audiences into binge-watching an entire series in a matter of hours.

As a subscription service, the aim of Netflix is to attract, sell and keep subscribers to the platform. To that end the organisation invests billions of dollars each year in new and existing content. *Netflix Original* series and movies have become synonymous with a very different approach to theme and subject matter that other media companies are desperate to emulate.

As such, Netflix is not simply on the leading-edge of media—a pioneer in the provision of media consumption—they are literally informing us on what we want to watch!

Gone are the days of the audience deciding on what they like or dislike—according to Netflix, we do not really understand what we like until we have watched the latest Netflix Original content.

The platform is so successful, it has taken to acquiring major film properties from studios such as *Paramount*. Unsure of box office success with titles such as *The Cloverfield Paradox* and *Annihilation*, Paramount sold the worldwide rights to Netflix.

This tempered the risk of losing money on problematic films, whilst providing Netflix with several cinematic-quality titles that audiences may not have ventured to movie theatres for, but were hungry to devour at home.

As storytellers in their content, Netflix storyselling is derived from the magic formula approach—they know how to enthral you in ways you did not even know you enjoyed. Content that would once be resigned to cult status attracts a mainstream audience, time and time again.

This consistency is not down to a veneer of *diverse fringe*, hiding a heart of mainstream culture—the shows *are* truly different.

The storyselling works by genuinely engaging us in the narrative, whilst offering us a unique experience. The techniques used in every Netflix production, to addict the viewer, create *mainstream*—one audience member at a time.

There is a vital understanding within the Netflix ethos that is often missed. It is easy to do what others are doing and wrap it up in something new. Every day we get regurgitated information, dressed up with a new acronym or ten-point plan.

To storysell in an effective way you absolutely *must* be different—you must stand out from everybody else. Standing out is three things: the dominion of true leaders, very easy to misinterpret and when done authentically, the most frightening thing you will ever do.

And if you are not unlearning everything you know, shaking loose every shackle and reference point—if this process does not make you quake with terror, you're not truly doing it!

Disney's Storyselling Ethos

Story, story, story. When it comes to engaging, compelling content that haunts the reader long after they have come into contact with it, none are more adept at developing story than Disney.

Where Apple demonstrates the core strategies of ecosystem and Adobe offers us insights into transmedia delivery of our content, when it comes to storytelling, Disney are beyond anybody else.

Disney turn fairy dust into a multi-billion-dollar enterprise each and every year. And whilst Mickey Mouse may encounter flak most of the time from the media and general populous, Disney's ability to convert so many franchises into staggering, income-engineering juggernauts is astounding.

Just focusing on their movie franchises, Disney have, in recent years, transformed both the Marvel and Star Wars universes into money-making machines, despite the aforementioned controversies.

Yet, rather than vacuous pits of profit, Disney understand that simply taking people's hard-earned cash and giving nothing is hardly a long-term strategy. So, for every dollar exchanged for product, Disney invest years of time in strategy, creation and perfecting each title.

They bring in the best creative teams and pay immense attention to every minute detail. They believe that if you create something wonderful, you turn customers into clients into advocates. Advocates will support your business no matter what.

At the very core of the Disney ethos is one simple thing: story!

Lift the lid on Disney's strategy and we see how the framework—or basic premise—of each idea is wrapped in layer upon layer of story until it is completely unrecognisable from the core premise.

Then you take the same basic workings and wrap them up differently to create something that offers a very different experience, from a foundation that is basically the same.

The leveraging of content and widgetising of attractions is achieved through the most important element of Disney's ethos—storytelling. At the heart of the storytelling process are the Disney imagineers. So named because they use imagination and engineering skills to dream up the impossible and then make it real.

If you want to understand how you can take your basic information and anecdotal content and turn it into an entire ecosystem of complex and interrelated products, you need look no further than the storytelling techniques of Disney.

Blue Sky - Brainstorming and concept design

Concept Development - ideas fleshed out and further developed

Architecture - concepts transition from design to reality

Models - development of scale models

Construction - physical construction and fabrication, test and adjust

This five-tiered foundation for dreaming up amazing titles, products and services, then turning them into realities, will offer you a means of presenting your business expertise with an equal level of authoring mastery. When you can weave a story like you can a business success, you will magnetise advocates to your business with an ecosystem of content-related products.

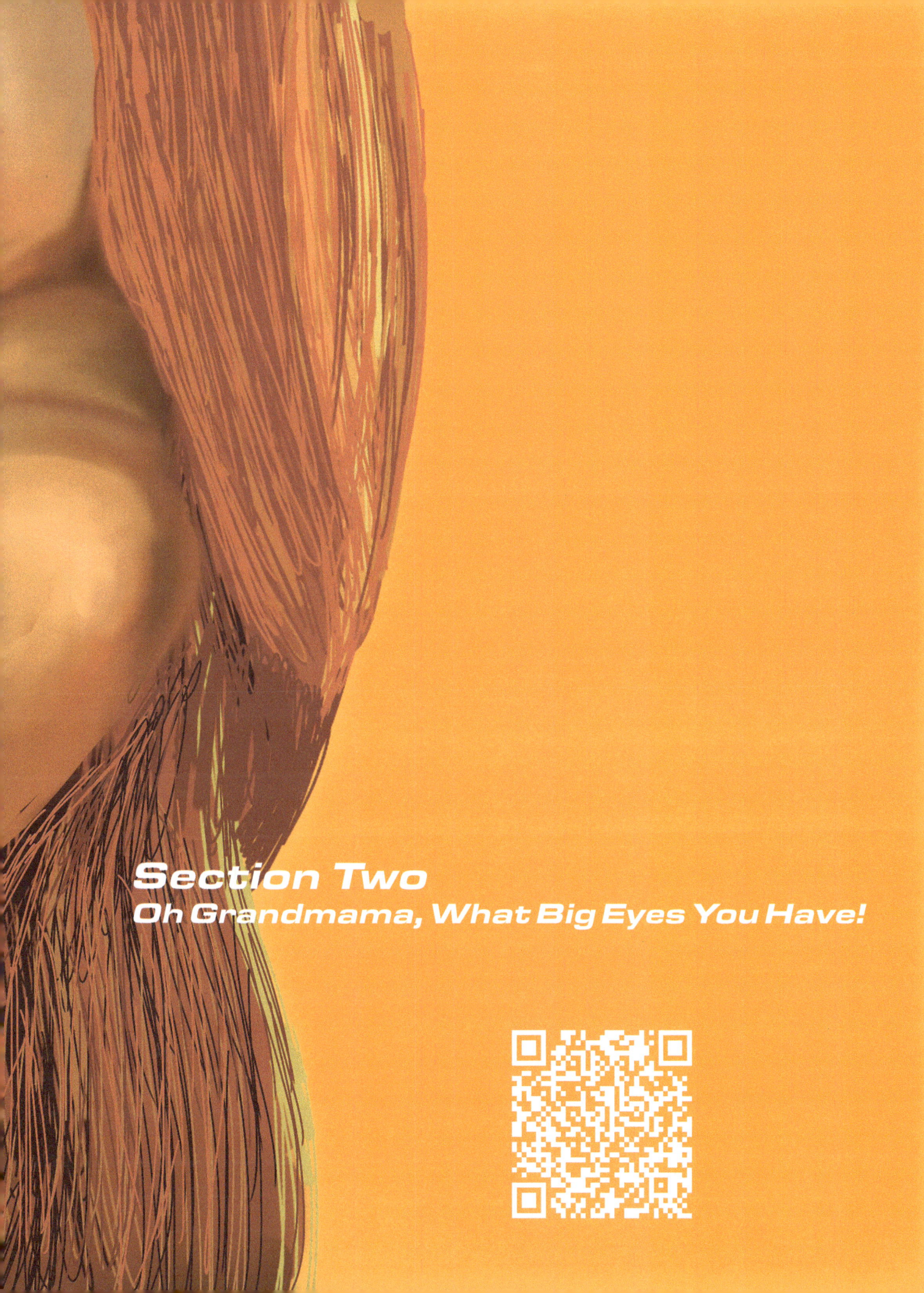

Section Two
Oh Grandmama, What Big Eyes You Have!

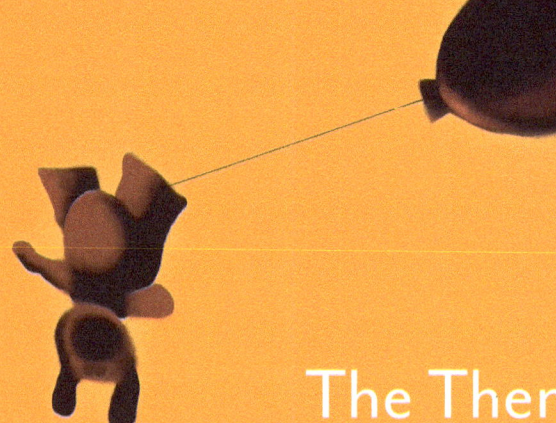

The Themes of Storyselling

Every book needs a theme or themes which act as a vehicle, transporting your audience from where they are to where they want (or need) to be. This vehicle is fuelled by emotion—their emotion—and cannot be, simply more information.

Whenever you give information about a specific thing, you activate a frame in the minds of your audience members. That frame contains the thing you mention. Selling your product by telling your audience there was this guy, who was middle-aged and lived in Borneo is just another frame of information to retain—information that detracts and dilutes the important information you want to give!

Chances are, rather than thinking of your product, audience members will be imagining the man of their dreams, worrying about getting older or thinking about orangutans! To effectively sell your product or service, you create a world and drive your audience through that world using the vehicle of theming (powered by emotion).

The British food retailer (and advocate for 1970's housewifery), *Iceland*, created an advertising campaign in conjunction with Greenpeace. It shows an animated baby orangutan displaced into a child's bedroom when the terrified creature's habitat is destroyed by men (some of whom could be middle-aged) deforesting in preparation for a palm oil plantation.

At no point are Iceland's products shown, but instead their message about striving to be palm oil free creates an emotional response with the audience. They are roused into alignment with the company and thus, more likely to shop there in the future.

When it comes to the themes you employ in your storyselling media, it is essential to have a strategic and creative effect on the real-world experience of your audience. So many attempts by businesses to present their products and services fall short. By slapping a story over the top of your product, you negate what you are selling in favour of the story.

The story's themes need to form alignment with the audience, so they position themselves in a buying position through a sense of kinship or community—in other words, trust.

The common, overused and bland approach employed by most businesspeople when authoring their book or developing other media products is to create thinly-veiled marketing materials and disguise these with a few anecdotal illustrations. These are just more information frames for the audience to inhabit, instead of genuinely caring about your message.

The frames you activate in your reader's or viewer's mind are windows into worlds—you need to be sure those worlds are of your creation. As every page in your book, video on your Vimeo channel and podcast in your audio collection is a gateway into your world, they need to align with the frames of your audience to fully-engage and offer unhindered access.

People within your audience will engage with your products in contrasting ways: they will respond differently and have their own individual motivations. Taking this into consideration when you write will ensure you broaden your niche market to encompass as many people (in that niche) as you can.

Keeping the scope of your niche as broad as possible is important—retaining your niche is also vital. Too many authors attempt to target large audiences or write for everybody. To be truly remarkable, you need *Marmite*, not bland!

How you deliver to your audience is an essential part of knowing how to get the most out of your product range and how you can achieve the most value for them. Understanding the nature of plot development and using this to *drip-feed* your information and anecdotes is vital to keep their interest.

Just as the purpose of your book and other forms of media is not to dump information upon your reader, it is absolutely not to tell them on the first page how to solve all their issues!

First, they need to remember what they think the problem is. Then you need to explain what the real problem is—the problem they did not know they had, but as an authority in your field, you are completely aware of. Finally, they need to know why this is such a major, business-threatening, life-diminishing challenge. Only then are they ready for the answers of how to solve their problems with your help.

The author needs to be a master of secrets and timely reveals. Placing each gem of information in an engaging, compelling and neatly-packaged thematic arc before their audience.

This endeavour is not designed to solve the audience member's problems, but to highlight what they think the problem is, explain what the REAL problem is and then detail in heart-wrenching ways, why this has such a devastating effect on the lives of the audience member.

In every moment of life, every one of us is hardwired to be solving the eternal and universal mystery of *what comes next*. Stories are and always have been the art of unwrapping what comes next. So, when your products, services, business, brand or ideals help people to contextualise and solve this mystery they will align with you.

Alleviating fears and worries, providing hope and excitement, stopping people in their tracks, breaking their patterns and disrupting their worldview—all elements of story.

And using stories to inspire emotion, authority and inspiration, you will be more than just another author—you will be the one who helped them change their life.

You will also find some of the covert storytelling tools useful as part of your repertoire. Knowing how memory, repetition and plot layering affect your reader will help you in the delivery of your information.

These and various other themes will help you storysell your products in extraordinary ways. More than this, they will help you to increase the impact you have and the value you offer.

And where better to explore themes than in a theme park...

The Narrative Landscape of Your Storyselling

By design or by default, each book has a narrative landscape. This landscape is the overall sculpture of the narrative from the first page, to the last, and it consists of two layers—the author voice you choose to present your narrative and your audience's reaction to your narrative.

Whilst these two aspects of the landscape exist in a fine balance, rather like two sides of a coin, they are very different from one another. Your voice as the world-building architect and thematic, storytelling vehicle that explores that world. And the audience's reaction, which creates a momentum that is fuelled by emotional tension and release.

In her Netflix special, *Nanette*, comedian Hannah Gadsby creates a stand-up comedy event of three acts. In which she explores how humour is the art of two acts—the building of tension in the telling of a joke and the release of tension through a punchline. These two layers of the comedic craft, Hannah explains, are missing the essential third act of storytelling...

And, after two acts of jokes and expected humour, the punchlines ebb away and we are propelled to the heartbreaking conclusion of how we use humour to give comfort to others.

mPowr Towrs

RESORT AND SPA

How we make them tense, with the intent of releasing that tension and triggering a shot of dopamine as a sign that all is right in the world. We hold up our pain, our sexuality, our gender, our mental illness, our deepest, hardest and coldest moments for the world to buy into and then laugh at for their own sense of well-being.

Then Hannah returns to the building of the tension, which was previously released thanks to a series of punchlines—and she gives the ending to her story. Now, what we were laughing at just a few minutes prior, becomes a tableau of the horrors of human behaviour. The hate, the abuse and the icy truth that make it okay for the perpetrators to *get away* with these atrocities (because the victim makes a joke of it), is not acceptable.

In her finale, Hannah starves us of punchlines—waiting, for the release that never comes. And in doing so, leaves the stage with an audience in tears and uncomfortable bewilderment.

Yet Hannah also offers us a profound insight into the art of storytelling—emotional tension, humour and finally heartbreak. Or, when we look a little deeper—emotional connection, intellectual realisation and eventually an integral, overwhelming sense of inspiration.

In the *mPowr Towrs Resort and Spa,* we shall adventure through the architecture of your narrative landscape from planning and strategising—exploring the actual writing and enhancement of what you have written.

As you sculpt layer upon layer of depth, scope and longevity into your book, you create a world for your reader to explore, learn and gain pleasure from in unknowable ways.

So, when you are ready, let us take a deep breath and enter through the gates, with a very warm—*Welcome to the Park...*

Discover Your Authoring Ethos

There are essentially four methods of authoring: through using your imagination, talking to other people, exploring your senses and writing by numbers. Depending on your individual personality, you will resonate with (and get better results from) one or possibly two of these approaches.

Focusing on one (or blending two of these approaches) will profoundly affect the method you use to plan your book, develop a video platform or author some other media product.

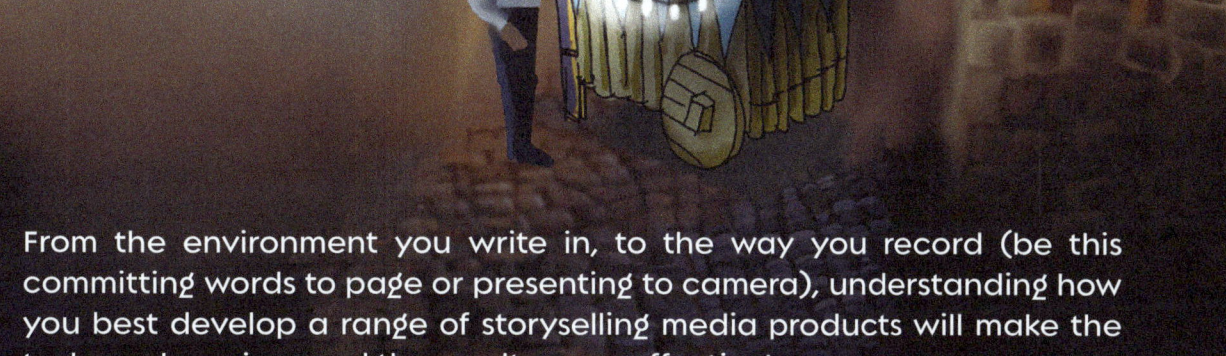

From the environment you write in, to the way you record (be this committing words to page or presenting to camera), understanding how you best develop a range of storyselling media products will make the task much easier... and the results more effective!

When it comes to book writing, our stereotypical image of an author is of someone shut away from the world, hurriedly typing away in front of a screen and summoning up words as they type. However, this method will only work if you are fundamentally creative by nature and can tap into your imagination in a very specific way.

If your feet tend to be on the ground or you prefer real-world experiences, rather than imaginary, if you are very social or (somewhat surprisingly) exceptionally introverted, the standard view of authoring will not yield the best results for you.

For you, another approach will enable you to write a better book and to discover greater pleasure in doing so. Using The Compass—the eight profiles that symbolise different behaviours or dynamics—you will be able to define what style of authoring to use when working through the following sections.

If you are very artistic in nature, you will want to experiment creatively and find your flow—this can involve other forms of artistic expression too, such as artwork and digital design,

The more social you are, the greater the need to involve others in the creation of your work. For example, you may test your thoughts on trusted friends and associates, because this will help you reconcile your idea and clarify your process. You may also want to include more video or interaction in your ecosystem.

Authors who tend towards a need for tangibility or real-world pragmatism can find pulling ideas or concepts *out of the air* challenging. So, focusing on what you know and creating your own perspective of the tried and tested will enable you to feel more authentic as an author.

The introverted author often prefers developing a very defined strategy they can complete step by step, whilst for somebody who is analytically minded, detailed instructions are often the most conducive way forward.

So, let us begin with a series of questions, each of which is colour coded. Without thinking too much about your answers, simply tick each answer that you answer *yes* to.

Red

Do you consider yourself to be artistic or imaginative?

Can you shut yourself away for hours on a creative task?

Do you have so many ideas that you could not develop all of them?

Do you have trouble finishing things?

Do you dislike doing the same thing over and over again?

Do you work through things and find answers through creative means?

Orange

Do you like to be centre stage?

Do you find it difficult to read lengthy reports?

Do you get excited by being the centre of attention?

Do you have a pretty clear idea of who you are?

Would you say you have a dynamic personality?

Do you like to inspire large groups of people with your message?

Yellow

Do you enjoy the company of other people more than being alone?

If you have an issue, do you like to talk this through with people?

Do you love networking and entertaining?

Do you find it easier to speak in person, rather than writing emails?

Are you a loyal person?

Do you enjoy inspiring others in a team environment?

Green

Do you relish a good bargain?

Do you prefer to speak one-to-one rather than to large groups?

Do you like to know what's going on around you?

Do you like to make deals?

Do you make connections in random things?

Would you prefer a quick win over a long-term investment?

Turquoise

Do you enjoy being of service to others?

Do you feel happier with the tried and trusted path?

Do you prefer what you can hold in your hand over fantasy?

Do you look to what you know, over what you can imagine?

Are you generally busy and running around?

Do you prefer facts over blue-sky thinking?

Cyan

Do you really enjoy working with data and spreadsheets?

Are you able to go over and over large amounts of data easily?

Do you notice spelling mistakes or errors in data all the time?

Do you want bullet points, more than the anecdote?

Are you better at activities when you have time to prepare?

Do you hate getting things wrong?

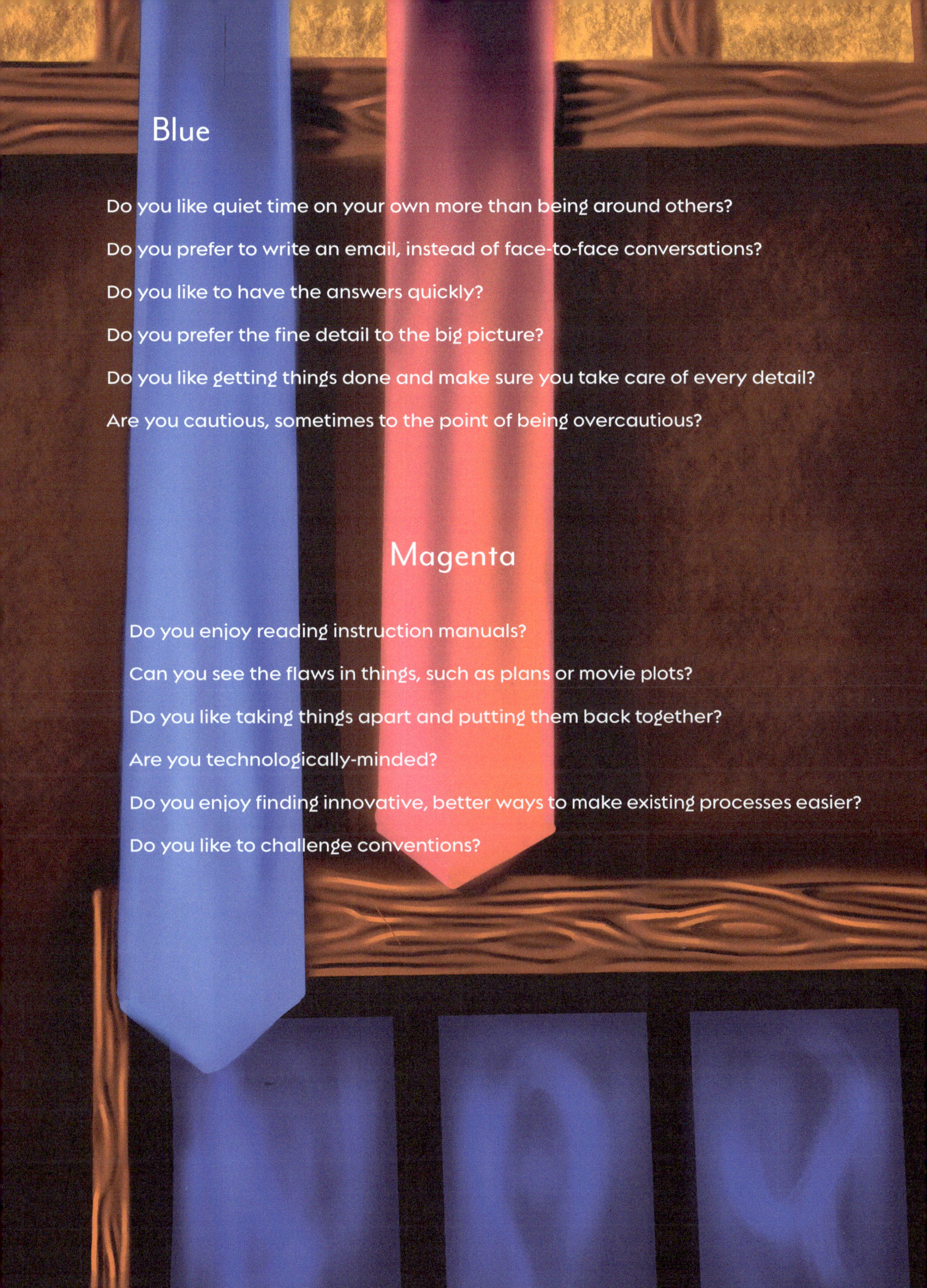

Blue

Do you like quiet time on your own more than being around others?

Do you prefer to write an email, instead of face-to-face conversations?

Do you like to have the answers quickly?

Do you prefer the fine detail to the big picture?

Do you like getting things done and make sure you take care of every detail?

Are you cautious, sometimes to the point of being overcautious?

Magenta

Do you enjoy reading instruction manuals?

Can you see the flaws in things, such as plans or movie plots?

Do you like taking things apart and putting them back together?

Are you technologically-minded?

Do you enjoy finding innovative, better ways to make existing processes easier?

Do you like to challenge conventions?

Now look at which group of questions contain the most ticks.

You may find that you have ticked a lot of questions in two or three neighbouring colour groups. If this is true for you, work with both groups to start with and find which works best for you. Alternatively pick the middle group where there are three possibilities.

If your selections appear to be completely random or widely distributed, ask yourself if you are more extroverted

Orange, Yellow and Green

or tend towards introversion

Cyan, Blue and Magenta.

If you are an ambivert (a mixture of both introvert and extrovert depending on context), you are either

Red

(highly imaginative and pioneering)

or

Turquoise

(prefer what you can hold in your hand, rather than what you cannot see).

As we explore the theme park, look out for notices that highlight advice for the different colour groups. These will help you work with the different tools and techniques in a way that best suits your own ethos.

Each tactic in our development process needs a different set of skills and if you attempt to approach every skill as it is written, you may come across challenges that disrupt your flow or throw you off task.

Some techniques will complement your own ethos, some will contrast and others will conflict with your way of taking action. Adapting the techniques in various ways, to match your skill set and ethos, will keep you immersed in the process of development and help you to finish your initial book and future projects.

Sometimes this will mean minor adaptations and at other times there will be alternative routes to complete that element in the creation process. You may have already discovered this in the creation of your living document!

For some people, this activity of information gathering, sorting and refinement is mind-numbing and for others it is an exciting, fascinating venture. As we develop more sophisticated ways of presenting your content, you will need to test your own abilities and expand your authoring skills. If you can do this in your own ethos, you will thrive as an author and content creator.

The Compass

Before you launch into the actual writing of your book and subsequent creation of your complete product range, there are some strategic aspects of your writing that will prove totally invaluable in the long-term development of your project.

As we enter the theme park, the first attraction we encounter is a colourful Ferris wheel that rotates guests around the high circle at a steady, measured pace. Here they can soak up the awe-inspiring panorama of the entire park and beyond as they peacefully glide around and around.

The attractive colour palette of the gondolas and plinky-plonk music of this ride present a rather misleading appearance, because whilst this big wheel is seemingly cinnamon-coated tranquillity at its finest, this Ferris wheel is actually 360 degrees of visceral terror!

Yes, this particular ride of cotton-candy death will have grown men cat-clasping the caged walls and primal screaming in a frenzied display of snot-bubbles, whilst the rest of the family laugh hysterically and film the scene with their mobile devices, ready for swift dispatch to YouTube.

The perfectly designed feat of engineering is designed to feel rickety and unsafe. Its minimal wire gondolas and a clever, yet innocuous pivot system were intentionally created to make the occupants feel as if they are going to plummet to certain oblivion at any moment!

Many who skip gleefully into the metal claws of this monstrosity never revisit a second time. Not because they were ever in any actual danger, but because they experienced something so traumatic that it caused an absolute aversion to anything vaguely circular from that juncture onwards.

Once you have wandered into the park a little further, you look back at the Ferris wheel and notice that on the side which faces into the park is a giant compass design. The letters NESW twinkle against the complementary-hued background and you realise just how well-thought-out strategy and design can achieve the most powerful results.

Those who think The Compass is going to be an easy ride are usually those who end up failing hard on social media, in networking, presentations and beyond. However, once you understand the structure behind The Compass, it will revolutionise the way you create your book, product range and business.

The Compass Points

The Compass has four primary points of NESW, which represent a purposeful action.

North = The creation of a product (this could be a book, YouTube channel video, CD, digital item and so on). This can also refer to creating a way of doing things in connection to ongoing development.

West = The creation of an ongoing paradigm (ownership of past results and designing a future plan of action based on these outcomes). Your paradigm is the complex, ever-expanding system through which you present your expertise as tools your audience members apply to their own context.

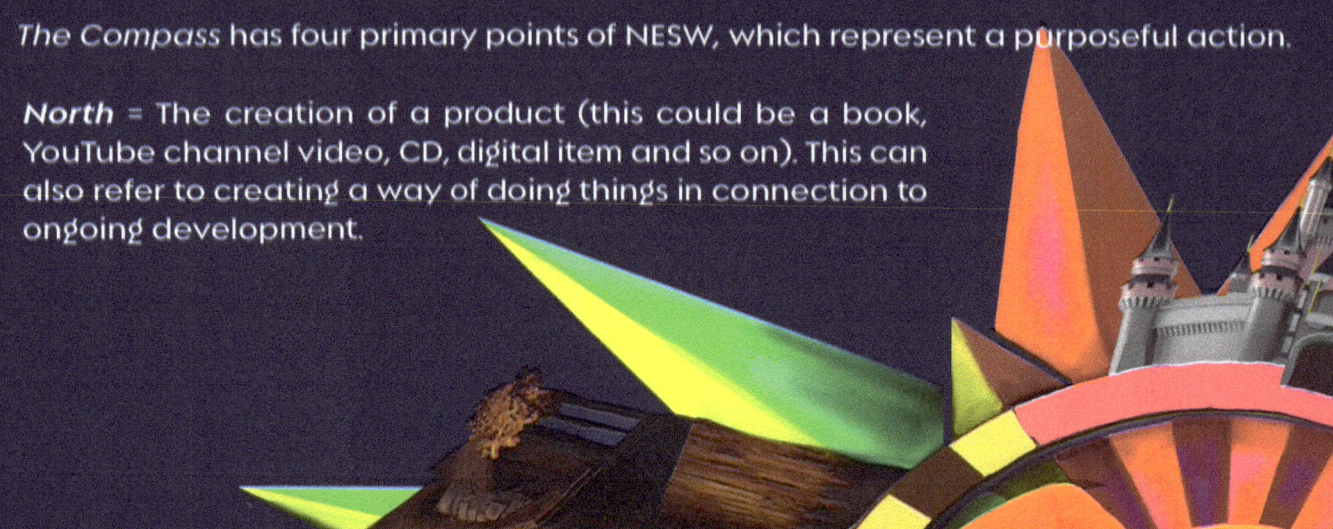

East = The creation of an audience (your readers, clients, advocates, etc.). The focus here is on the people you want professional relationships with—not demographics or market sectors, but people, individual people.

To maximise the degree of success you achieve overall, it is important to travel in a clockwise direction around The Compass. To transition from one point to the next, we need a mode of transport. There are different needs that enable a smooth journey around the four points of the circle.

These needs are:

North-East = To get from the north to the east, you need a brand to present yourself, your business, your products/services and your ideals to the world.

South-East = To travel from the east to the south you need a proposition to offer the world some deep, lasting change or transformation.

South-West = Continuing from the south to the west, you will need analytics that quantify everything from sales to the degree of success your products are having for your audience members.

North-West = Finally, the shift from west, back to north, requires improvements that are constantly ensuring a greater quality within your ecosystem and the results it achieves.

South = The creation of a transaction (this refers to the sales results of your audience relationship and other calls to action, such as a mailing list sign-up). Again, focus on the relationship and the products that create a journey for the relationship to evolve through.

When we apply this methodology to your context of writing a book, growing a video channel or developing big-ticket media products, it becomes apparent that before you author anything, you will need to construct a plan of action that will drastically alter the book or other media you thought you were going to create!

Where the instinct may be to copy what you have seen others do, to play it safe or to attempt something different by telling your audience how much you know—it is essential you *go bold*. To do this, you will need a paradigm—your unique system that adapts to the needs of your audience. Your media ecosystem will then become expressions of your paradigm.

While many of your competitors and the other experts of your field will be peddling their ten principles or newest series of acronyms, you are presenting your audience with a paradigm that adapts to their needs, based on who they are and how they experience the world.

Over the course of a single project, we travel around the circle many times; on each rotation we Create, Order, Refine and Expand our project to broader degrees of scope, greater levels of complexity and deeper experiences of value for readers, clients and advocates.

So, the first sweep of the circle involves creating a detailed plan of your paradigm and how this translates into a book and other media. This is only possible when you have a specific and defined audience in mind.

To reach this audience, you will need an author brand. When this brand is implemented into the plan, you will know how to build your audience and then need to initiate some type of transaction with them.

This transition will need a proposition, which is where you place your book in the context of a greater product range or relationship-building journey with your readers—that takes them from prospect to customer, customer to client and client to advocate.

Your proposition will eventually lead to your first transactions, which could be sales or some other form of transaction, such as an exchange of skills, etc. This initiates your client's journey using the product, experiencing the service or other factors, including aftercare and customer service.

At this point you must evaluate the journey so far—the strengths and any weaknesses—acknowledging both as the way forward. When gathering this information, you will also need to collect analytical data and study it. By doing so, you will know which aspects of your media cause the most interest and which are the least attractive to your audience.

Armed with this information, you will know how to widgetise your existing book/products for your current audience; direct your audience towards complementary products and understand whether you need to expand to a different audience by revamping your strategy.

You will also be informed on how to refine your existing product range; increasing client engagement, retention and satisfaction. This approach of ever-increasing detail in your improvement of current media products will ensure that future products are created more effectively first time. The skills you gain in refinement permeate through to your creation process and ensure better quality, as well as faster and easier creation.

To implement every aspect of your plan and create the next cycle of product development, you also need to develop systems or paradigms in the creation process—these will hone your overall results.

The storyselling does not stop with the client, even behind the scenes, a good storyteller will sculpt layers of story that immerse everybody in the business. From the character sculptures which adorn Pixar Studios to the design of Apple Campus. Including staff members and yourself in the web of storyselling will help your client-facing efforts to flourish.

When you better know your creative abilities, brand, audience, proposition, transaction, analytics, ownership (and improve your actions to mirror this knowledge both externally and internally to the organisation), you can create better and more compelling books, media product ranges, magnetic media channels and relationship marketing.

Before diving into the authoring of your media ecosystem, it is advisable to invest a little time in testing your proposition to see if your approach creates transactions (client interaction, relationships and sales). This could be as simple as writing blog posts, articles, etc. and deciding which subjects, tone of writing and mechanisms of publishing get the most transactions (likes, follows, comments and so on).

You may already have a following or audience, in which case, you will have a foundation in what your proposition may be. If you do not yet have a fan base, the focus of your endeavours needs to be audience building through relationship marketing and a core media product, usually a rapport book or an authority book.

These two items will transform you from yet another hungry entrepreneur or business owner looking to make a quick buck and into an expert in your field. This is not necessarily the solution to all your problems, because you will be competing with potentially thousands of other experts in your field.

To truly stand out, you need a unique, branded and completely original paradigm. Something that is your creation—and as the originator, your IP. This can then be storysold into something nobody else has. You are the pioneer, the expert above all other experts, the leader in your field.

The joy of creating your own paradigm and writing your book about this paradigm (within the context of the larger ecosystem) is: nothing you write is wasted! Every paragraph or snippet can be leveraged in some way.

From posting on social media to build your brand and develop an audience, to widgetising your book into a series of products that expand your proposition and increase your transactions, each word possesses potential value for you and your business.

Your starting place in the creative process is, therefore, to revisit your foundation manuscript and to use this as a basis for writing, posting and testing online. Continued analysis and honing of your overall strategy will help you create a better, more profitable book (and paradigm ecosystem in which to position your potential products).

With your foundation manuscript in hand, it is time to get down to the actual mechanics and creative processes of writing. And, regardless of whether you are authoring a factual or data-based educational book, a thriller novel or a business development series, there is one critical element you will need: a story!

"I'm not writing a fiction novel, why do I need a story?" you may ask.

Well, all authors, regardless of subject or field have one intent—to present their readers with information!

Now, throwing a mound of data at somebody and expecting them to engage with it (and want more) is like presenting somebody with a box of twenty doughnuts and then expecting them to scoff the lot in ten minutes. And then offering them another box of twenty and asking to purchase them from you. Not going to happen!

So, more experienced writers use anecdotes to wrap the information in supporting evidence—this is plutonium and it really does work. Because my great uncle Bill used it to glow in the dark at parties!

What nearly all, except the most talented authors, forget to do is present their anecdotally-wrapped information in the narrative of a story. This does not mean making stuff up. Instead, it is using story as a powerful methodology of information presentation. By understanding the mechanisms of storytelling as a vehicle which Engages, Compels, Haunts and Obsesses your readers so they are receptive for the information you present to them.

Whether your readers are off to wizarding school, space camp or accountancy college, if you do not engage their interest quickly and compel them to read onwards, most will never get more than a few pages into your book.

When you haunt and obsess your readers, they will not only glean immense value from your book, they will effect great change in their lives and come back for more, time and time again.

The science behind this approach is undeniably profound. Most new business (or otherwise) authors target the human (neocortex) region of the brain with logical information. Some focus purely on benefits, solutions and emotional responses, which affect the mammalian brain (the limbic cortex).

Whilst the storyseller goes directly for the lizard brain (the reptilian complex, including the cerebellum, pons, etc.), they seek to take a primal instinct, which is focused on making judgements, and ensure it makes the judgements that truly are best for the individual audience member.

Since the moment humans evolved, we have been making judgements that save our lives. Every single day you make judgements that inform your choices and make the difference between your survival and an untimely end. That you are reading this, suggests they were good choices!

An attempt to stop making judgements is impossible, our lizard brain won't allow it. And whilst we can choose not to judge; that, in itself, is a judgement upon our behaviour and the behaviour of others. When we stop attempting to be less judgemental and start leveraging this innate ability to make better judgements—beneficial, benevolent and bigger impact judgement—we become leaders. Leaders with better stories to tell!

As you amble further into the theme park, you happen upon *The Marvellous History of Theme Park Attractions Attraction* which is deemed marvellous, mainly because it marvellously shows up right when we need it most, which coincidentally is now.

Welcome to mPowr Towrs

The Clumpiest Place on Earth!

Red
Beware of
imitation, disguised
as innovation.
Research your ideas.

The Modern Cliché Machine

Just outside the entrance of The Marvellous History of Theme Park Attractions Attraction is an ornate wooden box, of a faded black and yellow. The crackled paint alludes to a better time in its history; a grander era when this unassuming box would have been a proud centrepiece, rather than an obsolete afterthought.

On three of the sides of the box is a large glass pane, each of which reveal the torso and head of a mannequin that, once upon a time, would have been a mechanical fortune teller. For a ha'penny, this automaton would jolt into life, light up with glowing red eyes and sway in a stuttering reverse twerk behind a glowing crystal ball, before popping out a tiny slip of paper with an enigmatic fortune scrawled upon it.

The Great Malevalo, as he was once known, is now clad in a *futuristic* neoprene turtleneck and has indigo hair, incongruous with the sculpted angular visage of his former self. This attempt to be modern and forward-thinking is merely a retrospective mind attempting to guess how somebody from the future might look. It fails miserably, being nothing more than a cliché.

The Modern Cliché Machine, for a two-pound coin, will jolt and light up just as he has always done, although his glowing crystal ball is now a strange LED-encrusted device that resembles (and so obviously is!) an old mobile phone.

The fragment of paper that appears from a slot below, instead of an ambiguous prophecy, is now a modern cliché, which, whilst more acceptable in the view of most than some obviously manufactured foible is actually just as worthless.

Phrases such as 'Show people the REAL you!', 'The FIVE-POINT PLAN will solve all your woes!' and 'Tell others how it REALLY is!' litter the ground in front of the box. With these lie various business cards and several index cards with *Marketing 101* tips scrawled upon them.

Modern platitudes and greeting card slogans are equally as trite and stereotypical as the messages of old, however, we are so culturally immersed in them, we have developed a perceptual blindness to them. It is not until we gain a certain amount of distance from them that we gain an insight into how vapid and nonsensical they are.

The Marvellous History of Theme Park Attractions Attraction

Have you ever been to a fairground?

You know, those travelling fairs that turn up on Bank Holiday weekends and feed small children copious amounts of sugar, before disappearing again in a puff of food wrappers and

unexpected

goldfish

attainment?

Well, the first display in this attraction demonstrates an old fairground ride that simply goes up and then, hopefully... fingers-crossed and touch wood... comes down again.

In this example you would pay for a single ticket, sit in one of the seats and, if you are fortunate enough, you may have a vaguely functional harness to strap yourself in with. If not, you just have to rely on gravity and the twenty doughnuts you ate earlier at that food stall that smelt so good, but now, not so much!

Once strapped in, you go up and you come down! You go up again and...

Once you have done this a few times, you release yourself from the seat and trot off to the next ride or that hoopla stand with the goldfish or the toilets.

Most people will not pay to do the ride again, they pass through on their way around the fair trying each attraction once, before heading to the next.

In this instance we are lucky, because we are heading to Florida and the next exhibit, *Dr Doom's Fearfall* in Universal's *Islands of Adventures* in Orlando.

This attraction goes up and down; very much the same as the previous ride, except here it goes up just under 200 feet in the air at a stomach-churning velocity and falls faster than gravity would normally allow!

The real difference in this ride is in its purpose. Whereas a fairground attraction is there to provide an income for the owner of the specific ride, Dr Doom's purpose is multifold.

As people in the park have already paid for their entrance, the purpose of this attraction is to offer value to guests, to gain potential additional purchases and also to give people something to occupy themselves with when the queue for the Harry Potter ride is beyond the three-hour mark.

With so many visitors to the park, guests will spend more time queuing for attractions than they do experiencing the actual rides. With this in mind, Dr Doom has been furnished with a vast queuing area where people wait in line from five minutes to forty-five minutes or longer.

When you are in a queue for the best part of an hour, it is very easy to get bored and walk back out of the attraction to see what's happening over at Hogwarts. With this behaviour in the park, it is not long before the perceived value for money that guests experience wanes and they become disgruntled.

To rectify this potential issue, the designers of Dr Doom decorated the queuing area with brightly-coloured murals of the Fantastic Four and Dr Doom. There are flashing lights and audio soundbites that offer some basic stimuli to those in the queue.

An occasional television screen presents a basic backstory and context to the ride, so that the few who are paying conscious attention know why they are going up and down again (although the reasoning is tentative at best).

Eventually, we arrive at the ride—we are strapped in, a safety check is completed and a highly-trained teenager bids us adieu as the door slides shut. A quick soundbite and we go up and we come down again.

We then leave through a gift shop that sells a variety of garish novelties and unrelated souvenirs, as well as a tsunami of confections to tempt every child, young or slightly older.

Most people will venture off to the next attraction on the path around the park. Hardly anybody purchases anything from the gift shop. A few people, however, will return to the queue and undertake a second, third or fourth ride of Dr Doom's Fearfall.

Our final exhibit in our exploration of theme parks is also in Orlando. This time at the *Walt Disney World Resort, Hollywood Studios*. Here, we visit the *Twilight Zone Tower of Terror*.

As we step into the park, our attention is immediately drawn to a massive edifice that appears to be a once-luxurious hotel. Now dilapidated and scarred with black scorch marks, this intriguing building dominates the park.

Within seconds of entering the park, two doors at the top of the building open up and, from afar, we are treated to a quick burst of screaming. We gaze over towards the sound, but the doors slam shut, muffling the screams and all we see is the fleeting image of people plummeting to their supposed deaths.

Driven on by curiosity, we make our way towards the building and as we approach we see a huge iron fence and elaborate gate that leads into the grounds. A maroon-clad cast member greets us with a sullen expression and bids us welcome to *The Hollywood Tower Hotel*.

We pass under the gated archway and walk up a twisted, contorted pathway. The angle is disorientating and causes us to feel a little bewildered. Yet, still we are drawn onwards, enveloped in the lavish, if slightly unkempt, gardens.

Nearing the hotel, the echoes of tinny 1930's music drifts towards us from the undergrowth and dusty windows dare us to peer in. Closer inspection only allows the faintest glimpse of dust and cobwebs.

At various points we are encouraged to interact in some way with our environment, be it through sight, sound or touch, so that by the time we reach the entrance to the hotel, we are excited and slightly nervous about what is to come next.

The lobby of the hotel is breathtaking, with ornate furniture and lavish decor that fills the huge reception area. Again, slightly tarnished and in disrepair, we are completely immersed in the sense of the faded grandeur of a once-opulent hotel.

A cast member on reception invites us to enter into a wood panelled room and as we pass through into this next chamber we catch a fleeting glimpse of a mangled lift that has been cordoned off—twisted metal and crumpled doors hint at the disaster that took place here and may be due to happen again!

As we make ourselves comfortable in this equally ornate room, the doors shut and the lights suddenly go off. There is a crack of lightning and thunder shatters the silence.

We are then treated to a short episode of *The Twilight Zone* that tells the story of the Hollywood Tower Hotel and how its once popular reputation as a playground of the rich and famous was shattered when a family plummeted to their deaths in a lightning-struck lift. Now they haunt the very rooms where we will be spending the night.

The presenter explains that the only way to our rooms is via a service elevator that we access through the basement, before informing us that we may never leave— The Twilight Zone!

When the lights come back on, a second set of doors opens and we are guided to the basement area. Here, huge furnaces steam and roar; creating devilish faces as we anthropomorphise our surroundings due to the very clever design. Pipes steam and we await our fate with other like-minded guests.

When we reach the service elevators, we may have been waiting in line for an hour or two, but it does not seem that long because of the carefully orchestrated and staged theming.

Getting into the lift and strapping ourselves into our seats, this is not the beginning of the ride. We've already been exploring it from the time we entered through the gate outside.

As the doors close and we are sent soaring upwards, we are fully engaged with the story—guests at a haunted, old hotel where disaster has already taken lives and may do so again.

We arrive at an upper floor and the doors open to reveal a corridor, several rooms leading our eyes to where a ghostly family wave at us. Lightning strikes and everything fades to blackness. The doors shut and we go higher, to a place where we are reminded that The Twilight Zone is at work here. And then unexpectedly we plummet downwards.

Then we ascend to the very top of the building, where doors open to release our screams to the outside world and with the flash of cameras we are dropped to our doom.

Even as the ride comes to its heart-pounding conclusion just two minutes after we sat down, the theming continues with the piercing sounds of grinding metal and flying debris. A short epilogue video and we exit into a service tunnel where we can purchase photographs of ourselves looking petrified and distinctly lacking in gravity!

However, the experience is not over, because rather than being simply dumped back out again into the humid Florida climate, we are led through a gift shop where every product is themed to the Hollywood Tower. Here we can purchase branded towels or stationery sets. Tee shirts with rapidly descending Mickey Mouse ears appearing at the bottom hem or picture frames with Donald Duck's weightless hat hovering in mid-air.

Each piece of merchandise maintains the illusion of this world and causes us to believe in the hotel and its history, even when we have left and are making our way back out through the gate.

This attraction virtually guarantees that at some point during their visit, guests will return for another or even multiple rides. More people are likely to buy a souvenir from the shop and a substantial number of guests will recommend the ride to family and friends when they get home.

Through a carefully measured strategy of theming, design and storytelling, The Tower of Terror immerses its victims in an ecosystem. A journey that begins with prospects entering the park and converts them into advocates who encourage others to visit the park in the future.

At a core level, the attraction is just an up and down ride, no different at a fundamental level to the fairground ride, nor more intense than Dr Doom's Fearfall. Yet, it engages visitors with an elegant storytelling world where even the mundane process of queuing for hours is part of the fun.

What is even more powerful is the realisation that by the time we have spent all that time in a queue, the experience has set us up to enjoy the ride more than we would have done without the queue. It builds a relationship with us: one that we will then advocate through additional purchases and recommendation to other people.

For Disney imagineers (the creators of the attraction) this is not a ride and a queuing system placed in concrete—it is an immersive attraction that envelops guests so deeply that they forget they are in a theme park and feel as if they have entered a haunted hotel with dodgy lifts!

It is this meticulous attention to every detail that has made Disney the biggest entertainment company in the world. The story is paramount to everything they do—making them a corporation that has literally built an empire out of fairy dust.

The Three APPROACHES of Authoring

The Marvellous History of Theme Park Attractions Attraction reminds us that there are three different types of presentation available to an author, which are:

Giving Information

Telling an Anecdote

Weaving a Story

The presentation of information can be clinical, but it is concise and offers the barebones of what an audience needs to know. Most people write to give information and, essentially, it is at the very core of your writing.

An anecdote or two will support the information you are presenting. So, here's a fact and these people will tell you the benefits of that fact, how it worked for them and why you need to invest time or money in attaining this fact for yourself. Anecdotal evidence can also be used to illustrate in greater detail or even to engage a reader with humour or some other emotion.

The weaving of a story offers context to the anecdotally-wrapped information. It engages, compels, haunts and obsesses your audience to the point where they absolutely must follow you and everything you have to say.

To illustrate this, let us explore the world of Peter.

Peter holds a stick that, when used a specific way, will cure disease and save the lives of all it touches.

This is the main information: all you need to make a judgement about Peter and his stick. At this point you have no supporting evidence or context, so there is a reasonable possibility that you do not believe in Peter or his sticky abilities.

Next, we meet Annabelle, Austin and Annalise, who wax lyrically about Peter and how they were dying and Peter, by waving his stick around and singing a special song, brought them back to life. Upon hearing this, you may believe the testimonials of these three people, but chances are you are even less likely to invest any real credence in the melodic Peter and his magical stick.

So, now we hear the story of Peter and how he studied hard at medical school, revising when others were partying or sleeping. How he put in long hours as a student doctor and honed his skills as a surgeon.

We smile as we learn how his mother used to sing him awake and now he sings that same song to his patients as they come round from anaesthesia, because he remembers how comforting it was to be sung to.

We then hear of his magic stick, which is made of the finest surgical steel. How the handle was designed to be held comfortably, how it is light and easy to manoeuvre and how the blade was sharpened to cut with absolute precision.

And suddenly Peter and his stick have a context that is not only plausible, it can instantly cause an emotional reaction that makes you feel more favourable to a character that only a moment ago you doubted.

These three types of presentation offer us in turn, three different approaches when it comes to the actual process of writing. These are:

The *Down-N-Dirty Approach*—this is quick to write and read; consists of brainstorming, bullets, paragraphs. In some circumstances the text may to too jargonistic and challenging to read. This may cause overwhelm or might not engage the reader, who simply skims through without any real interaction.

In book form, the Down-N-Dirty Approach usually contains padding, big text and blank pages, to give it more gravitas by seeming fuller than it actually is. It is bland, rarely stands out from other similar titles and is open to misinterpretation.

When we read a book that is swollen to give us a few extra millimetres of thickness, we tend to lose respect for the author, feeling cheated somehow and this encourages us not to value their information, learn new skills that are based upon the information or take much time over the book that contains the information!

The *Business-Writer Approach*—here, a carefully planned strategy is developed before a word is even written. And when the book is actually underway, it takes time and effort to write.

The Business-Writer Approach gets the information across and justifies its value through anecdotal evidence. In book form there are full pages of text and an adequate size so as to be a hearty, meaty read; it is well paced, clear to understand and builds the foundations of trust between reader and author.

The author who writes with this approach understands a rather valuable aspect of authoring: you may be an amazing entrepreneur, coach, trainer or expert in your field, but if your authoring skills do not match your professional expertise you diminish yourself. The perception of your audience will place your skills as a business person at the same level as your writing—therefore, in the world of book writing you are only ever as good a businessperson as you are an author!

The author needs to learn new authoring skills to bring their writing ability to the same level as their business/professional abilities. When you do this, you will be able to present your mastery of your profession, through your mastery of the written word and forms of media.

The *Storyteller Approach*—the storyteller gathers and researches the information they want to offer their readers; they collect anecdotal evidence and reminisce about experiences that offer support to the information, wrapping up data in first person tales that engage the reader.

They will then adapt everything they know, everything they are and everything they want to achieve in the world into an internally complex, outwardly simple to use paradigm. This is unique to them and represents the person or business in a standout way. They then deliver an exploration of their paradigm in a precise and measured story that propels the audience into the storyteller's world.

When conducted with flair, grace and a little technical knowhow, the storyteller creates a thing of beauty: emotionally driven and gut-wrenchingly transformative. Storytellers tell stories for many reasons, to entertain, to inform, to share their own history or knowledge. Yet, the art of a master storyteller is to inspire lasting change for the audience. They want to make an impact upon the world and firmly believe in something greater than themselves.

This can be achieved in a single book, but almost always requires ongoing experiences for the audience to remain engaged. Especially with so much content in the world, it is easy for a reader to be sidetracked or distracted by all that exponentially growing data and colour.

Hence, the storyteller views their book within the context of an ongoing journey of product creation. Through this approach, they form a new multiplication business that expands their time through product. Here the prospect embarks on a path to advocacy from blog to big-ticket, freebie item to continuity product.

This approach takes time and real effort as the author learns a range of new skills and crafts their work: layering information in anecdote and weaving the results throughout an engaging, compelling, haunting and obsessing range of products where each item stands alone and within a greater vision or ecosystem.

This develops their new business into one where each hour of time invested is multiplied and their business range expanded. Single products are leveraged into ranges, through widgetisation and extrapolation.

The Disney Imagineering Approach
(to Writing Your Business Book and Creating a Media Ecosystem)

The creative team at Disney Imagineering take a simple up and down fairground ride, where a couple of minutes of experience is matched with potentially hours of queuing, and develop a compelling and haunting experience.

Here, the queue is staged to form part of the overall experience, so guests feel the hours they have invested in the time from gate to gift shop are enchanting and valuable. The imagineers know that by investing the time and expense in developing the attraction strategically, they multiply the value of Disney's business by giving the guests an immersive experience.

Guests do not think, "Great ride, shame about the queue!" They tend towards, "Wow! I loved that attraction!"

By treating your media product ecosystem in this same way, you can use the mechanism of storytelling to immerse your readers through books, digital interaction, video channels and a huge range of other media (and live) products.

You are not writing a book—you are writing *the* go-to book. It is not your YouTube channel—it is *the* go-to YouTube channel. No, not just my online training—*the* go-to online training.

Investing your time in the plan behind a great paradigm, book and the strategy for an ongoing product range is worth more than just brainstorming a few ideas and then writing the information up.

The imagineering approach is meta. Not simply a five-step approach that works in a linear or cumulative fashion, but a paradigm where each tier reflects, relates to and stress-tests every other tier.

The tiers are:

Tier One—Foundations/Cornerstones
Tier Two—Guiding the Audience
Tier Three—Pervasive Elements
Tier Four—Reinforcing Ideas and Making Memories
Tier Five—Fundamentals

Together, these tiers are a pyramid of audience immersion. Each layer of tiers will give you a means to ensure that you are doing everything you can to create a storyselling approach nobody has experienced before. It is not just a book on your field of expertise, it is *the* go-to book in your field of leadership.

At first glance the pyramid approach may seem to be rather complex—a lot to think about when writing—but this is why your planning and initial strategy is so important.

By brainstorming every piece of information you want to be included and committing it to the page, you free up headspace to concentrate of the vehicle of storyselling. This begins with an exploration into the initial plan, through the filter of each element of the initial tier and adding to the detail as you go.

When you have completed this first sweep, you can then filter your expanded plan through every aspect of tier two, adding more points and so on. Being a meta process, your understanding of this system will also have an effect on you—over time you will intuitively know how to apply all the tiers to your information in a dynamic and adaptive way.

In the early stages of discovering the imagineering approach to story, take it step by step and really get to grips with each area of activity. Learn which you find easier, what is more challenging and where you need to focus for different results.

Eventually, your plan will reflect everything you need to offer through your writing, scripting and other forms of presentation. Thus, when you come to actually writing, the narrative and process of writing will flow, rather than attempting to consider everything you need to include in the authoring of your media ecosystem.

The Ecosystem...

This encompasses everything your reader experiences: what they see, hear, feel, touch, smell, taste, etc. From the overarching concepts to the finest details, the show interweaves storytelling, anecdotal presentation and sensory expression.

Your ecosystem consists of every single piece of media content, every sentence and every word, through to the overarching reality of the entire *world* you have created. It is the journey each audience member takes from their very first contact with your media, to the ongoing support you provide.

This is not simply a question of a blog post, a series of autoresponder emails, a small purchase and so on—the *ClickFunnel* model can work well for some, but it will not instil a sense of authority in your business. You are developing an emotional, visceral and experiential adventure in which the audience evolves in some way.

In the Disney theme parks, ecosystem is not only regarding the big picture or overview—it considers everything from the universe being created to the finest detail (and how guests will interact with those details to form their own perspective of the universe!).

You could view the *Magic Kingdom* as a park, created of different lands (Fantasyland, Frontier Land, Liberty Square, and so on), or you can take a minute detail, such as the gemstones that are embedded into the ground near the *Agrabah Bazaar*—a *diamond in the rough* reference for Aladdin fans.

You could try *The Grey Stuff* in the *Be Our Guest Restaurant* or get a warm glow at the *Hidden Donald* armchair in the Haunted Mansion. Every detail in the ecosystem is placed in exactly the perfect place, for exactly the perfect effect upon those who notice.

Even between the theme parks of Disney World, we see the ecosystem at work. Such as the Tower of Terror being designed to blend, from certain sightlines, into the Morocco pavilion of EPCOT. Ecosystem is a creation of the macro and the micro—the overarching concepts and finest, almost unnoticeable detail.

Every element, from words to graphics, audio/video to online interaction adds significance to your ecosystem. Your adventure can also include various elements, such as the colour story that transitions mood and atmosphere; the soundtrack, which heightens mood; or the method of delivery from print to digital and beyond.

Two key aspects to appreciate here are:

- Ecosystem or Ambient (in the product or in the reader's environment)
- Contractive and Expansive (does a product exclude or include a reader?)

As the author, you are the guardian of the creative and experiential intent of the ecosystem. This includes which information is presented, how you illustrate this information through anecdote and the specific storytelling methodology you choose to use.

Understanding where the audience members are when experiencing your ecosystem is essential—are they at home, on a train, in the office? Who is with them and what other stimuli are you competing with? Are they coming to you or you to them?

At any given moment are you including or excluding your reader/viewer? For example, are you referring to *those people (over there) who do that terrible, stupid thing?* Or are you presenting *yourself (who is right here with your reader), the one who truly changes the way you approach that super-amazing new paradigm?*

When an audience member voyages through your media, they will have expansive reactions to some areas and contractive to others. Use this to your advantage, ensure the behaviour you don't want is associated with contraction and the desired results are connected to the expansion.

Ask yourself:

- How does this *x* (topic, illustration, rich media element, etc.) enhance or support the reader's experience?
- Are you focusing on your target audience?
- Do you evaluate how each element contributes to the overall value?

Remember, the greatest idea in the world is both worthless and useless if you have yet to find an effective way to express it within the context of your ecosystem.

The Star Wars universe has become a fundamental aspect of the Disney canon. With main arc movies and stand-alone projects, the ecosystem is an entire galaxy of content. Content spills out into theme park attractions, merch, live events and a broader range of media in other forms, such as books and animated television shows.

Increasing Degrees of Focus…

From the overall big picture to the minutiae of each nuance and word, we start big and work towards ever-increasing degrees of focus. Defining the big picture, overall journey first and then heightening the details with every step forward.

This is like zooming a camera lens to focus on different regions of experience from the next step to the end result. We always move from the general to the specific; increasing the level of detail as we go.

View this as the landscape of your ecosystem: the broader the view the less focus your audience will have. The greater the detail, the closer it is to them. They need an overview to activate their physiology, but increasing detail to drive them forward.

At each step of your media ecosystem, explore which elements are immediately important and which are further away. The closer you are to an aspect of your narrative, the more detail it requires, whereas the elements that are further away need much less detail to maintain clarity.

Now there may be areas of your content that are more important to your overall message than those you are currently describing, however, always keep the detail in relation to the proximity. The most important point at the end of the book can be referred to at the beginning, but only with a minimal level of detail.

Ask yourself:

- Have you identified your establishing near and far foci?
- Are you presenting information in a way that moves from the general to the specific?
- Are you using different levels of detail to help guide your reader through your book in a manageable way?

In terms of media, a blog post needs less detail than an authority book. Online training needs even more nuance and complexity of form. Your website needs to pan out towards the horizon, giving broad strokes and high-impact messages.

From immense detail you can derive further products, using summarising techniques. Whilst a big-picture article could be the basis for an in-depth authority book.

Changing your focus when creating different media content enhances the journey and message for your ecosystem: presenting contrasting degrees of detail and depth in the field of vision.

The Pixar movie, *Inside Out*, demonstrates how effective focus can be when used in the appropriate way. The tiny glowing spheres of memories (and the emotions attached to them) are shown as a mass of glowing colour or a single sphere.

One presents the overall view of a happy (or sad) lifetime. The other hones in on the precious, powerful effects of a single moment in life. One is a backdrop to the action, the other is up front and centre. What does each moment of your content need to be?

The Devil is in the Detail...

Detail is only used when absolutely relevant to the story in one way or another. Lots of detail when contextually appropriate will engage and compel your audience, whereas superfluous details make your ecosystem seem cluttered and create overwhelm.

WELCOME TO
TRIASSIC PARKA

FASHION 65 MILLION YEARS IN THE MAKING AND RESURRECTED FOR COMEDIC PURPOSES!

The art of creating an ecosystem is not adding lots of detail to an overall idea; it is sculpting increasing degrees of detail that hone in on a result in a meticulous and measured way.

Details draw attention to themselves, so each detail needs to be relevant and in-theme. We must also ensure that the level of detail is appropriate for each region of our book or product range.

Remember to stay true to your message, avoid paradoxes between what you present and how you act. For example, never tell your readers to make *all-or-nothing statements*.

Ask yourself:

- Have you clarified the details in your planned media?
- Are you including too much/too little detail in relation to the focus of your narrative?
- Am I being true to my message through what I say and how I act?

Remember, every detail needs to be exactly right; if it is out of place or erroneous in some way, people will notice, even if they do not consciously notice.

In an early print of the Disney film, *The Rescuers,* someone placed a photo of a naked woman in a window of a background building. The image was minute and on screen for microseconds; as such it went unnoticed until the advent of video.

At home, people could pause the movie and watch frame by frame. Eventually this insignificant detail was noticed and is now an infamous piece of Disney trivia, firmly associated with the movie.

Theming...

Theme is the fundamental nature of a story. This is not merely the context of a theme, but the level of theming and maintaining cohesion within a theme. A cohesive theme creates immersion and when measured in degree, scope and continuity, can develop astounding levels of envelopment within your ecosystem.

However, if there is any form of contraction within theming the opposite effect will be achieved, when your readers will be pulled out of the trance and lose their way on the journey.

Many of the attractions in Disney's theme parks are perfect examples of the power of theming. However, this standard of excellence does highlight when they get it wrong.

When comparing the themes of *Disney's Animal Kingdom* and *EPCOT* (both a part of Disney World in Orlando) we see the power of bricks and cola bottles in one, versus the concrete stylings of 1970's futurism in the other.

Once upon a time, the theming in EPCOT would have been viewed as high standard, but now, compared to the newer parks, it simply pulls the guest out of the ecosystem.

Theming elements range from the imagery and circumstances you create through words, the imagery and design you use, the media you expand your product range into and the emotional experiences you inspire in your audience and so on.

Ask yourself:

- Are you being consistent in your voice?
- Are you staying true to the look and feel of your book?
- Is the theme of your ecosystem cohesive with your audience?

Here we explore:

- Theming from ecosystem to product, to chapter, to paragraph
- Creating a cohesive theme from language, terminology and tone of voice, to fonts, colour and design
- Effects of inconsistent use of design and voice

Creating a consistent, high-quality theme or themes for your media ecosystem will ensure a captivated audience. It is something that needs constant refinement and attention to detail, but when achieved your theming will enable you to replicate a single product into a series of products.

These stem from the same framework, but use different themes to offer value in their own right. This is particularly relevant in terms of paradigm creation. A single paradigm element can be themed and re-themed to give a completely different experience for the reader/viewer.

This can work in remarkable ways, however, be sure not to re-theme a classic brand in your ecosystem with a fad-brand, meme or transitory aspect of the zeitgeist. Sparkly is not always better, as demonstrated by Disney's divisive move to re-theme the Tower of Terror at *Disney California Adventure*.

After an extensive refit, this attraction re-opened in 2017 as *Guardians of the Galaxy—Mission: BREAKOUT!* All that had changed was the theming, yet a classic and timeless brand was gone and now a gleaming cash cow stood in its place.

The challenge here is the theme will date very quickly. A retro- or retro-futuristic theme lasts outside of time, but a modern (trying to be futuristic) theme will look dated very quickly.

Add to this the controversies surrounding the movie franchise, inevitable reboots and the eventual death knell as audiences scramble for something new and exciting (or a timeless classic) and we can see the power of a good (or bad) theme.

Story, Story, Story...

Story is the essential, fundamental principle when writing a successful book and creating a cohesive product range ecosystem. Story is not necessarily a narrative with a beginning, middle and end, but it is the contextual theme or method in which information is organised and presented.

A story can be seen as the context in which your reader's journey takes place.

Every region of your product range must be a story-region, which all interrelate into an identity that supports the ecosystem. The use of a powerful concept or core-idea informs the ecosystem in every detail.

Ask yourself:

- Do you keep the *big picture* in mind when developing content?
- Have you excluded *tangential* topics where appropriate and/or necessary?

Important aspects of this layer include:

- The primary theme or concept within which your products are to be created
- The purpose and goals of your products
- Eliminating unnecessary or tangential topics/details

Remember, story needs to be at the heart of everything you do in the creation of your product ecosystem. Be very sure to differentiate story from anecdote. An anecdote is information, presented in a human, often linear context.

Story is a narrative vehicle that uses various methods and tools to cause physiological, emotional and higher thought processes. These immerse the audience in a journey—one of relationship with the storyteller and the core wisdom at the centre of the story.

In every aspect of the Disney organisation, the question is asked, "What is the story?" From accounts offices that are named after animated characters to laundry services that have Mickey Mouse bubble logos, everything is imbued with narrative.

Story is often viewed as something businesses tell their clients. Stories *are* your business, from the financial statements to the boardroom, shop floor to the HR contracts. Stories told differently, but stories nevertheless. To truly master storytelling and therefore storyselling, you need to be conscious of the stories you are telling.

The stories you choose to create by design are under your control (rather than stories happening by default which you do not control). When you implement story with volition in every aspect of your organisation you transform how the vision of the organisation translates into the culture of the organisation and the results you get across the business.

Tier Two - Guiding the Audience (grabbing attention and leading them on a journey)

The Magnet...

The magnet is a singular, powerful force that pulls the reader from first word to last page and the viewer from the *play* to the *like* and *subscribe* buttons. It is the benefits, the rewards and intriguing little something that utterly possesses them with a will to discover more.

People are drawn to magnets, because they know they will be rewarded for the time and effort it takes to get to the source of the magnetic force. Hence, every magnet needs to be pitched to the degree of reader/viewer input—the more time they need to invest in your product, the more compelling the magnet needs to be.

Therefore, the benefits of a large, authority book need to be far more rewarding than those of a ten-minute podcast. Promising too much at the start of a simple piece of content will leave the audience feeling cheated. When the opening magnet of an authority book is weak, they will usually only get a few pages in—if that!

Magnets set the scene, establish mood and draw the eye. As introductions to the media element, magnets demonstrate how your readers, listeners or viewers will glean value from your media product(s). These narrative elements are not based in what you want to share with your audience, but instead, what they need to hear to keep them engaged.

The magnet of a particular region is vital when establishing the sequence of a story and organising the journey towards the magnet. These literally grab the viewer/reader and drag them to the end of the piece. Get it right and they will relish the journey and be completely addicted to it by the end.

Ask yourself:

- Do you provide compelling benefits for reading your book?
- Have you explained what fears will be alleviated from reading your book?
- Are there plenty of reasons for your readers to invest time and effort in your book?

Magnets include:

- Benefits and rewards
- Previews and examples of what is to come
- Promises and commitments
- Alleviation of certain fears/worries

The best known examples of magnets in the Disney theme parks are the princess castles. These iconic attractions have come to symbolise the parks and even adorn the Disney movie idents.

When entering the Magic Kingdom in Disney World, the castle leads you up Main Street, USA, and firmly into the park. As a hub to all the other regions of the park, the castle is not simply a draw in its appearance, but also a promise of what else awaits the guest as they get ever nearer.

Transitions...

Creating seamless transitions from one region to another will enable you to keep captivating your audience, whilst preserving the cohesion of each region. Moving from one topic to another can cause a jarring effect, but transitions will help smooth the journey from one context to another.

Again, back at the Magic Kingdom, the contrasting worlds which form different regions of the park would cause a stuttering or disengaging experience if not transitioned.

So, from *Fantasyland* to *Tomorrowland* or *Frontierland* to *Liberty Square*, the guest is treated to a very subtle and slow transition from one theme to another. The almost imperceptible change in architectural styles that blends features of storybook and science fiction. The same piece of music, yet played on a banjo or by an orchestra.

Transitions are multi-sensory hybrids that take the elements of two (or more) themes and transition us from one chapter, scene or world to the next.

Three-dimensional cross-dissolves are an excellent way of creating a transition, here you employ three different layers of experience that blend elements from the two regions being traversed. These provide subtle sensory clues that a change is occurring.

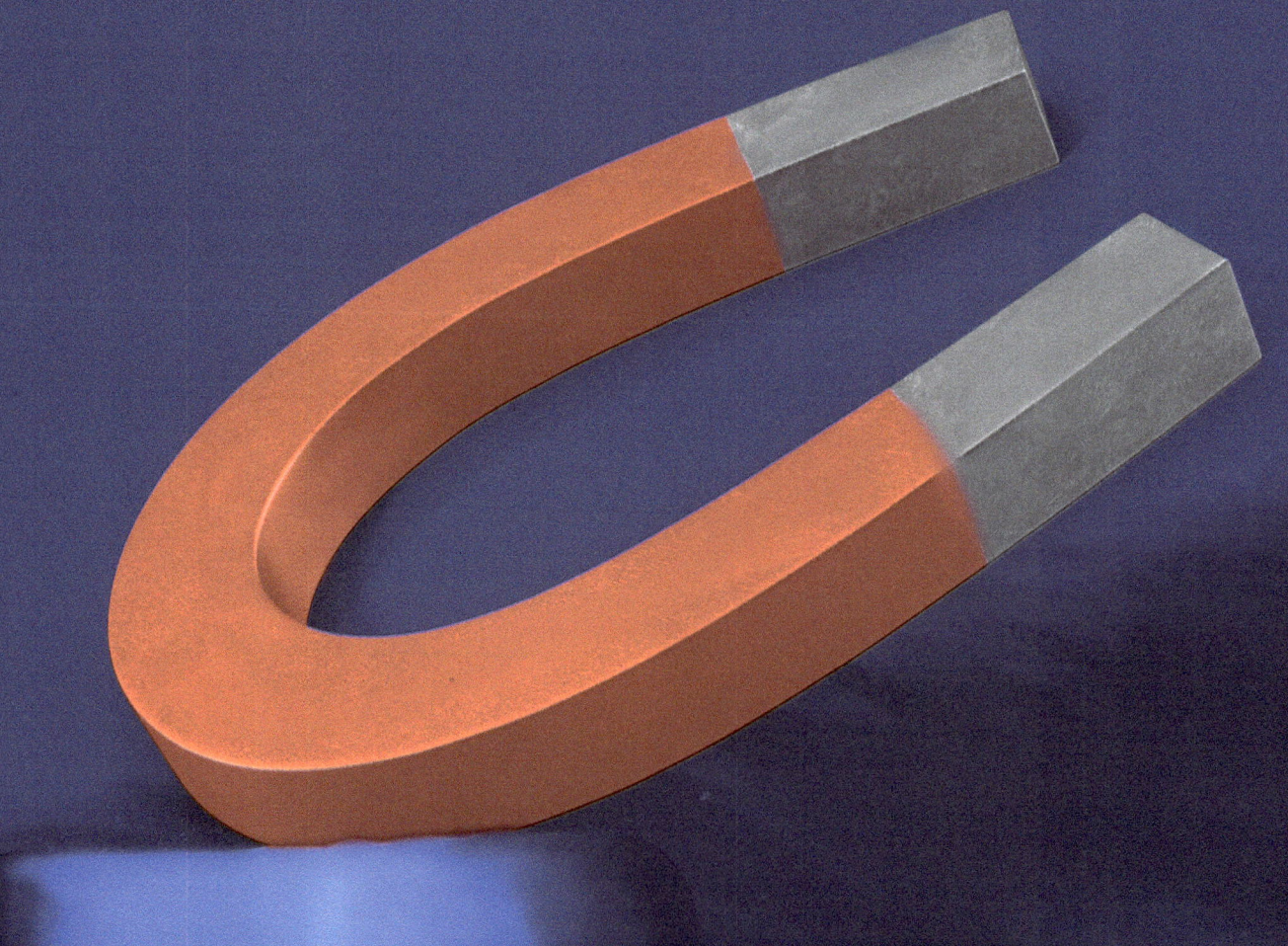

Ask yourself:

- Are you guiding your audience from subject to subject in a manner that benefits them?
- Have you identified areas where you need to use hypothetical, themed content rather than real-world content?
- Is your narrative seamless across a variety of different media and narrative?

Transitions include:

- Moving from general to specific
- Overarching to detailed
- General application before specific examples
- Hypothetical to real world

Disney and Pixar movies, such as *Big Hero Six*, use a colour story to transition us through the narrative from moment to moment, mood to mood. As a very subtle example of transitions, the hue of each scene changes over time to tell its own story; one which is meta to the narrative we are conscious of.

From the bright, bold colours of an exuberant life in San Fransokyo to the washed-out, colourless scenes of bereavement, the dark, *film-noir* hues of the movie's main mystery and finally, the balanced palette of the resolution scenes, we are transported through the film in colour as well as dialogue, action, etc.

Storyboards...

Storyboards are visual/textual points that outline nexus areas of a story. These are key points of interest, information or theming that are encountered by the reader.

In terms of movies, entire films are mapped out in storyboard forms, not only to give the creators a sense of what each frame will do within the context of the movie, but also to sell the idea of the movie, to get teams on board and to demonstrate alternative ways of achieving greater impact for the audience.

Storyboards are a means of communication, before we communicate a single word or image to our reader/viewers. They are a map, by which to navigate and a path that keeps us from getting lost in the overwhelm of a huge project.

A storyboard could be a mind map, a system chart, a word-processed document or a series of index cards. Storyboards cover every aspect of the story, from theme to specific products, so act as an excellent way of ensuring your entire ecosystem of products is coherent and seamless in its presentation.

Ask yourself:

- Have you outlined the entire ecosystem, product range and individual products?
- Have you stepped back to *view* the entire experience?
- Have you considered different ways to present the products?
- Is your first book a seamless and sculpted aspect of your entire ecosystem?

Storyboards include:

- Bullet points and summary lists of main themes/content
- Rough images and diagrams
- Pinterest boards that encompass experiential themes
- Mind maps, etc.
- Index cards, visual images of each step and so on

Pre- and Post-Shows...

Pre-shows are the six touches that we use to create engagement, whereas post-shows include areas of interaction, follow-ups, continuity products and so on.

Pre-shows identify what a reader needs to know before any given step on their journey and also present a summary of what is to be expected. Post-shows also summarise what has just been encountered, yet here it is a means of reinforcement and memorising.

The definition of a *touch* is a nexus point of transmedia elements or point of interaction between you and your readers. These include, online interactive content, images or diagrams, a piece of text that is highlighted by typography or style, a technique or tool, a stop-and-pause-for-thought moment or some other chunk of content that is differentiated from the main text in some way.

The Haunted Mansion and *Splash Mountain,* which are both found in the Magic Kingdom offer enthralling examples of pre- and post-shows. The six touches of the mansion's staging area include pun-laden tombstones and a musical mausoleum, as well as a morbidly-amusing pre-show room.

The post-show for Splash Mountain arrives after the journey has culminated in plummeting into a soaking pool of water and the ride vehicle is making its way back to the disembarkation area.

Here we are treated to a huge animatronic number on a riverboat, where we experience a final refrain of *Zip-a-Dee-Doo-Dah*. The colourful, musical finale is a fitting way to round off the story we have just journeyed through. However, more than just a final scene, it validates the story by saying the story matters, not simply the splash at the end.

Ask yourself:

- Do you have six touches that differ from each other and engage the reader?
- Do you introduce your magnet early on in your narrative?
- How are you accounting for post-show and ongoing interactions with your readers?

Pre- and Post-shows include:

- *The Six Touches*
- Interactive content that continues a chapter
- Techniques and tools that follow a chapter
- Continuity products

Forced Perspective...

Forced perspective is the relative adaptation of narrative to make the underlying concepts appear larger or smaller than they actually are. The creative concept is derived from Disney resorts, where certain buildings have first, second and third storey facades that are progressively smaller in height. Here the first storey is 90% of the full size, the second is 80% and so on.

The overall effect of the forced perspective process is to make the buildings seem larger than they actually are. The opposite effect can also be achieved to make an object appear larger.

In narrative you can use this same philosophy to make complex ideas seem simpler than they are, to highlight the importance of specific areas of information and to increase the value to your audience of certain choices, actions or behaviours.

By diminishing problems and resigning them to the fate of a smaller perspective, you lessen their impact on the audience. Conversely, when you use a greater

perspective on the effects of your paradigm, you enhance their value for the reader/viewer, by making the results greater than the initial challenges.

This is very effective at times when your paradigm, services or solutions entail activities that may challenge your audience—for example, writing a book takes time, commitment and effort. By using false perspective, you can outweigh the effort by introducing benefits so powerful they make the issue completely insignificant.

Ask yourself:

- Are you shifting the reader's perspective to affect them in some profound way, e.g. offering information or offering transformation?
- Are you using story to simplify complex ideas?
- How can you highlight the importance, value or benefits for your reader?

Forced Perspectives include:

- Descriptive details and layering techniques
- Overviews and big-picture analogies
- Metaphorical imagery
- Visual aids and transmedia sculpting

Touches

Touches are used to create points of connection and to demonstrate very quickly a whole plethora of ideas, concepts and definitions that would otherwise take a great deal of time and effort to present. They can also be used to suggest things you do not want to make obvious or known and in circumstances where you want to *divert the eye*.

A touch can be a clear point of interaction, where you have your reader complete an activity, ponder something within themselves or switch medium and so on. It may also be subtler than this, where you get the reader to notice something (consciously or unconsciously) without really paying it much attention.

So, you might create some form of incongruity, where some aspect of the narrative is out of place or odd. You could refer to an object, action or state that sums up an underlying theme, without mentioning the theme (they sat, facing away from each other), or you can use polarity language to evoke a mood that is in contention with the description.

There are several other forms of *touch* that you can use to extraordinary effect and you can even layer touches to increase your reader's level of engagement and immersion. This is most obvious in the six touches of engagement you use at the beginning of your book and at each new area of narrative.

The now iconic opening to the Pixar movie, *Up!*, contains touches which are so emotionally effective, they bring grown adults to tears. From scratch, the filmmakers take us from knowing nothing about the adventure to come, to being blubbering wrecks.

This response is created, not from the tragic conclusion of the pre-show, but from the layered impact of each touch. Bringing us closer and closer to these characters; extorting our care and need to relate with them. We click into sync with them and their journey, so when the horrible and inevitable events transpire, we feel the gut-punch with the protagonist.

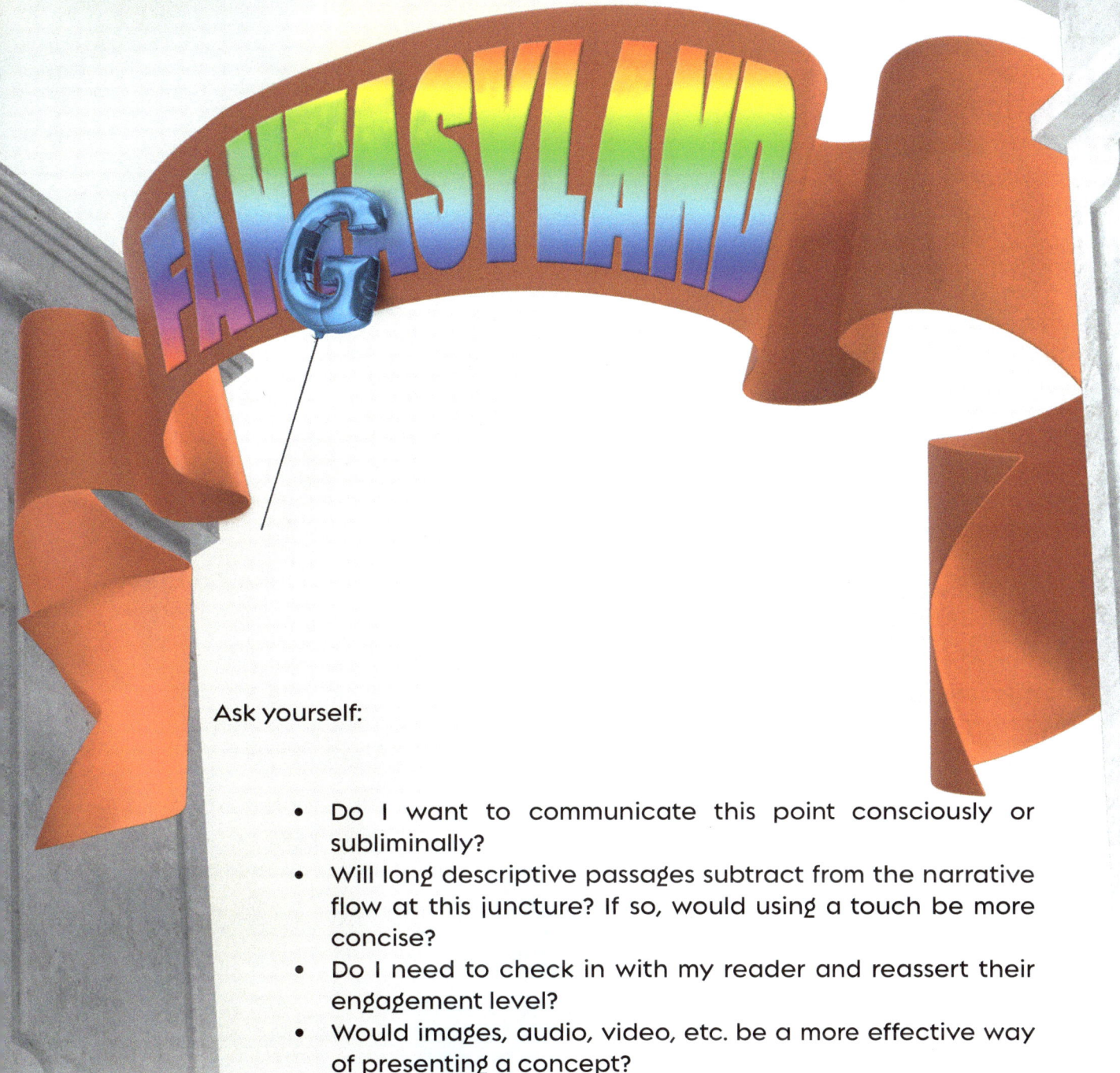

FANTASYLAND

Ask yourself:

- Do I want to communicate this point consciously or subliminally?
- Will long descriptive passages subtract from the narrative flow at this juncture? If so, would using a touch be more concise?
- Do I need to check in with my reader and reassert their engagement level?
- Would images, audio, video, etc. be a more effective way of presenting a concept?
- Is there value in misdirection or subliminal demonstration with this information? For example, rather than telling your reader about a mistake, you get them to make the mistake and then highlight that they just made the mistake.

Touches include:

- Design and media elements
- Narrative points of interest
- Exercises, tasks, note-taking, etc.
- Contrasting/conflicting, subliminal or demonstration-based descriptions

Kinetics...

Stillness loses engagement, halts momentum and creates inertia. This does not mean you cannot have points of quiet reflection in your narrative, but they must remain kinetic in nature. Kinetic narrative is about keeping the atmosphere vibrant and the reader engaged with your story.

As an author, you need to develop a sense for when the tension in each section of narrative is ebbing and immediately change some aspect of the journey.

Writers who are simply delivering information will frequently lose the kinetic drive in the narrative, because it is easy to get wrapped up in the textual equivalent of a monotone drone. In extreme examples, the reader may actually stumble over words, lose their place in the text or worst of all, suddenly realise they've read a page and do know what they just read!

Using kinetics in your narrative voice is about texture, as well as motion. Creating movement within stillness and differing the pace, style and layer of your narrative journey will surprise, shock and emotionally satisfy your reader/viewer.

Disney resorts contain various form of kinetic device, from flowing streams to constantly-piped music through hidden speakers. The emphasis on movement is not only visual, but aural, kinaesthetic and even olfactory (aroma-based).

As you walk through the parks, hotels and other areas on Disney property, your senses are bombarded constantly with movement and flow. The kinetics dance with each other. They combine and contrast to orchestrate a custom-built provocation to keep engaged with your surroundings.

Ask yourself:

- Is my narrative active, proactive and containing interactive content?
- Have I lingered on this topic in such detail that I need to adjust the style and kinetic dynamics I'm using?
- Is this region of narrative internally and externally kinetic?
- Is there an opportunity to overlap kinetics here?

Kinetics include:

- Constant dynamic of the narrative journey, even in stillness
- Momentum in narrative, style and content
- Practical exercises and interactivity
- Transmedia elements

Tier Four - Reinforcing Ideas and Making Memories

Repetition...

The use of repetition will reinforce ideas and concepts in very profound ways. You can simply repeat important facts at various points of your narrative or by slightly changing the way you repeat information (through phraseology and terminology) you can create a deeper, more nuanced effort.

When we are creating with transmedia, we can repeat across contrasting media to force powerful retention of memories. This can also be achieved through contrasting narrative styles and tone, as well as employing different design elements to nuance the repetition.

The most **effective** way to weave repetition into your narrative is not simply to repeat in a uniform and equal way. Choose what you want to emphasise carefully

and then add exponential spacing between the repetition, for example, to repeat a point made in chapter one, you may find the most effective means is to repeat twice again in chapter one, twice in chapter two, once in chapter four and again in chapter eight.

Too much repetition can confuse and actually be counter-productive, so be discerning and wise in your selection of aspects to repeat.

Ask yourself:

- Are you reinforcing key concepts and aspects of your information?
- Is there adequate spacing between repetition?
- How can you vary repetition for the most dramatic and effective result?

Repetition includes:

- Repeating content in contrasting and interesting ways
- Leveraging transmedia to repeat key points
- Adding different sensory modalities in the repetition process
- Mixing media with practical exercises to repeat a key piece of wisdom

Hidden Dynamics...

Hidden dynamics are ongoing themes throughout your book and ecosystem, which become noticed by those who know and love your work. These obscure, barely noticeable points of interest are scattered throughout your narrative, only recognised by your advocates.

A hidden dynamic could take the form of a treasure hunt, where readers look for bonus snippets of information or hidden features, such as the *Hidden Clumpy* motif woven through mPowr Publishing products.

You may also choose to withhold little gems of information and encourage your readers to figure out the missing pieces—although this information should never be vital to the overall understanding, simply extra or as an enhancement to the overall experience.

Ask yourself:

- What narrative *in-jokes* or *nudges* could I use to acknowledge my most dedicated readers or viewers? Something only they would notice.
- How can I make my audience dig deeper/look harder?
- How can I structure narrative so my reader is doing some of the work, without leaving out vital information or creating *knowledge gaps*?
- Am I asking questions that require students to think outside what they have been told?

Hidden dynamics include:

- Strategic questioning
- Graphical treasure hunts
- An ongoing thematic strand that is somehow hidden or obscured
- Elements that only become apparent across products

Tier Five - Fundamentals

Plussing...

Plussing is a continual process whereby you plus or add value to your books and other products. This requires many read-throughs of your work, each time adding extra value until you have the best finished product that you can create at this time.

Plussing does not always mean putting more content in or making things bigger—it could be a tighter editorial process, better stylistic strategies or a simplification of your narrative to develop a smoother experience.

Taking each part of the imagineering creation process and applying it layer by layer is part of the plussing regime. So, sculpting and crafting your work through the touches you place, followed by adding hidden dynamics, are two layers of plussing. You are constantly looking to hone each nuance and perfect each narrative region of your work. And don't forget the cherry on top!

Always seek to give your book and ecosystem that extra edge over the other content that is out there, try using different perspectives, getting second opinions and focusing on contrasting aspects of the overall creation. Do keep in mind, however, that this is your work and plussing mustn't become clumsy, random or a distraction from the specific magnet you are aiming towards.

Ask yourself:

- How can you make your book and other products better?
- What little things can you add, subtract or change in your work that might improve the experience for your audience?
- What finishing touches can you use to sculpt a more compelling and successful product/range of products?

Remember, the smallest change can make the biggest difference

Have your privacy invaded...

Using the Imagineering Model

The aspirations of a book (and ongoing ecosystem of products) is to present information, offer an entertaining experience and very often to create a lasting impact on your audience.

Every book we invest time and effort in changes us in some way, even if it is simply the enjoyment that we derive from its reading stays with us as the fond memory of a moment in time.

With self-publishing technology and services being so ubiquitous, the ability to publish a book is now easier and more economical than it has ever been.

This has resulted in forward-thinking business owners realising that they can leverage their expertise into book form and create a very potent business card. One that takes the necessary amount of time for a reader to develop a deep level of trust for the author.

by a group of telemarketers called Aileen!

As this trend has increased in popularity, the authoring of a book has become a prerequisite for any business owner or entrepreneur that wants to be successful. This has caused the market to be swamped with new business books. Books whose page texture is not the only thing they have in common with *Izal* toilet paper!

This comes down to competence as an author, not as an expert in a chosen profession. Very often, the most experienced and passionate business professionals fail to demonstrate their mastery because their degree of authoring experience does not match their business prowess.

Those with very little actual business savvy can be far more successful, purely because they present themselves in a certain way through their writing abilities. When writing your business book, your finesse as an author is more important than your skill as an entrepreneur.

The very fact that you are reading this book demonstrates your ability as a businessperson, because you are seeking to improve your expertise in authoring so that you are not just writing a book. You are writing *the* book that will come to symbolise how powerfully your wisdom can affect the lives of others for the better.

The key to engaging your reader and enabling them to absorb the information without devaluing or overwhelming it, is to appreciate that you are creating a story of your perspective now, percolated through the filter of the past—illustrating the information you want to present in a sculpted and dynamic way.

When you apply the tried and tested methods of the imagineers, you provide more than information. You deliver the potential for deeply affective and effective content that impacts your reader, stirs their emotions and creates lasting change for them. You can offer information or you can offer transformation, the choice is yours!

Beginning with the big picture of your ecosystem and where your book sits within that world is paramount to pinpointing your starting point. Using varying degrees of focus to shift from overview to the minutiae of detail will help you plan and structure your book in very potent ways. Then coming up with a compelling theme and exploring the story of your book will enable you to produce the blueprint for your book.

Tier two techniques will assist you in developing an awe-inspiring magnet that yanks your reader from their everyday life and thrusts them into your universe. Deciding on transitions for each region of your narrative will limit the harsh jolts that can occur from one section to another. This smoothing of the flow can be turned into storyboards, which are fully honed into a cohesive story through pre-and post-shows.

The third tier is where you add Forced Perspective, Touches and Kinetics to alter the way your information and anecdotes are received. By taking the complex and making it easy to understand, and strengthening areas where you have diluted your ethos, you will ensure your audience knows the value of what they are experiencing, whilst still being able to digest it and emotionally engage with it!

Touches and Kinetics keep the momentum of your narrative, whilst removing the potential points of inertia and blocks to the continuing flow. Keeping your narrative energised and gripping, whilst maintaining the emotional tension is a truly masterful way of authoring your book.

The next stage is to use reputation and hidden dynamics to absolutely send your message home. Using connective points under the surface and by appealing to your audience's sense of advocacy will not only ensure they experience the power of your words, but also that they remember that power.

Finally, the routine of multiple *plussing* sessions will perfect your product into the best it can be at this time. Whilst plussing is often the last aspect of your imagineering strategy, as each element can be brought into play concurrently and using a variety of sequences, you will need to *plus* your writing on a continual basis.

When combined, the imagineering tools will transform your writing from a slab of cold data and bare information to a vibrant and exuberant journey that is filled with life, joy and powerful change. A journey that impacts your readers' lives and leverages their emotion to the point where they create lasting change for themselves in a multitude of profound ways.

An Introduction to Breadcrumbing

The imagineering model can provide us with an exceptional way of distilling information and anecdote into an engaging and compelling read. When it comes to the delivery of your content there is another vital aspect to writing that many new writers are unaware of.

In the need to get the narrative out, they draw a direct line from beginning to end and walk that line through their narrative path. This results in a finished title that is lacklustre and rather bland.

With the vast majority of the thousands of books that are published every week consisting of bland, your book needs something more: a narrative journey that meanders and weaves around many points of interest.

It is these points of interest that will keep your reader immersed in your world and offer them the greatest value they have known from a single book.

The Trouble with Tryfan

The heart of a storytelling approach can be summed up by baking a loaf of bread. The loaf is the essential information, various anecdotes are the slices from which the overall loaf can be determined. The breadcrumbs lead the audience on a journey from first chapter to epilogue and then the ongoing series.

This journey guides a prospect in your audience to big-ticket item and onwards through continuity products. Thus, breadcrumbing is the most valuable aspect of storytelling to consider.

Blythe's Buns and Biscuits

Venturing back into the main park, we decide it's time to sit for a while and reflect on the art of breadcrumbing. So we make our way to a rather fabulous artisan bakery, *Blythe's Buns and Biscuits*.

The main street through the park, which leads from the entrance gate to the central hub is named *High Street, UK*, and features a rather enchanting array of shops, from bespoke eateries and coffee houses to souvenir boutiques and gift emporiums. There is, you will be very relieved to hear, a distinct lack of Primarni, which makes this particular street rather unlike any other high street in the UK!

Blythe's Buns and Biscuits makes the best buns anywhere and has a rather wonderful range of quality loose teas from around the world. So, we sit outside in the sunlight, watching the world go by for a while and wait for our drinks and baked goods to arrive.

As soon as a huge tray of piping hot tea and various buns is brought out to us and set down upon the table, a small group of sparrows appears and begins to flutter around the ground in front of where we sit. This little band of feathered opportunists chirp and flap, almost as if they are trying to get our attention or more specifically, trying to get a taste of those freshly baked buns.

I reach out and throw a whole bun to the birds, who scatter with alarm. Obviously, the sight of a huge, whole bun rocketing towards these little chaps was too much for them! So, I pick up the bun and return it to the table, waiting for the sparrows to return.

When they eventually discover the allure of these sweet temptations outweighs the fear of being pummelled by them, they gradually begin to flock around our table again. So this time I cut a slice off the bun and toss this over to them.

The sparrows dash over to the slice and peck and pull and fight over it, but the slice is still too large for them to manage, so they end up playing tug of war. So, I then crumble the remaining piece of bun into small crumbs and throw these out a few at a time, slowly and carefully leading the birds towards to us.

Soon this approach brings the sparrows *closer* and *closer*, until eventually one of the birds flies onto our table and hops up onto my hand. Here he nibbles and pecks a small pile of crumbs in my hand. This is the art of breadcrumbing.

In narrative terms, breadcrumbing is the gradual and paced dropping of breadcrumbs for your reader to follow. The greatest mistake that many inexperienced writers make is that they have something to tell you and they tell you, usually as quickly as possible!

Especially when it comes to writing business books—business professionals are so used to giving information as quickly and concisely as possible that their book will read like an instruction manual or monthly report, rather than an engaging and compelling narrative piece.

Even when an author employs the use of anecdote, it can be disjointed and a struggle to read for the usual audience. To illustrate the difference between information, anecdote and story, we could say that...

Julie was ill, she got better.

Julie is a patient of mine, who came to me with acute bunions and after six treatment sessions, she explained that she felt better than she had in years.

Have you ever experienced a situation in your life that seemed so devastating you could not see a way out, but everybody around you treated the challenge as if it were nothing but laughable? That is how it felt for Julie...

For years, Julie had suffered a crippling condition that had all but stopped her living her life. It had stripped her of her independence, diminished her self-esteem and robbed her of her will to go on. That was until she made a decision that would change her life in unknowable and profound ways.

We all remember those movies and television shows that began with a voiceover. The character would detail some exposition or important piece of information that gave us context for the narrative to come. This technique is still used today, however, a far more sophisticated form of storytelling is to give the information through the actions and events of the narrative.

Filmmaker Christopher Nolan is an expert at creating movies with very complex subject matter: plots told backwards, plots within plots within plots, multidimensional tesseracts created by humans in the future that affect the protagonist's past and so on.

Nolan breadcrumbs the story in such a measured and precise way that we, the audience, never feel bombarded with ideas. Instead, we become swept up in the various layers of narrative tapestry as it wraps around us.

From his vast canon of storytelling tools, Nolan will often introduce complicated concepts in the first act. These are reinforced or demonstrated in the second act and then collide into each other as a cascading finale in the third, final act.

With *Dunkirk*, Nolan's film about the evacuations of Allied troops in World War II, the narrative contains three speeds of time. Like a circle, the plot arced from beginning to end; the nearer the centre the less distanced travelled and the slower the pace.

The troops waiting on the beaches for days. The British fishermen who sailed their boats across the English Channel in a day. The heroic acts of an RAF pilot in just a couple of hours. Each layer is interspersed across the whole film, yet each in its own time frame.

The first act introduces our characters through the lens of their own time frame; inviting us into their world. The second act ratchets up the tension, creating a palpable sense of peril. In the third act, we see events smashing into each other from different perspectives, on the ground, at sea and in the air.

To write a captivating book you need to present information with anecdotal support, through the mechanisms of storytelling. Breadcrumbing is achieved by layering the information (entire loaf) into anecdotes (slices of bread) and then teasing each morsel (breadcrumb) by asking the question, what does my reader need to know at this point?

At any given moment in the reading of bewitching text, your audience will need enough information to sustain their journey; reminders of what you have told them and incitement to drive them forward.

You will also need to be aware of what information they need to understand the next step, before they make it. This can, in some circumstances, mean drip-feeding background information over several chapters so that when they get to the core material it is received easily and with clarity.

There are several methods of breadcrumbing your story, which expand greatly in depth, scope and length when you view your project in terms of a product range or ecosystem and when you add transmedia into the mix.

The Shell, The Onion and
The Strange Little Box

Adjacent to the central hub is a little play area for small children known as *Impossible Park*. Here, sugar-soaked and sticky-fingered tots, wired on bun-glut, regard their surroundings and each other with wide-eyed delight before detonating in a tumultuous brouhaha of squealing Armageddon.

Whilst the kids expend as much energy as they can muster, their parents relax with a hot beverage from Blythe's Bun and Biscuits. The pleasure of a revitalising coffee and basket of baked-novelties is almost as great as the precious moments of respite, away from the screeching, carb-infused cacophony of the cherubic hordes.

In this unassuming, almost secret section of the park, we find three miniature attractions: a colourful swing carousel whose shape is based upon that of a nautilus shell, an undulant, miniature rollercoaster that has model onions for cars, and a mysterious cube that is oddly bigger on the inside than it is on the outside!

Each curious attraction symbolises an approach to breadcrumbing:

> The Shell
>
> The Onion
>
> The Strange Little Box

The Shell

The lurid hues of *The Shell* clash and clatter against each other as incongruently as the track and carriages which traverse across it. The odd harmony derived from this vaguely aquatic attraction is somewhat hypnotic in effect, mainly because of an organic, natural beauty in the movement of the carriages.

The Shell is mesmerising because it is based upon a Fibonacci Spiral: an ever-increasing spiral that gets exponentially bigger with each quarter turn. At each quarter rotation, a car will spin 360 degrees on the track, so the occupying child can enjoy a gleeful (if somewhat blurred) panorama of their surrounds.

Of course, this may also cause issues if said child has consumed too many Blythe's buns and biscuits prior to embarking upon The Shell experience, so parental discernment is advised!

If we were to view this ride from above, as our sparrow friends often do, after also consuming rather large quantities of buns and biscuits, we would see a perfectly formed nautilus shell or Fibonacci Spiral.

If we were to place a numbered dot at every point where the cars stop and rotate, we would have a breadcrumb map where each numbered point refers to a section of your finished book.

Think back to the CORE strategy and specifically the Creation and Ordering process you completed earlier. You will have a collection of initial information that can be ordered into sections, let us say twelve chapter heading, for instance.

When you apply this ordered list to the corresponding numbers of the spiral, you will be able to gather, at a glance, which other pieces of information you can breadcrumb and when.

Once you have populated each point of the spiral with the items from your list, you will not only have a baseline path to your narrative, you will also have created a blueprint for referral points (both revisiting previous information and alluding to future narrative).

Contained in this blueprint you will additionally have a guide to what your reader needs to have breadcrumbed before reaching the subsequent chapters.

- Chapter One can allude to information that is included in Chapter Two and needs to give any background narrative to the regions that will be covered in that next chapter. This chapter can also tease benefits from Chapter Four.

- Chapter Two can reiterate knowledge covered in Chapter One, with the purpose of strengthening the readers' retention of any key points covered in the preceding chapter. It can also refer forward to Chapter Three and tease Chapter Six.
- Chapter Four can refer back to previous chapters, especially Chapter Three. It can also acknowledge future information and build towards concepts in Chapter Five, as well as teasing Chapter Eight. You should also make a special point of reiterating important aspects of Chapter One to offer a sense of familiarity with the content—if you can bring up information from the chapter humorously or adapt it some way, you will develop a stronger relationship with your reader.

Green
Plot paradigms are complex—focus on your audience and how they will 'walk the story'.

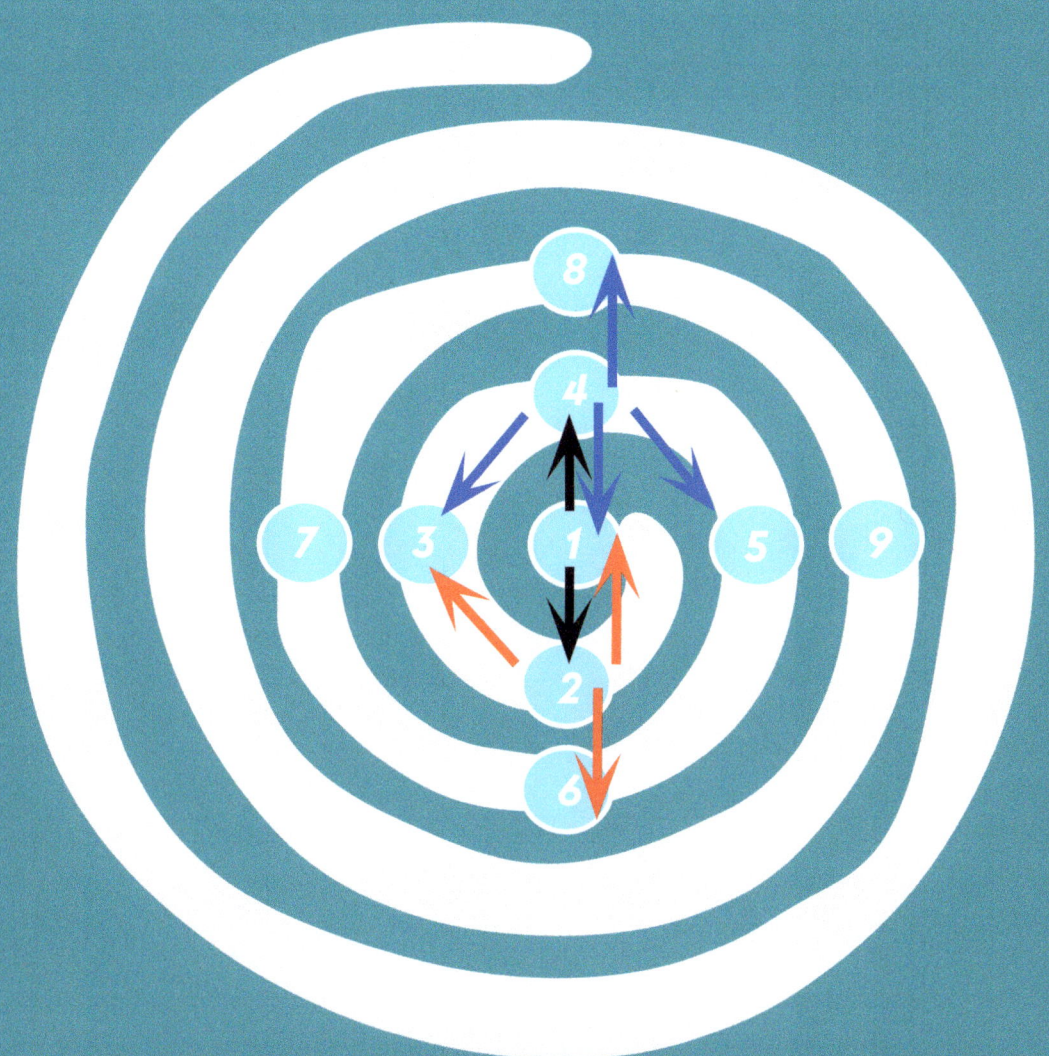

The Onion

Once The Shell has finished spinning each child around until suitably dizzy, they can move on to *The Onion*. This rather peculiar rollercoaster has eight straight tracks that are positioned around a circular framework, which looks like the rings of an onion. The tracks converge upon a central point, undulating over each ring of the frame as they go.

After slightly green-coloured children are strapped safely into place, in all of the eight onion-cars, the ride is ready to go. The cars then climb upwards towards the first hump on their respective tracks.

On reaching the crest, the cars then drop into the trough and back upwards to the next peak. This continues until all cars have reached the centre, when the often-wailing youngsters are treated to the whole ride again, backwards.

The overall effect of the ride is to create a rather odd sound, similar to a particularly out-of-tune and screechy choir of demonic children, practising their scales with added doppler effect. It is not the most pleasing noise. However, it does cause most of the people at Blythe's Buns and Biscuits to laugh hysterically when they hear it.

By gleaning a sparrow's-eye view of the ride, we would be looking at a series of ever-decreasing circles, with eight lines positioned along the compass points. If we then place a dot where the lines and circles meet, we would have a series of connecting points.

This pattern is excellent when applied to a story with many characters or themes. If you take each connection point as a moment of significance in your narrative, you can trace a number of different paths or schema across the ride.

To use The Onion method as a strategy tool, you need to assign a theme of your book, product or ecosystem to each rail. Each circle of the framework is now a section, with the first being the outermost ring and the last section attached to the central hub (the convergent point).

These sections are not discrete chapters, but the journey that your readers take from where they are to where they want to be; not knowing to knowing. Akin to the movie Dunkirk, you can play with what each ring of the onion represents and, within these rules, author your narrative piece by piece, layer by layer.

Once you have arranged your themes and planned content to each connection point, you can decipher a narrative journey by using:

- The rails join a series of steel rings, with the outermost ring encompassing the next inner ring and so on, ingressing to the last ring at the centre of the attraction

- The narrative traces all rings, through the nexus points with the rails. Section-one is traced full-circle, then section two and so on
- Use several formulaic paths to create complex narrative patterns for different outcomes

The Strange Little Box

The final ride the children embark upon is perhaps the most complex and mysterious. Yet, it guides us towards a master storytelling technique: The Tesseract.

For the little ones with the strongest stomachs and stardust constitutions, *The Strange Little Box* beckons. This enigmatic little cube, painted black and seeming rather nondescript is not as one may initially suppose, a vomitorium. It is actually an exceptionally enchanting attraction.

Those rather clever quantum architects behind the resort have developed a rather nifty little device that is actually two cubes, one inside the other and connected

at all eight corners. In three spatial dimensions, this simply appears to be a single box, covered in black paint and left in a corner of Impossible Park.

However, when we add a fourth spatial dimension the two boxes align with different spatial proportions and become eight separate cubes, with one cube as a central box and the other as the outer box.

The mind-bending thing is that the inner cube in four dimensions actually appears on the outside when viewed in three! So, once you step inside The Strange Little Box, the area inside is bigger than that of the outside!

Once they venture inside the box, our little children can explore the different rooms for hours, days, months or even years and, because time behaves differently in here, only a few seconds pass outside.

From different realms and worlds, to other times and ways of experiencing consciousness, within the context of this little box anything is possible. And when employed as a narrative tool, you will be able to create the most effective and masterful of books and products.

Of course, this may all seem a little too ambitious to start with, but as you develop your experience in authoring, you will soon feel more confident using the Tesseract approach to writing.

Placed in the simplest of terms, you create your narrative in four types of definition and present it in three. The four types of definition (dimensions) are in/out, backwards/forwards. up/down. left/right. The three dimensions you are presenting your narrative in are length, width and height or better still, time, scope and detail.

Everything you do to plan your narrative is in the out box, everything that goes into the final book, product or ecosystem is contained within the in box. With this in mind, let us label the *out*-cube *plan* and the *in*-cube *story*.

Now take four sheets of paper, one for each dimension. Label the first Plan/Story and slide this to one side for now. Next, label the other sheets left/right, up/down, backwards/forwards.

Take the left/right sheet and draw a line down the middle of the page. On the left, write down all the information you want to give to your readers, based upon your CORE notes. Then on the right-hand column, list an anecdote or story that you can narrate to illustrate or support each piece of information.

On the backwards/forwards sheet, draw a line diagonally from top left to bottom right. In the lower triangle write down all the benefits and results you would like your audience to achieve through reading your work. In the top triangle, list everything they will need to do in order to achieve their results.

Now, with the up/down, draw a line across the middle to create an upper and lower section to the page. On the upper section, jot down as much information as you can regarding your brand/voice. This refers to how you want to be perceived by your readers and how your narrative personality can best help them achieve your success through attaining theirs.

The next step is to brainstorm as much information as you can about your audience's behaviours, personalities and motivations. Get as much detail as you can about what makes them tick, how they respond and to what, what inspires and motivates them, what are the definite no-nos, etc.

Once you have completed this stage of your narrative planning, take the Plan/Story sheet and divide into three sections. Label these Time, Scope and Detail You may need to extend these sections across several sheets of paper, multiple cue cards or create a digital document.

Finally, list the chapter headings and summary in the Time category, the main themes and topics transferred from your other sheets in the Scope area, and lastly, makes notes in the Detail section on how you are going to deliver this.

The Guild of Nomads

Back on High Street, UK, we discover a small emporium that sells unique goods from around the world. These assorted items are created in small numbers, often by hand or using some rare artisan method. Every product line is usually only available in the area it was exported from and is not available online, which makes each piece rather exclusive.

From luxury leaf teas to handmade pottery items, wooden charms to sumptuous hand-creams, each shelf is crammed with boxes and jars, beautiful displays and lavish goods that you've never seen before. Combined with the heady aroma of incense and the ambience of the lighting, you feel transported to a faraway place.

Tucked away in a small alcove at the back of the shop, you see a range of hand painted postcards, one of which takes your attention. Imported from a small village in the Austrian Alps, the card depicts the *Plot Hills*. This small range of snow-peaked mountains has four summits, arranged neatly in a row, ever-increasing in height as the valley recedes into the distance.

In the foreground, the smallest of this alpine quartet creates a sharp crevasse known as *ECHO Valley*.

The Plot Hills: ECHO Valley

When authoring a book or any media content, the imperative is to understand what result you are seeking to achieve. This is the fundamental element when creating content and the most difficult for most to truly grasp.

Where many believe the purpose is to give this piece of information or to share those specific benefits, the sole purpose is to engage, compel, haunt and obsess your audience.

Before you even think about what you want to say or what your audience needs to hear, you must engage your readers into reading further. The faster you can get your reader to engage with the text, the more likely they are to continue reading.

Engagement is essential to activating the audience member's physiology in such a way as to get their lizard brain's attention. These changes are as simple as changing their breathing rhythm, but are indescribably powerful in result.

On webpages you have microseconds to engage your audience. In videos or audio you have a few seconds. In book form you have until the first page turn—often half a page of narrative.

Next, you want to *compel* your readers to venture further, initially by taking some action. The turn of a page, the settling down to watch or listen or to scroll down. The compulsion then continues with the turning of every page and every moment they are engaging with you.

ECHO VALLEY

ENGAGE
COMPEL
HAUNT
OBSESS

When done with mastery, compelling your audience will cause them to feel a pang of unwillingness when it comes to putting their copy of your book down (or completing the video, etc.). The ability to compel your audience is essential when building a relationship with them and needs to saturate every page, frame or word.

Throughout your content ecosystem you also need to *haunt* your reader in some way. This is usually achieved through emotional tension. Or in other words, getting your reader to invest emotion into the reading of your work.

The stronger they feel about your book, the deeper their trust for you and your voice becomes and the closer the relationship will be. Relationship is key here—you are seeking to form an intense bond with your audience, not to overwhelm with information and most certainly not to sell your wares!

Finally, comes a factor that is often not considered by authors and which leads to many titles being remembered (if they are remembered) as mediocre. The ability to *obsess* your readers will create advocates.

Obsession will not only have your audience clamouring for more, it will inspire them to share your message: telling their associates, friends and family members all about this amazing author(ity) they have found.

This is where the wisdom and experience comes to the forefront of your narrative. As you obsess your readers, focus less on the *how*, in favour of explaining what the problem is and why it is so important.

So many business authors protest against this vital aspect of authoring their content—proclaiming the need for quantifiable value to their audience. Surely, the *how* is why they buy the book or watch the video!? Why would anybody want to focus on the problem or the pain of the problem?

Ask yourself this, how worthwhile is your profession?

And how important is your offering within that profession?

If your field is not vital to the consumer, if the problem is not so terrible as to keep your audience member up at night and if your solution does not possess the ability to change their lives, why are you doing it?

To warrant your products and services existing in the first place, your audience needs to know that going it alone will usually cause them to fail—or at the very least, expend inordinate amounts of time and money in doing so (with copious risks round every corner).

If you truly believe in what you do and why you are doing it, why would you not see the value you can give to every single person in your audience?

When you appreciate the essence and essentials of your business—the heartbreaking, soul-destroying, gut-wrenching, all-encompassing devastation that you can help others avoid, you will storysell the what and why into a captivating solution.

The solution—the *how*—is that there is an answer and when you work with me, invest in my products and services, I will help you solve the problem. Even if, as is so often the case, you did not realise you had the problem (or thought you had a different problem) in the first place.

This is storyselling through a relationship with your reader, instead of a handshake and sales pitch!

Engage

The cultural history of humankind is imbued with storytelling. From the oral tradition and early cave drawings to the first manuscripts and printed book, we used story as a way of passing information from one person to another.

Whether it be valuable life lessons, morality tales or complex philosophical ideology, the use of symbolism and metaphor that storytelling employs is a perfect wrapper for the wisdom within.

In the twenty-first century, however, the need for stories, other than in fiction books or movies, may be called into question, especially when it comes to educational or business content. Why have a story when you can have headlines and bullet points?

The concise presentation of data is based in the attitudes and needs of the last century. With the advent of *big-data* and information overload that is already beyond our ancient brain's ability to comprehend, the need for valuable information to be found, delivered and consumed as quickly and easily as possible has never been more urgent.

The attention span of the average content consumer is now down to microseconds as we acknowledge a piece of data and decide whether or not to pay it conscious attention. As you attempt to present and build your author brand, based upon personal-professional values, you must also build trust and, just as vital, consider the immediacy with which that trust is developed.

This is an essential part of any author/reader relationship, because without an agile, initial engagement, the interaction will last no more than the briefest of glances. Yet, this is where the mechanisms of storytelling are more relevant now than they have ever been—because the art of any good story is that it engages the reader before it does anything else.

We are literally thrown into the action, feel emotional attachments to the protagonist or find our curiosity pushed to extremes when there is a master storyteller orchestrating the text. The key here is immersion: enveloping your reader in a narrative world as swiftly as you are able.

The best methods to engage your reader quickly is to place them in the middle of an emotionally powerful, humorous or inspiring anecdote. If you know your audience very well, you will appreciate what captivates them and how to sculpt the piece into textual entrapment!

Recognising at depth who your readers are, will help you to design for their journey. You will be more proficient at aligning with their experiences and strategies, because your readers' behaviour is paramount.

Having a client journey map of the emotional experience they have and understanding how they make choices will focus your writing and creative experience.

Of course, over time you will measure your audience's interactions and be able to track the effectiveness and overall experience they have. This will help you refine your writing and content development, expanding both its range and effectiveness.

As you start to magnify the scope and style of your interactions with your audience, you are seeking to change the way people interface with your ideas and information. Think about initiating engagement and creating transformation through delightful experiences. Ensure customers understand what you want them to understand and instinctively know how to interact with you as an author.

We often assume that a book is a one-way street when it comes to interaction, but now more than ever, delivering content as part of a greater context is about social interaction.

Writing a book is part of a wider strategy of content creation and loyalty marketing that builds a social community. A community that thrives on conversation, interaction and relationships.

The secret to engagement is not wildly trying to engage everybody in some blanket (and therefore diluted) catch-all statement. It is to identify the audience that is asking the questions you can answer.

Create a change in their existing physiological patterns in that moment and then target the fears, worries, benefits and rewards of finding the answers. Make them believe that you can give them those answers, then they will engage with you in a single line.

Compel

Storytelling can be compared to the links in a chain where each moment leads the audience on to the next. The importance of creating a compelling experience for your readers is demonstrated in the fact that if they don't feel the need to turn the page, your book may never be read cover to cover.

Each word leads to the next, every paragraph to the next, Chapter One takes us to Chapter Two and your first book inspires your clients to purchase your second and so on. The more you create an experience that utterly compels your readers, the greater the longevity of your relationship with them.

To maintain the continuity of any interaction between your audience and your product range, there need to be an imperative to continue reading. This does not mean you need a cliffhanger every few sentences, but there must be a driving force that impels them onwards.

On the YouTube Channel *OmarGoshTV*, our host, Omar, guides us on a series of videos that encompass dumpster diving, paranormal investigations and urban exploration. Whilst sharing many traits with similar channels on the platform, Omar has used compelling narrative to nurture an audience of over two million subscribers.

Whereas many comparable channels create content where the host will explore an abandoned asylum or venture out into a lonely wood, Omar imbues his media with story arcs and careful editing to showcase the overall storytelling.

Whether he is rowing out to an isolated island, losing the kayak and getting stranded or having his investigation partner venture off, getting lost in underground tunnels, the purpose of each narrative is to compel us to watch to the end.

In one masterstroke of compelling narrative, *We Were Followed,* Omar and his companion set out to explore a haunted sewer system. The tension is palpable at the beginning of the video and builds through random sounds from the tunnels, such as bangs and sounds of screams.

When a dark figure is caught moving in the shadows, we know they are not alone down there. Then, deep in the sewers, their torch fails and they are cast into darkness. For several minutes we are forced to listen to the lonely explorers conversing without any visuals other than a black screen.

Then, Omar's companion finds a lighter in his pocket and ignites the scene to reveal *something* standing directly behind him; close and menacing. The light dies again and we are left utterly transfixed. A second viewing reveals the thing to be a person in a head-to-toe black body-stocking—nevertheless the proximity the figure and suddenness of the reveal create a jump-scare most Hollywood directors would envy.

With simple equipment, an ideal setting, great editing and a compelling story, you can absolutely grasp your audience and keep them with you every step of the way. Whether you are producing videos, audio, digital or written word, compelling your audience is the key.

An extremely potent means of keeping your audience momentum at a high level is to speak with authority. The more powerfully you present, the greater your expertise and the deeper your readers' trust, the less resistance there will be.

Not only is there a need to permeate your book with demonstrations of your authority, you must also interweave each segment with trust-building rapport. Leading your reader through inspiring content exists in a fine balance with avoiding the appearance of being too egotistical.

If you present yourself as perfect, unflawed and unwavering in your self-congratulation, you may alienate your audience. So be humble in what you say about yourself and allow the authority and power to flow through anecdotes where your greatness is implicit, not explicit!

To ensure a compelling experience for your audience, you will also need to make certain your content moves the narrative on. As some writers develop their breadcrumbing style, they can stray into rambling for rambling's sake.

Even when you are leading your readers away from the eventual destination, always be ruthless when it comes to staying on task and moving the story onwards.

Haunt

The ability to truly *haunt* a person through business or educational materials takes a lot of skill. For the haunting experience requires a high level of emotion that is measured in a specific way to pace and undulate the way a reader feels.

Starting with a real appreciation for what it is to haunt a reader, you can construct a narrative journey that leads your audience from a compelling experience in each moment to an adventure that stays with them long after your book has been completely devoured.

The haunting is a tangible force that magnetises your audience back to your content when they are away from it. When haunted by your narrative, they will hunt you down online, hit that subscribe button and click for notifications or be searching on *Amazon* to buy your other books.

This force is a part of their everyday life—it permeates their experiences to the point where they keep coming back to you at unexpected, random moments each day. That *something you said* plays in their head like a vinyl album, stuck on a particular lyric and repeating on a loop.

For this is the nature of haunting your readers—tapping into their emotions to provoke reactions of particular types and motivations. Be aware, however, that when you are plugging your reader into their feelings, it may affect how they interact with your content. So, this can mean you will need to employ some emotional savvy.

Traditionally there are seven human emotions, which are: anger, fear, worry, pensiveness, joy, shock, sadness. No emotion is *good* or *bad*; they simply motivate us in different ways.

For instance, anger is the best motivational force—people often create irrevocable change because they are angry about the existing state of affairs in their life or community. Fear is a protective force that stops us from coming to harm in some way. Without fear our life expectancy could be a lot shorter.

Pensiveness is a consuming force, often associated with addiction, an emotion that keeps us fixated with a thought or circumstance. This emotion keeps us engaged with a task until completion. Joy, which many people strive for above all else, could be viewed as a state of high-agitation or excitement. One that keeps us at a high level of alertness and ready to react quickly.

Sometimes, we become so focused on something (due to experiencing pensiveness) we need a complete change of course to stop us from getting lost. Shock is the ultimate pattern interrupt. It stops us dead in our tracks and insists on an immediate course change! Worry is regularly confused with pensiveness, but rather than a focusing emotion, it is a paralysing one. Proceed with caution, it tells us, guiding us through treacherous terrain where terrible outcomes may come to claim us.

And finally, we have sadness: a cleansing, still force that motivates us to be quiet and gain clarity. Sadness also provides a defining influence on our lives, giving context, depth and meaning to experiences that we find pleasurable, whilst providing us with reasons to avoid the situations that we do not find pleasurable.

Much of the time, we experience a mixture of emotions that sculpt our perspective in life and hence, our behaviour. Every emotion adds nuance and complexity to how we feel, think and act.

From the poignant, to the idyllic, melancholy to the awe-inspiring, these seven emotions create seemingly chaotic, yet beautifully orchestrated interactions, which in turn drive our sense of being and personality.

If you set out to make your readers angry, sad or worried, they may resent you for doing so and lose interest in your book or other content. A more effective strategy might be to combine emotional terrain through your narrative.

Highlighting and inverting their existing worries so your reader feels obliged to take action, then shocking them with a carefully concocted scenario that leaves them confused, sad and slightly angry, whilst offering a joyous outcome... This is the foundation of a haunting, lasting adventure.

Obsess

When we refer to the art of obsession, we are not referring to your readers hunting down your home address and turning up in the middle of the night to watch you sleep and steal your laundry items! We are focused on the process of continually absorbing your readers back into the world or ecosystem you have created.

This is more than the words you write or content you create. It is a series of anchors that compel your audience to want the environment that you have defined for them. As such, it is not simply a case of buying your next book, it is about living their lives within the context of your ecosystem.

You are converting your clients into advocates, who will live according to an ethos that you have introduced them to: one that makes a real and dramatic impact on them. That inspires them to be more, live with greater fulfilment and achieve something greater than themselves.

If you are thinking in terms of a helpful guide or a feel-good message, then you are spending time trying to create something life-changing and, in reality, giving your audience another mediocre example of a writer who did not seek to match their mastery of authoring to their professional and personal achievements.

Writing a book and framing it within a carefully sculpted ecosystem is a huge investment of your life. The task is a heart-pounding adventure that will dare you to recognise your own greatness. All the while, hungrily grasping at your time, energy and commitments.

It will thrust you into exploring aspects of your mind and personality you have not ventured into before and demand you learn a plethora of new skills. This relates to hours, upon hours of your time. And these are expended over weeks, months and years of your life.

So, if you are going to step up to this immense challenge, surely you don't just want to write a book. You want to craft a great book: a legacy to leave behind and a phenomenal heritage for those who are just waiting for you to make a difference in their lives.

If you are like a lot of business owners, you may find that balancing professional time with family, social and personal time is a carefully considered balancing act. Frequently, these demands on your time conflict and vie for your attention.

In situations such as these, many business people who seek to write their book, just want to get the words out as quickly and easily as possible. They don't have time to learn new skills or to fashion their work into something special—they just want to tick another box on the list of what's expected of them.

Yet, think about this, in two hundred years, long after you are gone, a person may discover your book in a library, shop or online. They may read your words, your message and become obsessed by it. Your book and the greater context it exists within, could encourage them to make an impact on the world according to your passion and perspective.

Throughout the expanse of time, your lasting legacy always has the opportunity of effecting change in the lives of other people and this is one of the greatest achievements we can invest our lifetime in. That six months you channel away from other activities will always possess the possibility of being meaningful to others, now and for many aeons to come.

And over the lifetime of a single book, you audience will potentially invest more time in your content than all the hours and moments of your entire lifetime. Your lifetime will most likely extend to less than a thousand months. It is not much, especially when you consider how many of those months have already been spent.

Through your content—your books and media ecosystem—you can leverage a value from your life that cannot be gleaned on a moment to moment basis. If J K Rowling continued to author Harry Potter novels until she was a hundred years old, she could never put more time, thought and emotion into those titles than her audience have already invested in the very first book.

This is the core undertaking of transforming your book into a masterpiece—how you consider the purpose of your work, your writing and your ecosystem. You are not seeking to provoke a few chuckles or something that helps out now and again. You are forging a message that will illuminate the path of those who are lost, to where you have the answer they so desperately desire.

You are gathering your skills and expertise and leveraging them into a method of lasting change for your audience; a considered and powerful canon of work, which makes a far greater impact on the world, than you could ever hope to achieve through your business alone.

Implementing ECHO Valley in Your Authoring Strategy

Holding the postcard from ECHO Valley in your hand, you ponder how this method could help you to perfect a plan of action. You turn the card around and read the caption on the back, it reads, "To traverse the ECHO Valley, you'll need to use SPELCHEK."

"Indeed!" you think to yourself and as you purchase the card, you ask the woman standing behind the cash register if she knows where you can access a spellchecker. She replies that she does not know, but they may be able to give you advice at *The Shoppe of Intangible Things*, which is located three shops down in High Street, UK.

So, with a head full of questions, you tuck the postcard into your pocket and set off in search of the next clue in this particular conundrum.

The Shoppe of Intangible Things

At first glance The Shoppe of Intangible Things is surprising. As you step through the glass doors of the shop, you are expecting a weird and wonderful emporium of curios and unusual things. What greets you, however, is a clean and crisp space with white shiny surfaces, sleek edges and minimal design.

Thin, elegant computers sit atop clean, uncluttered desks and the smartly-dressed staff smile as you step forward towards them. This is a place of service and virtual things which have little or no actual presence in the physical word.

From education and knowledge to electronic media, coaching and counselling, to professional services, this is the hub of all things that augment our reality, without actually existing in it. Here, we experience the product, not by directly holding it in our hands, but through witnessing the results it has in our lives.

One of the reception staff asks if he may be of service, at which you produce the postcard and ask if he can help you to do some spellchecking on this most peculiar piece of stationery.

Without a glimmer of condescension, he takes the card from you and replies that you are looking not for spellchecking, but to SPELCHEK the postcard.

You give him a bemused look, which provokes him to explain...

SPELCHEK

To traverse the ECHO Valley, we need to engage with Speed, compel with Power, haunt with Emotion and obsess with Lasting Change (Habits, Experiences or Knowledge).

In other words, we SPELCHEK.

The faster you can establish a stable rapport with your readers through narrative impact, the more likely they are to be compelled to read onwards. In fiction writing, we engage by creating tension and/or using humour, introducing likeable characters, encountering dramatic events and so on.

In an educational or business book, however, it is not always appropriate to have characters and fictional dialogue, yet we need to create a connection and quickly. Narrative tension, humour or desire are three great ways of achieving this.

Spelling out how reading the book will fulfil a desire, want or need that your reader has will demonstrate why they should invest their precious time and effort in reading your book cover to cover. By highlighting where they are and where they want to be (or what they want to have, etc.), you create tension. The tension between the dissatisfaction of how your reader feels now and their pleasure when projecting your narrative/solution onto their situation.

Humour comes with its own framework that, when mastered, can be used to create almost instant engagement. If you can make your reader laugh heartily within a few sentences, you will have developed powerful engagement. (If you would like to know more about comedy writing, please see the mPowr book, *Transmedia*.)

Creating narrative tension can be achieved through anecdote, especially when you employ storytelling techniques to enhance and ratchet-up the drama of your piece. The pitfall that many inexperienced writers make is to begin an anecdote, with factual information, when actually this is presented much later in the process.

Orange
When writing for rapport, think of your narrative as a stage performance.

Narrative tension is when you throw something completely unexpected or dramatic into the mix. So, rather than writing, "It was 1992 and I went on holiday..." you may choose to present your reader with, "We were told that the riots were coming and to stay in our hotel rooms. The US Navy were moored offshore, but it would take them an hour to arrive and begin the evacuation of tourists. The mob were only minutes away..."

We can weave humour and tension throughout our narrative, constantly maintaining the momentum. Yet using these to engage our readers within a page or two (and depending on your audience this could be reduced to a single paragraph) is worth investing real time into.

Perfecting your opening chapter is vital if you want to create a book that captivates and delights your audience right from the outset. And whilst this same level of effort is advisable throughout your title, it is particularly important at the start of the narrative.

When shifting your focus from the initial rapport to maintaining—and even increasing—the degree of engagement through a compelling narrative, you will need to express yourself with power. In other words, you compel through demonstrating your authority, experience and wisdom.

This does not mean you need to tell people that you are an authority, in actual fact, this approach is best avoided! The presentation of your expertise will be much more effective if you demonstrate *how* you became an authority.

Through the words you choose to place on a page, the rhythm those words form across sentences and the linguistic patterns that emerge from paragraphs, you demonstrate your authority. Using story, you can surprise your reader, enthral them and illustrate how your actions and behaviour differ from those who do not have your expertise.

As you suggest challenges, blindside with unconventional solutions or describe complicated situations where your knowledge has helped create a resolution in a way that most people would not even think about, you will be revealing why you are a master in your field.

Your narrative will suggest an approach that is direct and without hesitation. This in itself will help to stop any dilution of your business and brand. It is surprising how many dilute their authority, just through the amount of uncertain language they use. For instance:

It is possible that maybe you might like to listen to what I say, perhaps, because it could help you to write what some people I have worked with previously have suggested is a potentially great book. I remember the kinds of struggle I sometimes faced in writing my own books and you could benefit from what I humbly call my experience as a fairly successful author.

After 250 rejection letters, my first book was finally published! It was a great achievement and an embarrassment. It took me three decades of journalism, writing copy and ghostwriting bestsellers for others to grow my confidence. It took authoring over thirty of my own books and creating years of transmedia training courses worth thousands of dollars in product.

It took mentoring many businesspeople in writing books that made them tens of thousands of pounds in sales of up-sell products, before I could say this...

When I advise you on your authoring and you do the work, you will write and publish a number one Amazon bestseller that grows your business.

Once you have established your own authority, you will need to use the same ethos of demonstration to assert and reassert the power of your material. Whether you are offering education, personal or professional development, advice on a specific topic or field or some other type of information, you will consistently need to make your content valuable, inspirational and uniquely *you*.

Remember that you are not sharing with your readers *the truth*, the *real you* or how things *really happened*. You are presenting your current wisdom and knowledge, enveloped in the memories and anecdotes as you understand them now, through the narrative medium of your past.

A business author can approach the book with a mentality of *this* happened, then *this* and then *that*. However, it does not matter what really happened when it comes to your narrative story.

Go to the most dramatic part of the story and make this your first breadcrumb. And then build the tension from there, undulating from unbearable anxiety to humour to suffocating claustrophobia to joyous resolution.

You are focusing on the vehicle—the engage, compel, haunt and obsess—and using this to transport your reader to your world. Here, they will get immense value from your knowledge by seeing the world differently, as you see it.

In comparison to this, the mundane nature of life events, presented as a checklist will fade into nothingness. Because no matter how interesting you think that time you saved a person's life is, in the authoring, it will never have the impact on your audience unless you use story to tell it and sell it.

As this process continues, you will begin to haunt your reader in a deeply impactful way. We haunt others through emotion: visceral, potent emotions that act as the mechanism for life-changing thought.

People make decisions on emotional responses. Even when we attempt to be completely logical and rational, it is much easier to be influenced in some way by emotions, than it is to be absolutely and exclusively mind-centred. And while many think they are making a choice based on pure logic, they are actually being influenced by a core emotional response.

Yet, emotion is not an autonomous thing, it is fluid and ever-changing. Emotions blend and undulate, change and transform from one to another. We can use this liquid state of emotion to influence our reader's journey.

This can be through injecting joy to pull them towards an outcome or fear to push them away from what we don't want them to know at this point. We can introduce worry to stop unhelpful behaviours and anger to motivate them into action.

The rich and diverse tapestry of emotions enables us to create immeasurable depth and scope to our writing, adding layer upon layer to narrative and the experience the reader encounters. This complexity and gravity will cause them to develop indefinable bonds with you as an author, your books and your business.

When you orchestrate your content in a powerful and emotionally charged way, the haunting will continue throughout the reading experience and for a short while afterwards. To ensure the connection you share with your audience lasts much longer—into advocacy and in some cases, a lifetime—you will need to turn their emotional adventure into an obsession.

The idea of obsession is not the pensive and compulsive view of obsession that we assume. To obsess your reader is to spark a passion within them, some lasting change that stays with them for a long period of time.

Now you may be planning to write a book on how to get the most from a suite of apps or cake-baking or accounts. You may also feel that the topic of your book, whilst informative and valuable, is probably not going to change the lives of your audience.

Except, whilst your readers are purchasing your book because they want information, if you author your book using storytelling, you can develop a relationship that goes beyond the information. It is that relationship that is the life-changing aspect of your book.

When writing a coaching book—be this personal or business development or one where the emphasis is on lasting change—the importance of obsessing your readers is obvious. The more obsessed they are with your work, the greater the impact and lasting effect will be.

However, it is vital to remember the change comes through knowing you (your author persona), not through the actual information. Information can be found online: transformation comes through a trusted, deeply persuasive and emotional narrative.

To create obsession, we want to support our reader in the development of new habits, lasting experiences or knowledge that sticks in some very real and tangible way. You are aiming to shift their perspective in some profound way. Where getting to know you through your words (and other media touches) develops trust, enjoyment and eventually a deep connection.

Obsess your audience by guiding them through a journey of what the problem is, why it is such a major issue and how to solve it. The emphasis of the journey needs to focus on the *what* and *why*, taking time to detail these in a complete and emotionally-grounded way.

Media creators use emotional motivators all the time to provoke a response within their audiences. This has become so extreme, modern audiences are utterly fatigued from the marketing and selling of everything from products and services to people and ideals.

The traditional forms of emotional motivation are tried and tested, but now have to outdo each other by increasingly extreme promises or consequences. The carrot that tempts an audience towards some visceral desire or stick that beats them to a pulp—repeatedly—are mostly ineffective.

We have been lured and pummelled so much, only to find this product is not the answer to all our woes or that service will not make us millionaires. The golden carrot is merely tarnished plating and the eternally damning threat is hollow.

The solution to this is shifting your audience to a different perspective: one where they truly appreciate what the problem is and why it is such a big problem. They will then be more receptive to a solution that is matched to the real issue and quantifiable in the results.

The what and why of your narrative will Engage, Compel and Haunt. The *how to* segment of the story brings the obsession—the aspect of your narrative that stays with your readers for a very, very long time.

The *how* needs to be profound and focused, initially, seeking to explore abstract or third-person changes. Then emphasise how to change and guide readers through this change/the changes they will experience.

When we imagine an experience, our body reacts as if we are living that experience. We may stay perfectly still, but there are subtle physiological reactions occurring whilst we visualise ourselves doing an activity.

Walk somebody through the experience of changing their lives and those same fundamental mechanisms will sow the seeds of change within your reader's mind. This method may appear to be vague or too soft an approach, but it will usually work much more powerfully than bluntly telling your reader what to do.

When you tell people what to do or how they need to change, they will often question or resist, unless you have a near perfect rapport with them. Ask a person to run a mile and they will ask, 'Why?' However, ask someone to think about running a mile or show them a video of somebody running that mile and their muscles and skeleton will twitch and move as if they are actually running it.

All this from a postcard you think to yourself, as you regard the little rectangle of card between your fingertips. You glance up at the man from reception as he finishes explaining the SPELCHEK philosophy to you.

"This, however, is only half the story," the enigmatic shopkeeper murmurs in an unassuming tone that both underestimates the gravitas of his words and compounds the importance of them. "ECHO Valley is merely the gateway to a much longer journey. To create a book with true authority and majesty, you will need to traverse the narrative landscape!"

Blue
Share your wisdom through a systemic paradigm that adapts to your audience.

A concerto is never one note. A painting is never one colour. A good story cannot be flat. For a narrative to grip your reader, for it to develop a trusting, emotional relationship that haunts them and has them coming back for more, you need ups and downs. You need a rugged and ever-changing landscape.

Every story will be different, unique to you, your authoring style and narrative choices. However, we can use themes which have a proven track record of enthralling an audience. Indeed, the following theme appears in most books, plays and movies—it has made media outlets and writers very, very rich!

All storytelling has a purpose—be it to entertain, enchant or educate. The purpose of storyselling is to sell your reader on a specific product, service or idea. Knowing the purpose of your narrative at every juncture of the story is imperative, because the purpose drives the story.

When authors focus on characterisation, wording and the story, without appreciating the purpose, a narrative will ramble, become confused and eventually lose the reader's attention. The purpose of ECHO Valley is to get the reader into your world and keep them there, regardless of whether they are actually reading your book, have put it down to do some other activity or have finished reading your book.

You want to get them in, keep them in and have them wanting to come back for more. This is the result of an effective ECHO—the focus of your book at the beginning and a consistent point of reiteration throughout your narrative.

Deconstructing ECHO Valley into paragraphs and pages will offer an idea of when to focus on engagement, when to concentrate on compelling the reader onwards, when to start ramping up the haunting and when to introduce the seeds of obsession. However, there is a significant point in any story that enables us to evolve beyond ECHO Valley.

The Point of No Return is a moment in the narrative when your reader is pushed to the edge of the first peak in dramatic tension and is then pushed over the edge into the initial release of emotion (tension).

At this point, the momentum from their descent will compel them into the second upward building of tension. From this moment onwards, they will find it much harder to put your book down and this, in turn, creates a rather unique opportunity.

This second tension-building element in the overall story arc is known as *The Impossible Climb*. Here, you are focused on identifying every pain your reader has and leveraging them. You are actively seeking to push their buttons and to pound them with challenge after challenge.

On this face of the second mountain, your aim is to keep piling on the pain, stating why the pain will yield such disastrous outcomes for your reader. By the end of this section, your purpose is to have arrived at the summit of *Hilltop Mountain*—Hope Is Lost Little Triumph Occurs... Perhaps.

Your reader is now so immersed in their own pain points, only one option is left—another emotional release. This time, offer them hope. That little triumph in the name of this mountain is the glimmer of hope in the answers you will provide your reader—providing they keep reading.

Use the ECHO method to engage your reader in the possibility of a solution to all their woes. Compel them in the pursuit of discovering more about your solution. Haunt them with the emotions of their pain and the pleasure they will achieve when those pains are resolved. Finally, obsess them with the power and transformative results you will help them achieve.

Turquoise
If you're having challenges with inspiration, focus on what you know.

This release of tension will take us to the midway mark of your book—*The Turning Point*. It is here you seek to turn everything on its head; both narratively and in the purpose of your core message/purpose.

From this point onwards, you are seeking to demonstrate to the reader how they have been approaching their problems from the wrong perspective and how they require a dramatic and revolutionary shift in their ethos. This is not just a surface layer claim of something radically new, which is just the same old, same old. No, here you want to offer them a fundamentally different way of thinking.

You are also focused on changing the narrative style in some way. This could be switching from telling the reader about their issues, to getting them to think about their problems in a practical way. Perhaps presenting them with a series of exercises or developing a major shift in tone.

The Cutt—Crank Up The Tension—is the third peak we encounter on our journey and the first climb of act two. Stories are often divided into acts that offer a change in pace, style and purpose. If act one exists to bring your reader into your world, by reminding them of their pain and giving them hope of resolution, act two ramps up the tension.

Whether your story has two or three acts, this area of the narrative journey guides the reader from the midway point and therefore contains the portion of the journey where you are at greatest risk of forming a lag in the narrative.

The middle of any story requires more finesse and magnetism than both the beginning and end combined. For it is here the story is in danger of becoming too cumbersome.

Authors easily lose their way here, relying on filler or padding to bulk up the story, when they must be presenting key wisdom. This requires the cranking up of tension to gather an upward momentum, followed by utter devastation.

As you put the reader over this third peak, everything comes crashing down around them. This *Disaster Point* is the juncture where you present them with impossible odds. You demonstrate in pragmatic, cold and perhaps even cruel ways just how difficult the road ahead is going to be.

However, at this point, you also need to be planting the seeds of success—teasing how the danger can be averted and what the reader needs to be doing to prepare themselves. Here you become the trusted guide: the expert and the leader who will ensure their safety.

In this endeavour you provide your reader with an *Alternative Route*. One that transitions them from the pain to pleasure. As you build them up, ready to receive the wonders your service, products or ideas can bestow upon them, the excitement grows to its most extreme level yet.

As we reach *Crap N Calm Peak*, the reader faces Complete Ruin Almost Permanent Now Completely Averted (at) Last Minute. The peak of the mountain is where you introduce the *Double Disaster Point*. Here lies the sting in the tail or the twist that completely changes everything. This is the crescendo of the piece and the final blow before you make everything better.

As you leap over the edge of this summit, entering *Resolution Pass*, you systematically tie up every problem with a solution, ease each pain with a pleasure and soothe every woe.

Ensure you wrap up all loose ends and close any nested loops you have opened. In summary, present your reader with an absolute and neatly-packaged conclusion. This *Concluding Point* finishes the journey in a satisfying, truly profound way, which—if you have storysold effectively—will leave your audience wanting to go back to the beginning and do it all again.

ECHO VALLEY

HILLTOP MOUNTAIN

THE IMPOSSIBLE CLIMB

THE POINT
OF NO RETURN

THE TURNING POINT

STARTING POINT

ENGAGE
COMPELL
HAUNT
OBSESS

HOPE
IS
LOST,
LITTLE
TRIUMPH
OCCURS...
PERHAPS

THE CUTT

CRAP N CALM PEAK

DISASTER POINT

DOUBLE DISASTER POINT

RESOLUTION PASS

ALTERNATE ROUTE

CONCLUDING POINT

CRANK
UP
THE
TENSION

COMPLETE
RUIN,
ALMOST
PERMANENT,

NOW

COMPLETELY
AVERTED (AT)
LAST
MINUTE

When storyselling through a book, extended narrative or other forms of media, you will need to use emotion to create and release tension for the reader. This emotional journey creates an undulating landscape that peaks and troughs; compelling your reader onwards.

As the author, you have carte blanche as far as the different types of emotion you provoke in your audience, however tension is key. With every narrative step in one direction you pull the reader in the opposite direction.

This develops themes of conflict, paradox and impossible odds that keep the reader enthralled. For this to truly take effect upon your reader, you ned to know their pain and pleasure points. What pushes their buttons? What inspires them? What throws them into the depths of misery and lifts them to the heights of joy?

Creating a sense of conflict between what they want and what they have is a very effective way of instilling doubt within your reader— doubt in themselves and their ability to go it alone. Conversely, every step up in tension has a reflected step down that releases the tension.

As you build tension by pressing on pain points, you will need to ensure that at key points you release the tension by offering the promise of resolution. It is important not to give a solution, but to promise a solution. The solutions will arrive in the last act of the book.

The overall landscape needs to create peaks, where each successive peak is higher than the last. The higher the tension causes the reader to climb, the further they will fall into a trough when the tension is released. Emotions will strengthen and be more profound the further into the book your reader travels.

A great way to build tension is to use nested loops, where you open a can of worms and then, before any resolution is offered, you drop the reader into a second can of worms. A third, fourth or even fifth can of worms or loop, follows. It is only when you have opened every loop, that you begin to close them again by offering a solution or closure.

Like a mountain reflected in a lake, treat every aspect of your narrative as if it were a mirror. Contrast words, statements and whole sections of text to stretch the reader between pleasure and pain. They dare not release or let go, for fear of missing something. Your language from words to entire chapters must create polarity.

If you have an emotive word when describing a concept, follow it shortly after with an opposing word. Create disparity between the beginning and the end of a paragraph. Start a chapter by introducing a problem and then finish it by demonstrating how the problem cannot be solved (except it can with your service, product or idea).

A way of releasing tension is to introduce comedy, switching viewpoint between characters or methods and dramatic crescendos of action. The key is not to introduce any real solutions or support until the end of the final act of the book—just keep reminding your reader that you will help them, before piling on another obstacle or challenge.

This may seem harsh. However, your intent is to help your reader; to guide them to the success they want and deserve. You are not using tension to cause them pain or stress, you are just reminding them of the pain and stress they already have; getting them to truly recognise the mistakes they are making and the dangerous pitfalls around them, then offering help when they are most receptive to it.

You look to the shopkeeper as he finishes explaining the narrative landscape to you. All this information seems somewhat overwhelming and you are not sure you will remember it all. You lower your head and find yourself regressing into your own thoughts and concerns—where to begin? What to do next? How can you solve your own problems when there is so much to remember?

At this precise moment, he smiles a rather mysterious smile and offers you a brightly-coloured book.

"We offer a range of live author coaching services, writers' training materials and immersive online courses for broadening your storytelling techniques," he chirps. "This fully illustrated guide will help you get started and offer you all the knowledge you'll need to begin."

You run your thumb over the pages of the book he has just given you and think about how much you have learnt about the structure and purpose of your narrative.

You thank him and he swings open the pristine glass door to the ambient sounds of High Street, UK. As you step forward to leave, he recommends that you visit the park's newest attraction, *The Memory Loop*. For this is the best place to further your adventures in authoring.

STARTING POINT – STORY SETUP & ENGAGEMENT

THE POINT OF NO RETURN

COMPEL THROUGH DOUBT, TENSION, AND CONFLICT

FOR EVERY STEP UP...

...THERE IS A REFLECTED STEP DOWN.

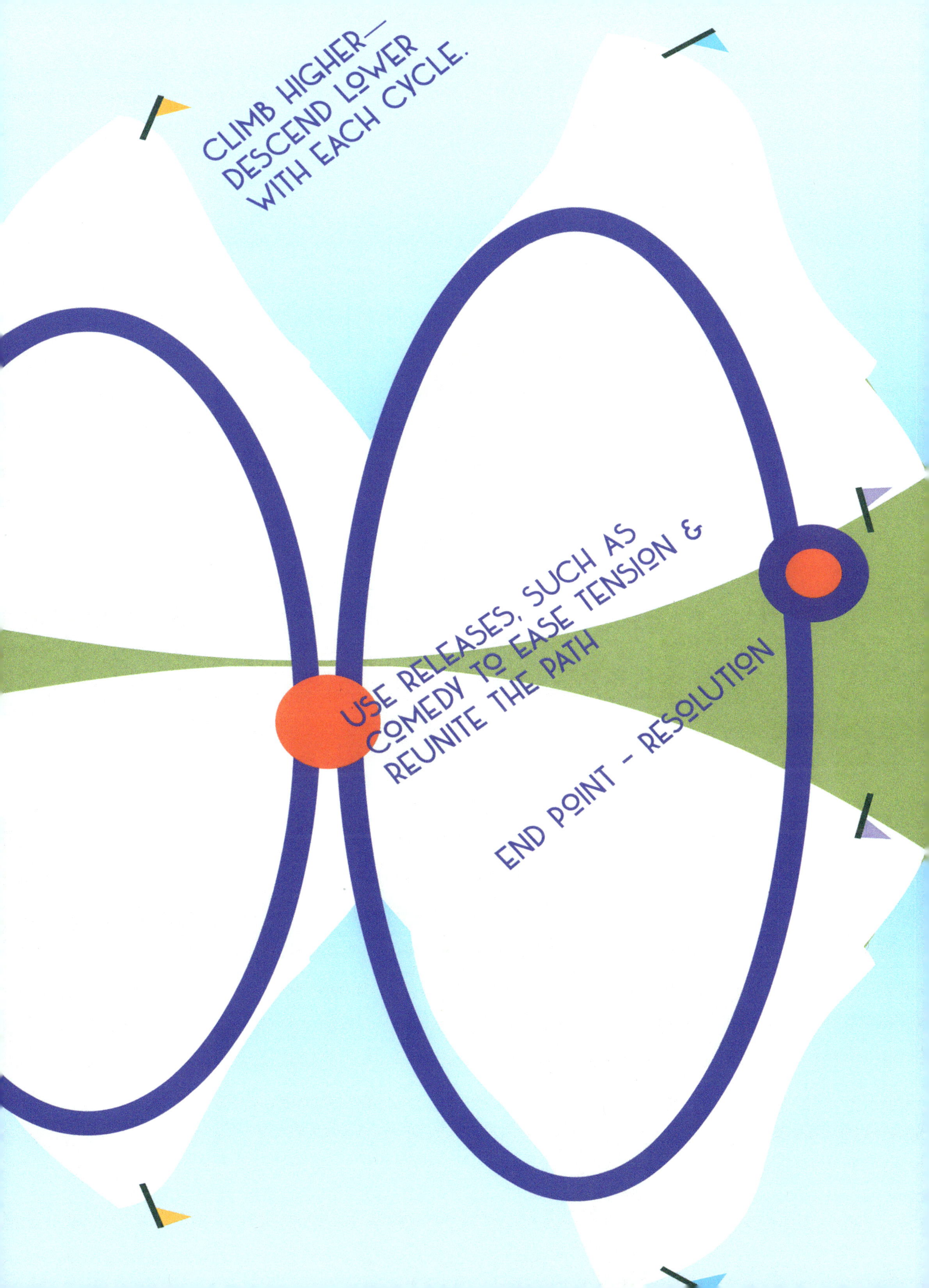

CLIMB HIGHER—
DESCEND LOWER
WITH EACH CYCLE.

USE RELEASES, SUCH AS
COMEDY TO EASE TENSION &
REUNITE THE PATH

END POINT – RESOLUTION

The Memory Loop

As you approach The Memory Loop, you find yourself in what looks like a fairy-tale village. Wooden houses with exaggerated features line a cobbled street. From these thatched abodes you hear the sounds of fires crackling and children giggling. A warm, almost romantic glow emanates from the windows as small lamps twinkle within each home.

In the tiny gardens that decorate the front of each house, animatronic chickens cluck and squawk, whilst an occasional scarecrow seems to follow you with its button eyes. The aromas of home cooking and flowers intertwine as you are guided towards a darker, more foreboding sight.

At the end of the village is a shadowy woodland, which appears from the outside to be more like a forgotten cemetery. It stands malevolent and quiet; seeming to regard you with an air of contempt.

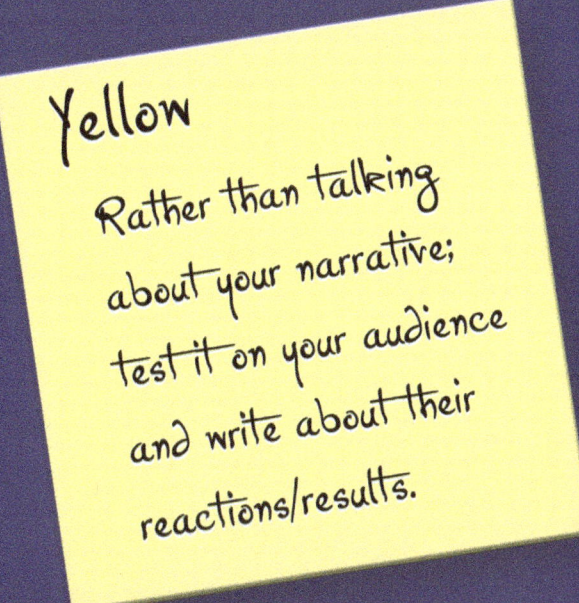

As you arrive before this gloomy forest, wrought-iron gates block your path forward. Here a small group of people have gathered and you wait with them until a short pre-show jumps into life. Tiny marionettes, projected imagery and all-enveloping sound narrate the tale of a little girl who became lost in the woods.

As she wanders deeper into the forest, she becomes disorientated and increasingly frightened. In her anxious state she trips over the gnarled root of an oak tree and plummets down the open maw of a badger set. As she tumbles through a strange, swirling void, the little girl is transported to a strange forgotten world.

Here, she is in danger of forgetting all she knows. For this realm is stalked by the *McGuffin*, a terrible monster that sends all who venture here into a maelstrom of memories that are not their own, pounding them with false reminiscences—they forget once and for all who they are.

The story ends with the desolate howl of the McGuffin's laugh and a voice that explains it is now down to you to find the little girl and return her to her parents before she is lost forever.

With this, the gates shudder open and you are free to enter the woodland via a narrow, cobbled path. The tension is palpable as you venture into the darkness. A strange disorientation that starts with a tightness in your throat and causes your heart to race.

The sound of hooting owls and strange ghostly whispers herald an ominous silence as you turn around a dark corner. You expect to meet a horrible fate, so terrible you hardly dare take a breath in case whatever lurks here hears you.

What you actually see is a rollercoaster carriage, ready to take you on a 90-second thrill ride. As you tuck yourself into a seat and fasten your safety-belt, the ride propels you through the woodland and then drops you into a black tunnel, plummeting you past nightmarish images and oddly distorted faces.

You are then thrown into a three-loop spin, travelling round and around various flashes of the girl's adventures through this mysterious place. The final loop is accompanied with that fearsome laughter of the McGuffin, as you see the little girl, teddy bear in hand, above you and reaching out towards you. You lift your arms up to catch her, but she is snatched away at the last moment.

As the ride slows, you are treated to a final scene which depicts the little girl being reunited with her family: a smaller version of the village you passed through earlier is filled with people celebrating her safe return. The rich orange glow of the twinkly lights is somehow reassuring, everything is perfectly as it should be.

The exit steps you through to a wonderfully themed gift shop, you hear the laughter of the McGuffin echo through the corridor, seeming to follow you, even though the ride is now but a memory.

The Memory Loop demonstrates various storytelling techniques from both a structural and narrative perspective. From the plot devices and delivery mechanisms and the concept of flexing your imagination, to the McGuffin and Nested Loops. we explore ways of presenting information in a very cohesive and sticky way.

In works of fiction, the need for a plot is somewhat self-explanatory, however, non-fiction titles also require a plot, albeit one that closely emulates reality.

The information you want to offer in your book needs to be accurate and as authentic as possible. Anecdotes are used to support this information, illustrate its value and make it both engaging and compelling.

The story is a plot—a specific means of presenting the information and anecdote so that your reader is deeply affected and influenced by your book as an overall experience.

The plot is not what actually happened or true portrayal of you as a person. It is a story-based delivery mechanism that frames the information/anecdote in the most valuable way for your audience.

The plot creates a kinetic flow throughout your book and greater product range, it gives your audience something to hold on to and be guided by as they journey through your ecosystem.

So, here is a stick that magically transports you to faraway places. It seems so small and fragile, yet this little piece of wood allows you to experience different points in time. It can enable you to witness enchanting, life-changing and sometimes dramatic events from the furthest reaches of imagination.

If I told you this as cold, hard facts, you probably wouldn't believe that a mere stick is capable of this feat.

I might choose to bring forward a group of people who can testify to the power of the stick from personal experience. They could present you with anecdotal accounts of how this stick transported them away to different settings and elaborate on the contextual circumstances of their encounters.

Their explanations may interest you and in some cases they may convince you that they believe what they are saying, but would they convince you that a magical stick really exists?

Chances are that you will finish reading their tales unswayed from your initial scepticism. Anecdotes may convince some; they will leave others unmoved. Mostly, anecdotes convince us the teller believes what they are saying.

There once was a tree that stood in a wide meadow, overlooking the little village of Littleknowes (one of the three Knowes of Thrysden Hyde). In the village lived a little girl who loved that tree.

Each morning she would run giggling across the meadow, her heart pounding with excitement as the thought of climbing her solitary friend filled her being. Her family did not have much money, despite her mother and father working so hard.

And, whilst the other children in the village would spit at her and call her Penniless Penny, she still found the ability to smile when she saw the tree's outstretched branches, inviting her into his ancient embrace.

It was late one summer when Penny breathlessly climbed across the meadow, her lungs burning and knees smarting at what was once such a flat piece of land. She leant heavily on her stick, feeling the weight in each finger and the pain in every joint.

Everybody she had ever known was now gone. Her parents died long ago and even those name-calling, spit-flinging urchins had all grown up and left or gone the way we all go one day.

As she reached the crest of the slight incline, she gasped as she saw the tree shattered on the ground. Cloven in half, from a lightning strike so severe, her arboreal friend had fallen: one sliver jutting into the air, whilst his heavy trunk and ever-embracing branches now lay upon the ground.

Now you have heard the story of this magical little stick, are you not only convinced of this little stick's magic, but have you not also travelled a little into your own imagination?

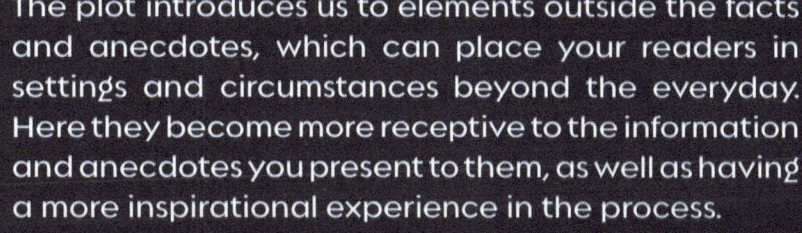

The plot introduces us to elements outside the facts and anecdotes, which can place your readers in settings and circumstances beyond the everyday. Here they become more receptive to the information and anecdotes you present to them, as well as having a more inspirational experience in the process.

Information is head-centric, anecdote is emotional and therefore of the heart, but story involves two things—the gut (our need to survive and how best to achieve that) and the imagination. Anything which leverages our imaginative abilities is limitless.

The Memory Loop serves us in various different regions of storytelling, many of which we explored in the imagineering ethos. However, there are three specific areas of interest that benefit you as a business or educational storyteller.

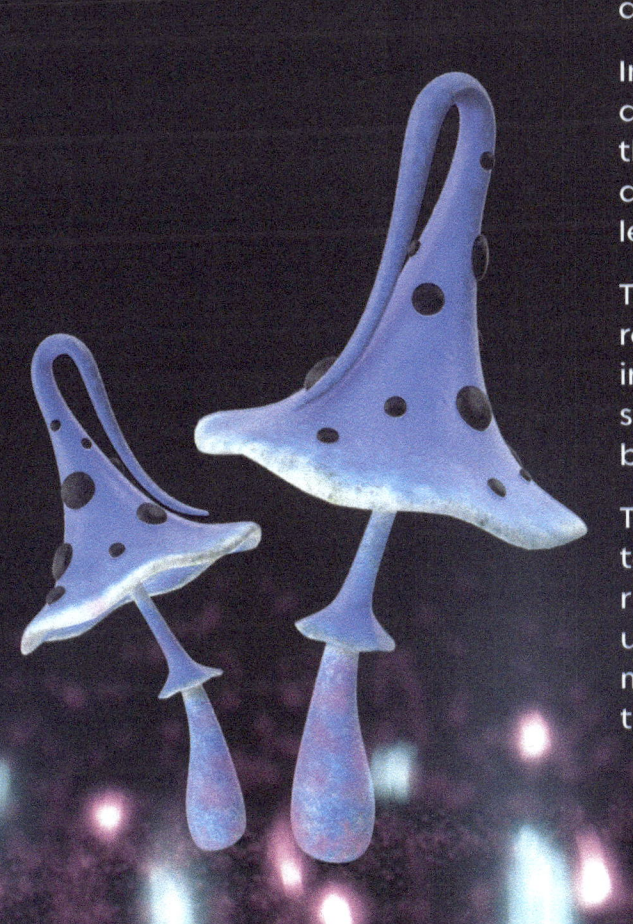

The attraction invites us to use our imagination by taking us on a journey from village to woodland to ride. It uses the concept of the McGuffin to compel us with an imperative force or time-sensitive, motivational peril—in this instance, a major threat to the survival of a child.

The attraction then uses nested loops to deliver the information within multiple layers of story. These three elements combine with pre- and post-shows, transitions, repetitions, touches, hidden dynamics and so on, to create a cohesive, immersive and neatly contained experience that entertains, emotionally engages and educates.

When you get to grips with weaving your own stories in this manner, you will stand out from the masses in your own field of expertise and demonstrate your actual expertise, by matching it with your writing expertise.

As businesspeople we may not think of our imaginations as the most powerful tool in our entrepreneurial arsenal. However, the infinite potential of your imagination is what inspired you to take the leap where so many are held back by fear.

We all know the depths and darkness of how things could go wrong or where we may end up. From the trauma of our own birth to

the monsters under the bed, it is easy to take the fear of the unknown (and how it jeopardises our survival) and tie it to any situation.

Most people spend time worrying about what might be and only ever travel to the limits of those worries. Some of us can expand our imaginations beyond the limits that life has shown us and begin to experience the successes we have not encountered before.

We can project our imaginations beyond the immediate challenges and troubles to a time when we succeed in ways that we cannot actually know from *real life*.

It is this ability in yourself and others that will enable you to create the story of your readers' success: be it educational, financial, personal or professional. Understanding where they are now

and where they will end up if they allow themselves to be guided by you, will enable you to lay down a journey before them.

Knowing them well enough to appreciate what interests them, what compels them, what they desire, will trigger your imagination to the worlds and realms that will work best for them.

What works best for your audience, what inspires them and changes their lives for the better, is an ideal you must hold sacred as the storyseller. The benevolence of something greater than any one lifetime—a true lasting legacy is vital when using these tools.

Too many politicians, and the media in general, leverage people's survival instinct and machinations of what might happen. They do so without regard for the individual person and how it is affecting their life. To avoid manipulation and control, you need

to stick to the mission of what is best for your audience.

And just as Disney can use fluffies, fairies, princesses and superheroes to consistently maintain a multi-billion-dollar, pan-global corporation, you can develop your own successful, multiplication business in your own field of expertise.

The most effective and valuable way of developing your innate ability for imagination is to nurture a sense of quirk in your imaginative experiences and expand these to extremes. Going as far as you can is the challenge, pulling back to an appropriate level is easy, so push ever onwards. And leave the editorial to the end of the process.

Finding, identifying and intensifying your own quirkiness will help you to stand out as well as enabling you to devise the perfect story envelope for your information/ anecdotal content.

Thus, when you are about to deliver a piece of information to your readers, you will be able to imagine a perfect story that delivers not only what you want, but also does it in a way that goes deeply into your reader's psyche: pervading and permeating their experience in ways that haunt and obsess them for a long time to come.

Keep in mind that story is based in the NOW—even if the narrative is set in the future or past. You author or record a story in this moment and your audience reads, watches or listens in this moment. Even when this moment is separated by centuries.

With this in mind, keep your narrative current—future-proofed if possible—and never be bound by the limitations of linear convention. Identify the most dramatic or gut-wrenching moments in your story and breadcrumb these whenever you are engaging and compelling.

Take the most inspiring and important pieces of wisdom and position these at moments in the narrative when you are haunting and obsessing. Jump from setting to setting, era to era, moment to moment, thinking ECHO at every point and not what happened and the order the events unfolded.

Your imagination is not only focused on narrative, but the visual, audio, sensual and interactive texture of your piece. By imbuing with quirk, all sensations, every moment and each layer, you will form a multifaceted adventure for your reader—one that is both valuable and enjoyable.

Absorb the everyday, things, events, thoughts, etc. and expand them into something more. Turn the simplest image or sight into a work of art, contort objects into other objects, turn scenery upside down and play with colour, texture and form.

Weave sound into an orchestral piece by blending the mundane or everyday noise into a perfectly synchronised piece of tone, melody and pitch. Make the cacophony into a concerto and the single sound into the most breathtaking solo.

Transform smells into the most exquisite perfumes. Play with the different *notes* of aroma and compose these into an olfactory journey that is both sensual and visceral. Treat every taste as you would a gourmet meal, taking each initial flavour and coalescing them into a menu of contrasting, conflicting and complementary experiences.

Get into the habit of making unusual connections, taking the mundane and making it peculiar or eccentric in some way and then amp it up. Push your own limits and go where most would fear to tread. When it comes to imagination there is a time and a place to censor yourself and it is *not* now.

For there are plenty of voices that will tell you that you *can't do that* or that *it won't work*. Your voice needs to be the one that is heard by your audience, because they have already heard those other voices too!

Your media ecosystem—your books, video channel and digital experiences—is yours and uniquely yours. Everybody else will have an opinion on what they would do. But it is what *they* would do, and you cannot really do that. You can only do what *you* can do—you can only walk your own path. So, never get bogged down in the advice of others, unless it truly inspires you.

As a pioneer of your own content, you need to go where nobody else has been before— there are often no maps or trails left by other people. You are originating something that is purely yours and as such, will have its own unique audience.

Dare to be different, be courageous and proactive, be prepared to get lost in the woods, because it is at that point, you will find your truth, rather than the voices of others you have simply learnt to mimic.

The McGuffin

The McGuffin is a plot element that initiates the story, builds momentum and creates a sense of urgency in the narrative, without necessarily being part of the main themes or core message.

The Golden Goose is a morality tale about human greed, not one of geese that lay golden eggs. Where would Indiana Jones be without the Ark of the Covenant? And without that crystal shard, we would never have pondered what a Gelfling smells like!

In many cases the McGuffin will be used as the layer of your story that motivates your reader to read on, however there may be times when the McGuffin is actually the thing you hold most dear: the apparent subject of your book and product range.

For example, some books are about NLP. Others are about the application of NLP in real-world scenarios. And then there are those books that are about the challenges people face and how they can use the way they think, feel and act to transcend those challenges.

You may have expertise in a specific field, but strip back the information that you know and you will get to the wisdom that is uniquely yours. This is the true nature of your book and ecosystem, not the labels and ideals that people may assume they are going to get by reading your book.

This is your knowledge, your personality and your book—the McGuffin is there to initiate a relationship and get the conversation going. When we delve deeper into what you are truly creating, the subject matter is the motivation to develop further interaction between you and your audience.

In this regard it is vital to write about what you know in an instinctual and imaginative way—not to promote somebody else's system or brand, but to wrap up everything you advocate into your own system or paradigm.

You make your own McGuffin, in which the hard-earned knowledge you possess is held. Each day you compete with thousands of other people who have similar training, expertise and skills in other people's ideology. By developing your own paradigm, you stand out as the only authority in your paradigm. And you will always be the greatest authority in your own paradigm!

It is very easy to pluck the McGuffin out of nothing and apply it to your paradigm (and the narrative that surrounds it). What is excruciatingly difficult is recognising the things we hold most dear. The sacred and the precious aspects of our lives are merely the McGuffin that provokes the telling of our own stories.

When writing your narrative, be very clear on what the McGuffin is and be aware that this is used to move the story along and motivate discourse with your audience, but it is not the essential foundation of your story. Avoid becoming bogged down or fixated by the McGuffin, always keep your attention on the important message that will most benefit your audience.

The Nested Loop is one of the most profound and powerful methods in the art of storytelling. A nested loop starts with a series of open-ended stories and anecdotes, each one transitioning to the next. Once we have introduced several stories, we present the important information to our readers, before closing each story in reverse order to the initial telling.

For instance, we begin with Story One, which builds to a cliffhanger and then transitions to Story Two. This ratchets up the tension to a further cliffhanger and then onto Story Three. Upon a third cliffhanger we detail each piece of valuable information we want to present in that section, before concluding Stories Three, Two and One, thus closing the loop.

The purpose of communicating in this way is that with each layer of storytelling, the reader becomes more receptive to the wrapped wisdom you place in the middle. With each successive cliffhanger, the suspense drives them forward to the next, until they are so absorbed that the information becomes firmly lodged in their memory.

Master storytellers use nested loops with ever-increasing degrees of complexity, wrapping stories across chapters, books and even an entire ecosystem.

They create nested loops within hidden dynamics as a running commentary or in-joke that builds advocacy amongst their audience. They will even design nested loops within nested loops within nested loops, to prepare the reader for vast amounts of incomprehensible data, overcome scepticism or challenge convention.

Be sure to build your expertise with nested loops through practice, before attempting various complex styles, as this can cause a story to collapse into chaos. When you become increasingly adept at constructing loops and strategising your information delivery, you will hone the art of the nested loop to awe-inspiring effect; thrilling and transforming your reader in one, very neat and rather special package.

Back at Blythe's—
a Summary of the Storytelling Adventure

In the warmth of the sun, you meander back towards Blythe's Buns, ready to reconcile everything you have learnt on this journey. As the afternoon draws to a close, you sit back down at a familiar table, surrounded by the delightful giggle of children and chirping of the ever-hungry birds.

You glance to The Compass and The Memory Loop, you reminisce about your travels through the park, from The Marvellous History of Theme Park Attractions Attraction and the children's' play area, to the various emporiums of High Street, UK, and the plentiful gems of value they held within.

You take a sip of your favourite hot beverage and you begin to jot down notes in your notebook.

Brainstorming Content/Action & Overall Strategy

The first and most important aspect of creating your book is to get as much content recorded as you possibly can. This will often involve a notebook; voice memos, online tools and other forms of capturing ideas are equally useful.

It is so important to get the information out, through brainstorming, making notes in the middle of the night, collating bullet points in an ongoing spreadsheet or document, keeping a journal and writing down everything of importance as soon as possible. Too many ideas are lost because a writer ignores an idea, believing they will remember it later!

You can also collect photos, images, audio soundbites, videos, everything that gives you ideas, develops themes or adds to the content of your book in some way.

Online resources such as *Evernote*, *Pinterest* or *Trello* are excellent ways of gathering and retaining information in a rich and visually stimulating way. And never underestimate the power of index cards that can be mixed into a storyboard at a later date.

Collate your information into an overall strategy that is simple, yet also acts as a detailed foundation to your planned title. Then add anecdotal evidence to each piece of information to illustrate and add depth to every point. Be sure to make meta-level notes whenever you have ideas on nested loops, themes, transitions, McGuffin and so on.

The Compass—
Create, Voice, Audience, Proposition, Transaction

The strategising of content is an integral element of the Creation of your book and ongoing ecosystem of products. However, it is equally important to remember the other regions of The Compass when planning your titles.

Characterisation and the attractive voice that form your author brand are essential to understanding how you will write your book. This is tied to a deep appreciation of your audience. If you do not know who your reader is and how they communicate, how can you hope to speak to them?

Knowing your readers is vital. Not through the cliché of demographics, but by really getting to grips with who they are, what they look like, what makes them laugh, how they perceive the world, what is important to them, where they hang out and what moves them, etc.

As you gain increasing clarity about who your readers are individually, you will discover more and more effective ways of interacting with them through your chosen voice and author brand.

Once you have defined and detailed both your voice and your audience, you will need to establish a firm plan and strategy for the proposition you are going to offer them. When you understand the greater overview of your proposition (ecosystem), you can create your current book in relation to that overarching world. This will form a cohesive first step in building a larger, more complex range of products.

As you write your first title, you will not only understand how it integrates into a larger product range ecosystem, but also be able to summarise topics and themes for articles and blogs, as well as developing greater detail for leveraging and widgetising products.

The Marvellous History of Theme Park Attractions
Attraction—Types & Tiers of Creation

Knowing the difference and relationships between information, anecdote and story is essential to the skill of taking raw information and turning it into a persuasive, transformative piece of narrative.

Taking a functional framework and developing it into persuasive prose is just the beginning. To create the transformational power of immersive products you will need to become an expert in storytelling.

Just as Disney turn a basic up/down ride into an advocate-making experience, you can take your wisdom and produce something that is truly remarkable. Using the imagineering philosophies, you can author a rich and expansive narrative that takes your reader on a journey and presents information and anecdote at precisely the right moment for maximum effect.

As you run every section of your text through each tier of the imagineering process, you will hone and perfect your writing into something that not only enchants and captivates—it will also turn a potential one-time customer into a servant advocate of you, your message and your business.

Breadcrumbing & Plot Strategy

When thinking about how to tell your story, you will need to consider how the art of breadcrumbing gradually unveils an engaging, compelling, haunting and obsessing story. As you decide on each crumb to place in front of your audience, you will guide them on a journey: an adventure that meanders and weaves an interesting path, rather than simply marching directly to a destination.

Exploring plot, voice, texture and action, you will begin to develop a very unique way of telling your story, with a rhythm and melody, colour and form, as well as various other elements that are special to you as an author.

In business and education we are trained into being concise and quick, but this just throws more information at the reader in a world that is already too full of information. Breadcrumbing will get your writing noticed and keep your audience's interest piqued throughout the book.

Using different plot maps you can develop an overarching theme with ambient themes and subplots. Each contrasting style of plot mapping will indicate when to introduce a theme, when to preview and review themes and how to interweave themes for the greatest effect.

As you deliver your information and anecdotes through the theme, using a plot strategy, you can imbue your narrative with increasing levels of storytelling to not only control what and when your reader is experiencing, but how they experience it. This degree of environmental precision is paramount to captivating your audience.

ECHO Valley & SPELCHEK

You will need to master how to:

- Engage your readers with Speed using humour, dramatic tension, etc.
- Compel your readers with the Power of your authority and gravitas
- Haunt your readers with Emotion, using emotive anecdotes and authoring flare to tug at their hearts
- Obsess with Lasting Change of Habits, Experiences or Knowledge, so that your reader takes your words with them into the future, in some profound way

Understanding how to combine these two processes will support you as an author in the narrative purpose of each section of your book. Knowing that the first task is to engage, followed swiftly with a compelling theme that maintains and builds the momentum throughout is vital.

Crafting your ability as an author to haunt and obsess your audience will differentiate you from other writers in your field of expertise.

The more you plus your work with ECHO Valley (and SPELCHEK) the more noticeable the results will be overall—not only to this book, but with your entire product range.

The Memory Loop—Imagination, McGuffin, Nested Loops

When it comes to imagination, you will need to practise, practise, practise! In the same way you could not run a marathon or sing an opera without first training yourself how, you need to use your imagination muscles until they become very strong.

Imagination is not necessarily about fantasy or being unrealistic. It is about the quirk that you instil in your narrative. The quirk that gets you noticed and enables your message to stand out as different.

Create a magnet that instinctually, emotionally and imaginatively informs your readers of just how different your approach is. However, if you prime them to expect something unique and then simply rehash the same stuff as everybody else in your field you are not going to develop trust.

Standing out through the intricacies and foibles of your own, particular imagination will serve you very well as an author and be greatly enjoyed by your readers.

Discerning the McGuffin as a motivating factor that drives your reader to the really important aspects of your work (your wisdom, rather than the mechanism) will help you keep the level of momentum high, even when breadcrumbing or taking time to explore greater themes.

The more accurately you can distinguish the McGuffin and use it purely to motivate, the more on-topic you will stay and the louder your message will become. Additionally, the clearer your wisdom will sound through the text of your book.

Finally, the use of nested loops will ensure that the information of the greatest value and effect is presented in the most life-changing ways to your reader. As you wrap information in anecdote and breadcrumb through layer upon layer of story, you will be able to pinpoint exactly what to offer and when.

As the Sun Sets...

...over the theme park and the magical twinkle of lights sparkle around you like ubiquitous fireflies, it is time to expand your authoring abilities even further. With your creation process now well underway, it is time to focus on the greater context of your product ecosystem.

From the creation of your unique, branded paradigm to the authoring of a rapport or authority book, it is time to understand how you can expand these into an entire world of media platforms. With every aspect of your digital and online activities, perfectly sculpted with your real-world products, services and events, you develop a cohesive journey for your audience.

It is this journey that builds relationships, enables you to stand out from every competitor and achieves an overarching, life-changing impact for yourself and others. For the true nature of storytelling is legacy— leaving a message that is greater than your own lifetime.

Section Three
And He Huffed And He Puffed...

Advanced Storyselling...
Going Beyond the Curve

When an audience trusts your ability as a storyteller, they will trust you as a businessperson and they will buy from you. This is storyselling!

The more effective you make your storytelling craft, the more you will combat many of the objections and obstacles businesses face from prospective clients.

Therefore, honing your skills as an author and mastering your expertise in storyselling is as valuable to your company as your professional knowledge in your chosen field.

However, storytelling your products and services is only the first tier of storyselling your business. To achieve the ethos of companies such as Apple, Tesla and Disney, you need to tell the story of your business from the inside out.

Great businesses have behind-the-scenes narrative that ensure the paradigm of a business is working effectively and magically. It is not enough to simply have your audience buy into the story. You too need to be enthralled by it. Your colleagues, businesses associates and anybody who comes anywhere near your business must experience it also.

We are all storytellers; some tell their stories through reports, minutes, accounts or presentations. Others do it through performance, creativity, graphic design or marketing materials. From HR to data entry, accounts to the leadership team, the story must be long enough, wide enough and deep enough to scale the entire organisation and beyond.

When you coalesce the innate value within your organisation, brand and offerings with the craft of storytelling, you start storyselling your business. When you grip your employees, partners and your audience with storyselling, you will create success in vast new areas of business.

This is not simply about negating information overload or even increasing one-off sales. Storyselling is about relationship, changing minds and hearts, to help those within and without fulfil their needs in transformative and profound ways.

Story is the interaction between a brand and its audience. As a basic need, stories fill the divide between a company and an individual, helping them to trust, build and grow together. By immersing your clients in the realms of story (and media products created by the stories you share) you will captivate them with your brand.

Many businesspeople who turn to storyselling as a quick win or to cover up weaknesses in their brand will usually make do with lazy storytelling. This fools very few people and is more likely to turn an audience away.

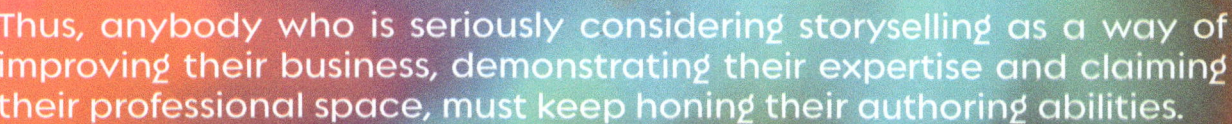

Thus, anybody who is seriously considering storyselling as a way of improving their business, demonstrating their expertise and claiming their professional space, must keep honing their authoring abilities.

Here, advanced storyselling techniques can not only help you conquer the market, but also place you ahead of any competitor. As a pioneer storyseller, you will put in place an ecosystem of media content that enthrals the clients of tomorrow.

Internally, storytelling inspires your teams into a perspective of enthusiasm—everybody buys into the ethos. This increases the overall mental and emotional health of those working for the organisation, in addition to halting the dreaded silo effect.

This also ensures you are not running at full pelt to keep up with advances in marketing and audience building, but are creating the ironclad content that others do not even know exists.

When we look to the most successful and popular storytelling of the teens, we see complex and deeply involved ecosystems. Fictional worlds that require attention, engagement and time. The multiple story arcs of the MCU, *Game of Thrones* and *The Walking Dead*, have addicted audiences across the globe.

You too can use these same narrative strategies to build a loyal and proactive audience for your business, although you need to use storytelling wisely.

Looking closely at the multi-strand stories of the MCU, we see how simple storytelling with a few key characters have gained momentum and complexity. Now each movie cascades into every other movie, with multiple storylines, a huge array of characters and very fast-paced plot development.

The Marvel television shows on Netflix also embrace this complexity, with pivotal characters appearing across the different shows to add continuity.

The behemoths of *HBO*, such as Game of Thrones and *Westworld*, use breadcrumbing, foreshadowing and in-episode turning points to develop slick, multifaceted stories which hook people very quickly.

The way many content producers in cinematic and television media addict their viewers is by using the six touches. As we explored with the Disney imagineers in their pre- and post-shows, these touches deepen relationships between the brand and the audience. On the seventh touch, if the audience are still engaged and compelled, they will begin the process of being haunted.

This remains true for all forms of media. However, it is particularly effective in multiple-thread storytelling. When various touches are triggering a range of sensory experiences, the effect is amplified.

To achieve this very quickly and effectively, the use of multiple forms of media, across a curated ecosystem of content yields amazing results. As the audience member is immersed in product after product, from a blog post to a little book, an authority title to a six-month online training programme, they become utterly transfixed and loyal to your brand.

This trusting relationship is sure-fire if the storytelling and selling is conducted in a way that is best for your audience. Hence, knowing your clients better than anybody else is a great foundation. Knowing how your brand offers them an

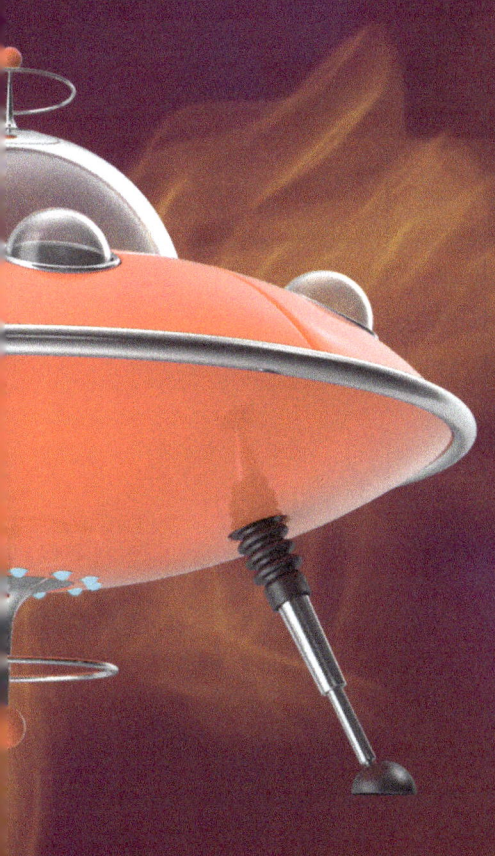

addictive proposition is even better. When you consider this is all achieved with stories, your ability to author great content needs to operate at an extraordinary level of mastery.

So, when it comes to advanced storytelling, it is not about learning more techniques or delving deeper into challenging narrative tools: it is a question of how you craft your narrative over a huge canvas of blank space.

When potentially looking at hundreds or even thousands of autonomous and discrete items of content, from reader discovery to last page, you need to hold the vision, whilst you expertly develop the ecosystem.

This product creation journey is done in linear fashion, yet involves multiple perspectives and an all-time approach. You need to know, regardless of the audience journey, what they will encounter when they are walking their path through your world.

If they encounter *that* book after listening to *this* audio file, how will this differ from reading that same book after watching *this* video?

If one reader has learnt a technique from another book in your canon, how do you stop them suffering reader fatigue when you need to repeat the technique for new audience members?

These are just two examples of many, many factors that come into play when storyselling through an entire product range. The solution is found in the creation, brand, audience, proposition, transaction, analysis, strategy and development of your ecosystem.

Product Creation Journey

Armed with the skills you have developed thus far, you will now be able to create captivating products. As you author books, scripts and other media, you will develop an ever-increasing ecosystem of valuable titles that transform clients into advocates of you and your business.

To be successful in your multiplication-of-time business, you will need to develop a cohesive range of titles on an ongoing basis. Your audience will hunger for more, so whilst new clients will be entering your content funnel, it is vital to offer further products and bigger-ticket items to your existing advocates. Their loyalty is your success.

The first step to honing the ideal product range for your business is to understand how products differ depending on the type of business you currently run. Service-based businesses, such as coaching and consultancy companies, will need different products to those who sell physical products.

Companies that offer physical products will differentiate their offerings depending upon whether they originate the products themselves or buy items for resale. Knowing how your specific business changes your ecosystem will be of real help in the creation and ongoing development of your range.

A product range or, better still, an ecosystem of products is a systemic thing. A world that your audience enters, browses and makes purchases within. Each title you create, promotion you launch or event you hold will affect this system.

Many content creators release titles that reinforce problematic aspects of the overall ecosystem. This could be that a product will attract clients that are detrimental to the author's brand or, equally as damaging, a product that will counteract/negate some other region of the range.

This is an endemic issue with many of the most viewed YouTubers. They build a channel on the platform, never expecting to be as successful as they are and end up with major flaws in their ecosystem.

Beginning with a specific subject or theme, the channel will become so popular the YouTuber themselves becomes the focus, rather than the subject matter. Here, they will often diversify into meme content (such as the latest *challenge* or microwaving fairy lights) or create videos about themselves and what they are cooking for dinner.

In extreme examples, the media creators will resort to clickbait content that fabricates a whole life for the YouTube celebrity or will team up with other channels in the scrabble to offer subscribers something new.

Knowing how an ecosystem functions from a systemic point of view will help you smooth out issues such as this, while enhancing the features that make you and your business successful. With a strong paradigm, method and legacy vision for your ecosystem, you will always have a fresh supply of new ideas and content for your audience.

Your ecosystem requires you to offer various forms of media that augment your audience's reality, so the more *au fait* you are with transmedia and what it can do for your business, the better your overall product range will be.

Here, in the Resort and Spa, we kick back, relax and take some time to reflect on how to turn your expertise into products that sell, both from the perspective of your existing business and the new content-related business you are developing.

Your Business—Your Products

There are many business models: including retail, franchise and subscription-based approaches. In the theme park, we visited three different types of business on High Street, UK, each of which uses elements of these models. The businesses were:

- *Blythe's Buns and Biscuits*—A cake shop specialising in handcrafted bakery items, created by the owner, Ms Blythe
- *The Shoppe of Intangible Things*—A business that delivers services such as coaching, training, consultancy and so on
- *The Guild of Nomads*—An emporium which sells artisan products made by other people (making The Guild a reseller or middleman)

Of course, there is a certain degree of blending between these three styles of business, for instance, Blythe's Buns has barista service. Here the results are obvious, but the service is not a physical product in itself.

The Shoppe of Intangible Things has physical products for sale, such as their own course materials and third-party resources, such as books. The Guild of Nomads sources the goods it sells (a service) and has a range of self-branded products, such as postcards and tee shirts.

Leaving aside these crossover areas of business, let us investigate these three types of business and how they can each create a range of content-related, multiplication products.

So, the three types of business we visited are:

- Those which sell in-house made products
- Those which sell services and intangibles
- Those which sell externally produced products

Blythe's Buns and Biscuits—
A Baking Extravaganza

Ms Blythe prides herself in the products she creates for sale and she knows that the retail experience does not stop at buns and other baked goods. For people to keep coming back for more, to sit in the café space and to recommend her business to their friends, she needs to offer good service and a pleasing environment.

The selling of baked goods is akin to the up and down ride, introduced in The Marvellous History of Theme Park Attractions Attraction—it creates customers.

Placing those baked goods in a specific setting and being aware of how this affects the customers is rather like Dr Doom's Fearfall attraction, creating clients who may return for more sweet indulgences.

However, Ms Blythe wants advocates. Those loyal people who not only return time and time again, but those who are exclusive and go the extra mile by promoting her business and getting involved.

To nurture an advocate relationship with her clients, Ms Blythe will need to introduce the Disney approach, such as that used to construct The Tower of Terror attraction. This is when a book and related ecosystem of products can really build her business. For in these new products, she becomes not merely a baker, but a friend that her advocates know and trust.

So, Ms Blythe writes a book of recipes; each one comes from a traditional item that is also available in her shop. As she writes, she includes stories from her life: sharing with

her readers anecdotes about her own grandmother and how she passed on the old ways of baking.

The book also includes tips and advice for achieving a better bake: from warming the ingredients to room temperature to icing techniques for different finishes. It is sumptuously themed with a rustic, homely style that harks back to a time when baking was a staple of hearty living.

Once this initial book is published, Ms Blythe takes the fifty or so tips that are scattered throughout the book and places these into their own pocket book.

This compact companion book offers each gem of wisdom in a concise and easy to find way, so rather than hunting through the big recipe book, a reader can locate the desired nugget of advice quickly.

She then creates laminated recipe cards for each recipe in the book and these become a more expensive, luxury item. Then she records audio for a CD set and digital download, in which she guides her audience in the baking of selected recipes. As she walks them step by step through each bun and cake, she chats about herself and her life as a friend might give an insight into who they are.

These audio products are presented as mentoring and cause the listener to feel they are baking alongside a trusted companion and wise master. As they listen and bake, they trust Ms Blythe ever more; they begin to feel as if they know her. And what's more, they hark back to their experiences in her shop and want to spend time there again very soon.

This is only the beginning. For Ms Blythe soon starts developing one-day workshops, each one covering a different type of baked produce, from pastries to buns, bread to gateaux and pies to biscuits. These foundation days lead to a week retreat and then an online home baker mastery course.

All the while, Ms Blythe is adding more scope, detail and types of product to her range. Whether it is collecting new recipes, developing books that go into greater, but more specific detail or even diversifying into pre-mixed, bake-at-home ingredient packs, which come with a downloadable audio of Ms Blythe meandering the listener through the history, method and other fun titbits of this particular item.

The baking of a hundred cakes takes Ms Blythe an hour; she cannot bake any faster than that. Those hundred cakes bring Ms Blythe a certain, finite income, which she could increase by raising the price, but there are limits to how much and how often she can do this.

For every product this master baker authors, leverages and widgetises, she can create ongoing income that multiplies her time across various products and multiple purchases. Hence, by growing her business through content-related products she actually develops a whole new business that uses her expertise in a different way.

The Shoppe of Intangible Things—
At Your Service

All sparse surfaces and crisp lines, the open-plan layout of The Shoppe of Intangible Things is very different from the frenetic atmosphere of Blythe's. Whereas the café and bakery's shelves are crammed full of tasty morsels, here the walls offer concepts rather than physical consumables.

Beautifully designed posters present various courses, events and services that all at once can make the most profound changes to one's life, yet cannot be quantified or held in one's hand.

Here, a team of knowledgeable individuals use their expertise and skills to help others attain a better life in some way. From the personal-development strategies of coaches to therapy training or marketing consultancy, each service is both invisible by nature, yet totally apparent in effect.

Often, the prospective client may not even know what they are purchasing here, because what they want to achieve on the face of it is not actually what they want to achieve. For example, a person may enrol on a business success course, which is actually about marketing, sales and accountancy.

These three topics are not business success in themselves, but when conducted in certain ways, can improve the chances of business success. Hence, the client is not buying what they want, but what they need.

On every occasion that a coach, trainer or consultant from this business sits down with a client, they do so on a time-for-money basis. An hour of service equals an hour of payment, reflecting the customer-driven ethos of the up and down fairground ride.

Every professional who presents their services through this business also has a book, which distils helpful aspects of their expertise into a paperback toolkit for the reader. Each book introduces the reader to a journey of several hours in duration, where they are guided through the specific topic in great detail.

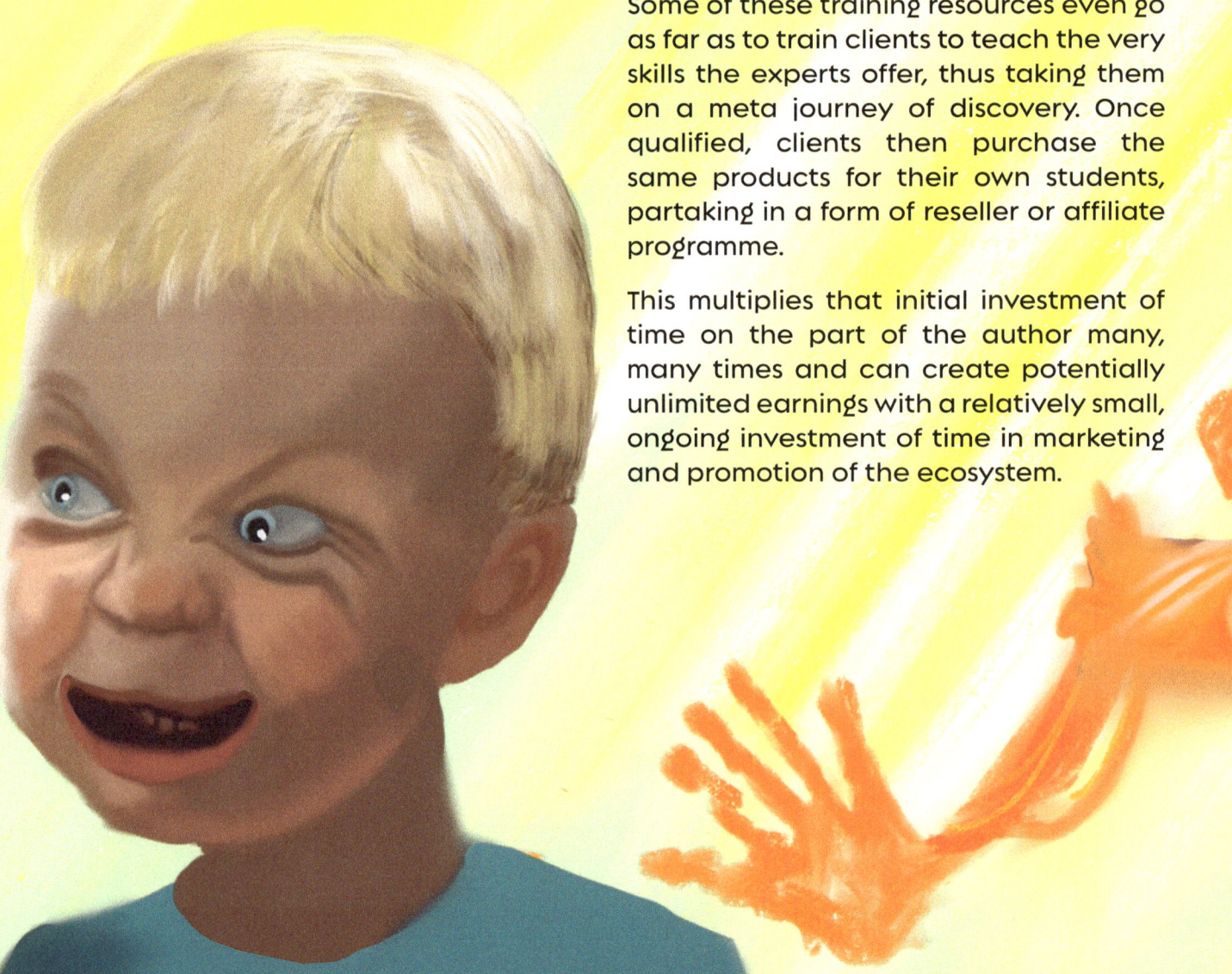

This not only increases the value of an hour of the writer's time, but also builds a relationship of trust and respect for the expertise and mastery of the author's knowledge. Here, the initial time invested in writing the book is multiplied by the number of clients who buy the book, but also gives a greater length of time in value to each reader.

This mirrors the approach of Universal with Dr Doom's Fearfall. The books on display are client-creating resources that bring repeat purchases and increase the value of training, coaching and consulting services offered.

The products do not stop here, however, as the intangible is made even more tangible through online training and home-study courses. These give regular, automated tutorials and self-motivated study resources, along with a range of up- and side-sell ranges. All presented in an ecosystem that is perfectly themed to the field of a particular expert.

The Disney approach of story does not simply bombard clients with products, it creates a world of products that clients are invited to explore and, by doing so, they become advocates.

Some of these training resources even go as far as to train clients to teach the very skills the experts offer, thus taking them on a meta journey of discovery. Once qualified, clients then purchase the same products for their own students, partaking in a form of reseller or affiliate programme.

This multiplies that initial investment of time on the part of the author many, many times and can create potentially unlimited earnings with a relatively small, ongoing investment of time in marketing and promotion of the ecosystem.

The Guild of Nomads—
A Whole New World

This cornucopia of shelves, crammed full of products from around the world may seem random and chaotic at first glance, but it has a highly defined niche. Here, available products are sourced locally, but not nationally or online. You cannot find the products in supermarkets and the manufacturers do not even have online stores.

Therefore, every artisan product can be bought only from the Guild or by going to where it is made. The products range from fine beverages and luxury chocolates, to beauty treatments, handmade pottery, candles, jewellery, clothing and art work. In fact, some of the items on these shelves are so obscure you would not even know what they are!

Some pieces are everyday, whilst others are truly unusual. There are those which cause the owner to feel happier about themselves, their day and life in general. There are some items that come wrapped in mystery and are a little darker than the rest.

Brightly decorated walls lead to dark corners. Twinkling lights enchant and odd angles unnerve. This is a very odd place indeed.

Nevertheless, for the weird and wonderful miscellany of stock, here is a successful and strong business. The proprietors know how to achieve profits, whilst offering excellent customer service. Their use of IT for stock processing and clever employment of systems ensures the day-to-day running is fluid and smooth, whilst a flair for picking desirable goods and displaying them to maximise sales is legendary.

The owners of this shop bring with them a wealth of business skills that most crave to possess. And it is these underlying business skills that present opportunities for an ecosystem of products.

Whilst not many people would want books on hand-sculpted clay fairies or the blending prices of English Breakfast tea, there is a huge market for people who want to explore business growth from people who build their businesses every day.

With real-world knowledge of the different aspects of business practice, the concept of the product ecosystem could be: multiple courses and education products on branding, marketing, sales and systems. These can then be supported with books and digital stand-alone products that present a client journey from first sale to big-ticket and continuity product.

Where the product ranges of Blythe's and The Shoppe of Intangible Things are extensions of the existing business, this style of ecosystem creation actually forms a completely separate business. This business not only leverages existing and provable business skills, but enables the creator to have a self-made catalogue of content and original intellectual property.

Whilst the existing business continues to flourish, they can build a whole new business from the ground up. One that transitions them from the reseller or middleman framework, to that of the content creator/owner.

The journey from customer to advocate begins with the selling of artisan products, which creates customers and some clients. If the owners of this type of business were to simply write books on those products, it would maintain a business in a similar single-item space and maintain a customer/client relationship, with an emphasis on the client relationship.

To focus a new business on the business skills they have would catapult their clients into the advocate arena, with clients coming back for more, time and time again. *Along with* converting information into transformation—a sure method of attaining loyalty from your audience.

The Nature of Ecosystem

The development of a successful product range is a feat of inspiring creation, great branding, knowledgeable marketing strategies, a magnetic proposition and accessible sales tactics. From there on in it is down to your customers whether they buy or not.

However, analysis of all sales and future planning based upon those transaction statistics are also essential to the ongoing refinement of your range. Even tried and trusted brands need to adapt over time to keep an edge over competitors and, more importantly, to ensure the relationship with clients is maintained.

Traditionally, businesses have viewed a product range as a very simple series of products that are either positioned at the same level of value and cost or advance from entry product to big-ticket item and continuity product.

In modern product-related strategy, the focus is on replacing this basic linear process with a customer to advocate journey that changes and adapts to the needs of each client.

Each and every person that purchases one of your products will have slightly different needs and perceptions. If you can present them with a tailored path through your catalogue, they will gradually form a lasting trust and attachment to your brand.

This is where a paradigm is an absolute must! Your own unique system transitions the generic, catch-all solution to a highly-adaptable method that the audience member applies to their own life. Rather than shouting quick fixes into the void, you offer a machine that takes problems and adapts solutions for the individual needs of your client.

Armed with your paradigm, they will not only make repeat purchases and recommend your business to their family, friends and colleagues, they will also step up when you need them to. A request for support, suggestions, testimonials is just the beginning.

Advocates will protect your brand, will adjust their behaviour to fit in with your ethos and even rearrange their whole life to place your business at the centre of it.

A bit far-fetched, you ask?

Just think about the Disney advocates who move to Florida to be nearer the theme parks and resorts or change jobs to get more time off for their Disney vacations! Reflect on the Apple advocates who set aside money from their wages every week of the year to buy products that they do not even know exist.

Every day, relationships are forged and ended, careers made and changed, fortunes made and squandered, because of the advocacies we develop in our own lives.

As customers we buy things, as clients we actively seek out purchases, yet as advocates, we partner with the businesses of our choosing—and those partnerships have deep-rooted and lasting effects on the widest reaches of our lives.

If you're not thinking ecosystem, you're not thinking business. For every product you create is merely a hobby; one that many will compliment you on, some will actually buy and a few will genuinely make use of. But, it will have no real longevity or lasting impact on their lives.

At its heart, an ecosystem has a precisely defined purpose or scope, it has emotional depth and it has longevity—the power to remain in a person's life for a long, long time. These three dimensions of ecosystem create a solidity to your products, one that increases the impact upon your advocates.

Additionally, there are various other factors that we must consider in the creation of an ecosystem. We are essentially constructing a world that we invite clients into, so they can find their own way through your range of products and services. Rather than adapting your products to each and every person, you present them with the scope and flexibility to make their own path from product to product, in the media form they most want.

This involves a great degree of planning and a definitive strategy, though in the long term it will pay off in ways that far outreach linear-product-range thinking.

Let us now explore the factors to consider when forming an ecosystem approach to your multiplication business and its products.

We could refer to an ecosystem as holographic, because whilst every detail is housed within the big picture, every detail reflects every other detail of the big picture. When you write a book, you want to gather each important theme from every other title in some basic form. You then seed this throughout your book, so it feeds an ongoing journey to your reader.

Therefore, focus on each detail, in addition to big picture and also know how each single product is positioned in relation to the whole. The goal of this is to achieve a naturally balanced ecosystem—or product homeostasis.

When a product is in homeostasis, it will smoothly guide a client from beginning, to end, to next product. It is not an end result or stand-alone—it is a link in the chain or step on the staircase.

If you include products in your ecosystem that are not in homeostasis, they will form

a vicious cycle that snaps your clients out of the world and directly into the marketing range of your competitors. This disengagement from your titles can stop a relationship dead, so it is vital that you are aware of any vicious cycles in your range.

Each product forms a virtuous cycle or a vicious cycle. The skill is in ensuring each product forms part of an overall virtuous cycle, in addition to identifying any vicious cycles that are underpinning this.

Hence, when creating a particular product, it is important that you keep your focus on the entire ecosystem and to specify a title's position within it, rather than becoming lost in the intricacies of that one position. We focus on the vision, not just individual goals. On something for a greater purpose than ourselves and not just what it will bring you in its own right.

As a product range, we view a book, a CD, a digital download, as things that are just there to be purchased. In an ecosystem, it is a living and evolving system with dynamic patterns of behaviour.

It is essential to understand these underlying patterns; to identify the behind-the-scenes structure. You absolutely must know how this structure both affects your client's journey through the ecosystem and how the construction of individual products will change and adapt the overall world.

When you can leverage change in the discrete patterns of each title to the overall enhancement of your ecosystem, its profitability and your client's journey from customer to advocate, you will possess a powerful means of identifying new products and how to revise older titles.

Being able to leverage changes in the whole ecosystem relies on your understanding of the relationships between products, rather than each title in isolation. We are taught in life to break things down into component parts, in order to understand complexity.

Unfortunately, when we break an ecosystem into chunks, we break it full stop! Conversely, starting with chunks or building blocks creates a rigid and inflexible structure, which falls apart when

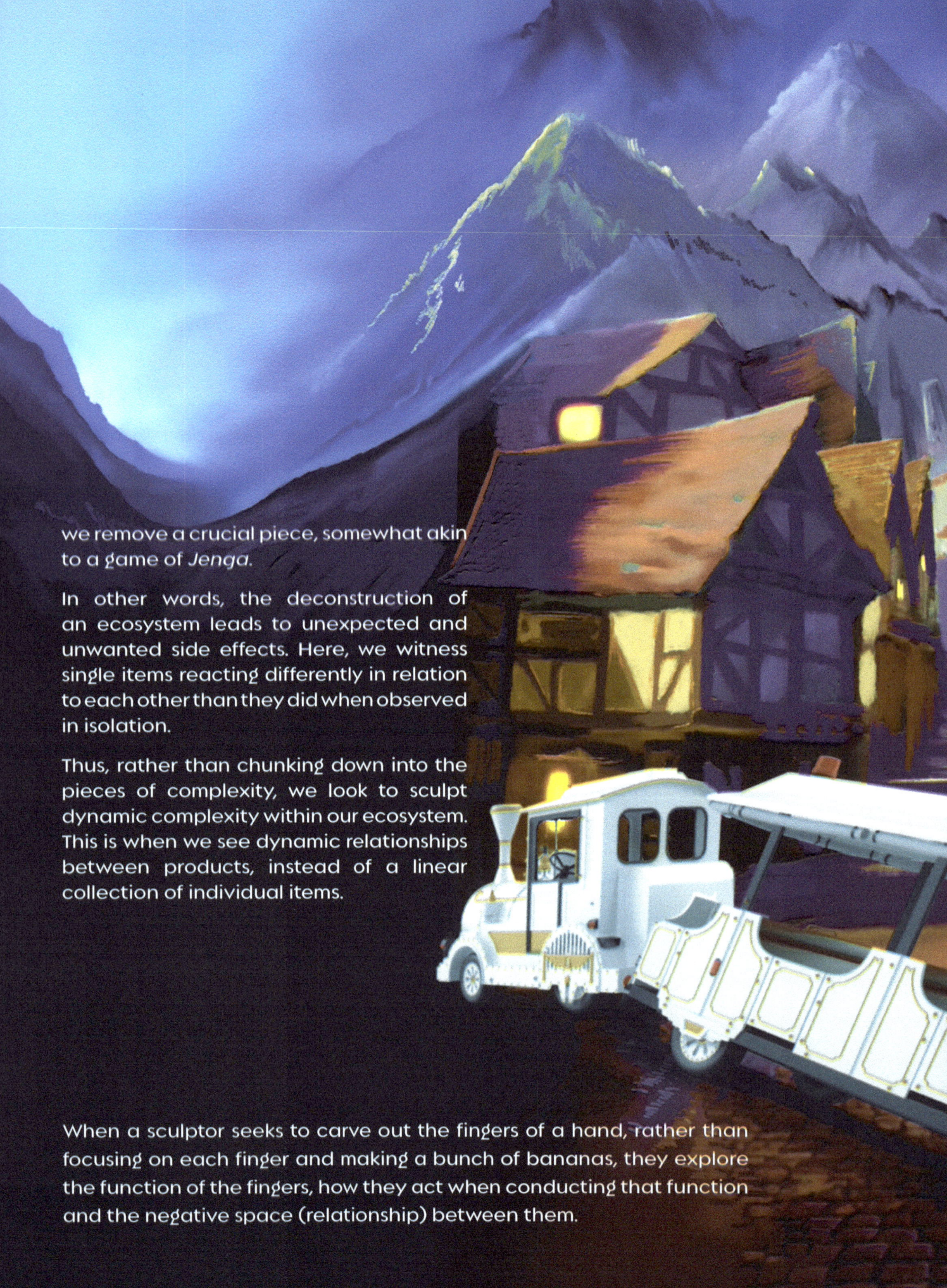

we remove a crucial piece, somewhat akin to a game of *Jenga*.

In other words, the deconstruction of an ecosystem leads to unexpected and unwanted side effects. Here, we witness single items reacting differently in relation to each other than they did when observed in isolation.

Thus, rather than chunking down into the pieces of complexity, we look to sculpt dynamic complexity within our ecosystem. This is when we see dynamic relationships between products, instead of a linear collection of individual items.

When a sculptor seeks to carve out the fingers of a hand, rather than focusing on each finger and making a bunch of bananas, they explore the function of the fingers, how they act when conducting that function and the negative space (relationship) between them.

THE TROUBLE
WITH TRYFAN

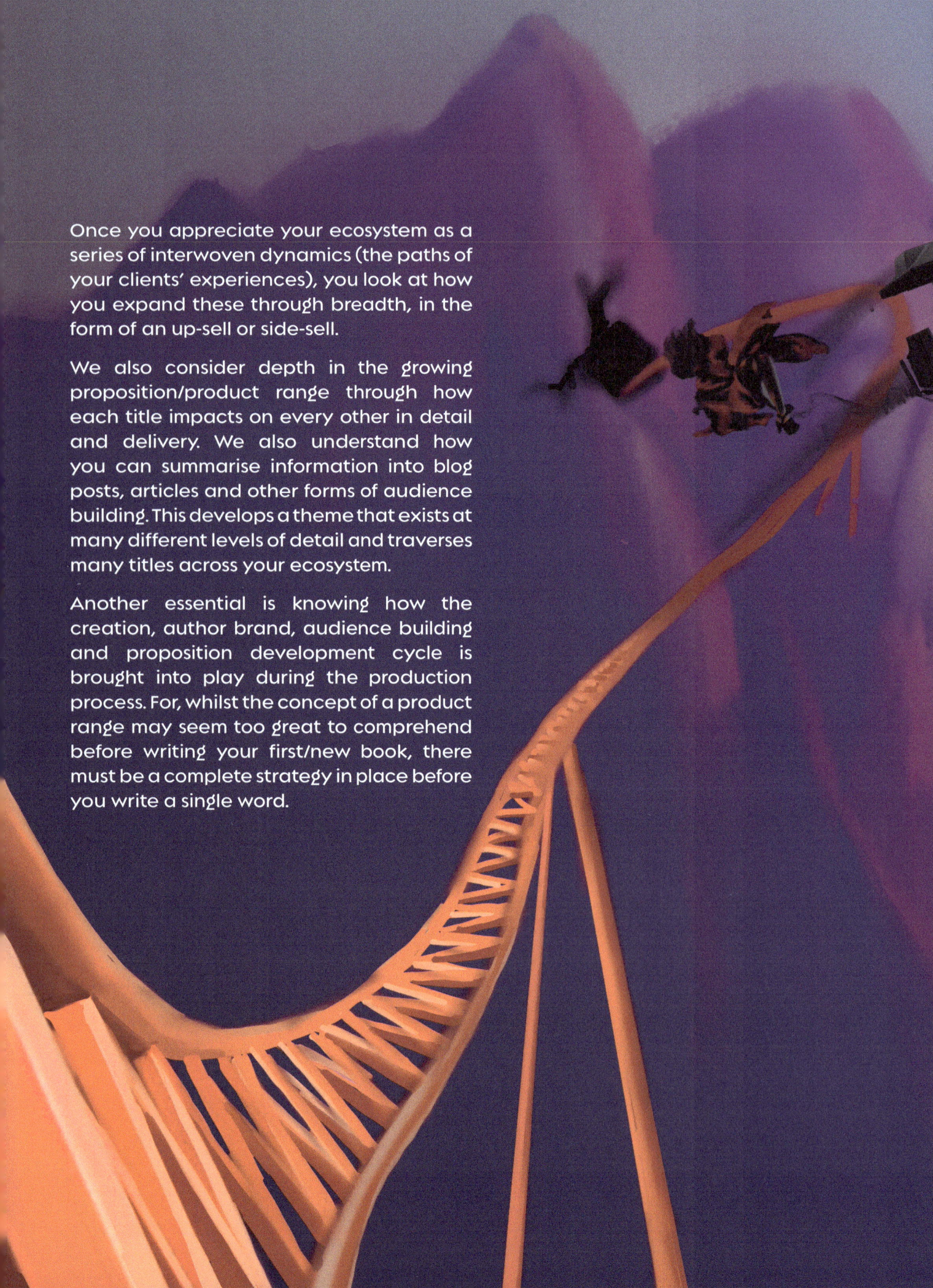

Once you appreciate your ecosystem as a series of interwoven dynamics (the paths of your clients' experiences), you look at how you expand these through breadth, in the form of an up-sell or side-sell.

We also consider depth in the growing proposition/product range through how each title impacts on every other in detail and delivery. We also understand how you can summarise information into blog posts, articles and other forms of audience building. This develops a theme that exists at many different levels of detail and traverses many titles across your ecosystem.

Another essential is knowing how the creation, author brand, audience building and proposition development cycle is brought into play during the production process. For, whilst the concept of a product range may seem too great to comprehend before writing your first/new book, there must be a complete strategy in place before you write a single word.

Forging Your First Ecosystem

When it comes to developing your first ecosystem of products, you need to set out with a very clear understanding that this is not a book or blog or YouTube channel or website or business report. It is a world. And more importantly it is *your* world!

Here, you will present your audience with an in-depth understanding of how you will help them transform their lives through use of your paradigm. You will guide them on a journey that is uniquely yours to create. You will demonstrate how your experience and expertise can impact their lives in profound ways. And you'll have an opportunity to invite them to step back into your world time and time again.

With this in mind, it is important that you begin with a very clear vision of where you are going with your ecosystem and how it will represent you in the best way for your audience to reach you.

Most view this through the lens of five or ten years. Some modern businesspeople think in terms of a lifetime or even centuries of value for the audience. If you really want to be the authority in your field, claim your territory and storysell your way to success, you will need to think a bit bigger—in terms of thousands of years!

Human society, with the help of politicians and the media, thinks in the *short now* and the *little here*. So, we tend to focus on our own little piece of the world and act in terms of the immediate future (including that five or ten-year period).

The short-term, quick-fix, navel-gazing answers to problems we do not actually face have swamped us to the degree of not even realising the importance of our own lifetime.

Sure, we may think in terms of pension and funeral planning, but what about the meaning and result of your lifetime?

What will you achieve, in every moment you have, to change the lives of others for the better?

If you are only looking after your tiny piece of the world and within the context of your own lifetime, you are wasting your life! Your content will be around for centuries and potentially for thousands of years, so why are you not planning for that?

If thousands of years seems too much too cope with, think about this. You take 960 breaths on average, every hour. This is very roughly the estimated number of months you will live on this Earth.

If your lifetime is an hour, this time next week will be 10,000 years in the future!

Despite seeming too huge to comprehend, an epoch is no time at all. When you invest your lifetime (or what you have left of your lifetime) in the creation of a system that changes the world over a ten-thousand-year period, then you are doing something truly worthwhile.

With this in mind, ask yourself:

- What do I truly care about?

Followed closely by:

- What do I want my life to be about?

And:

- How can I use this vision to help other people—my clients/audience?

Then finally:

- How wide can I make my influence and for how long?

Creating an ecosystem based in transformation, rather than information, is focused on self-actualisation and seeing one's life as a creative work that develops something greater than oneself—a legacy.

Your ecosystem stems from you and your uniqueness, but its focus has to be the needs of your audience wherever and whenever they are—if you cannot attract and sustain clients through the benefits of your products, any success will be short-lived.

Thus, in asking these questions, you are seeking to identify the challenges and issues that your clients encounter on a regular basis—and how your niche expertise can help solve those issues.

By appreciating the ways in which you can help them and holding a vision of what their lives will be like with your support, you are developing a creative tension.

Remember, in all situations there is the current reality, which is different from/at odds with your vision of the future. Every vision has a resolution which is derived from holding your vision until it is realised, or by lowering your vision into the reality you currently are experiencing.

If you hold fast to your vision, the creative tension brings reality to your vision. However, there are other factors at work here: pervasive mediocrity and information smog get most people to buy into emotional tension, which diminishes a vision for the future to the expectations of the present reality.

So:

Vision + Reality = Creative Tension.

Why is this important in the pursuit of your ecosystem of products?

Most businesspeople (and new authors in general) discover that when they begin to create their titles, the creative tension feels strange. And strange in a way that is not comfortable. This can lead to a loss of motivation, distraction exercises and eventually forgetting about the task at hand.

New authors will often make excuses or experience a failing of confidence the deeper they venture into the process. But this is creative tension—the very thing that needs to be there for any worthwhile product to exist. The more creative tension associated with a product, the more uncomfortable it can feel!

Global reach and epoch-defining thought is a whole lot of creative tension! It invites you to think about the greater worldview or the immediate pain, because upon feeling the sensations caused by creative tension, most new authors confuse the experience with emotional tension.

They react as they might if they felt fear, pain or anguish: by moving away from it! Personal mastery is knowing the distinction between creative tension and emotional tension; leveraging the former to make a difference, whilst transcending the latter.

Personal mastery is what you need to develop your ecosystem. Along with new skills, strength of character, steadfast commitment and courage. Combine this with the consistent, conscious act of doing the work and you begin to bring reality closer to your vision of it.

It is worth noting that emotions need to be there, they are just a part of current reality and everyday experience. These add to creative tension, which acknowledges reality and shifts it towards your vision. Yet succumbing to those emotions will pull you towards the current reality, without ever changing it into your vision. So, when it comes to emotions, use them, but do not be distracted by them.

The strategy for developing your ecosystem is your personal and professional vision. To build a fully-actualised and real-world ecosystem of products you require a shared vision between you and your clients/advocates.

They will hold and support your vision with you, making it a powerful brand. This shared vision is not a physical or real thing, more a shared identity or set of values—a community.

Shared vision is not about telling people what they should do or buy. It is their choice. This choice is more than enrolment into your brand and business. It is a joint responsibility for the overall success of the ecosystem and its cause.

This is your fan base and your advocates will behave like fans, when they subscribe to the shared vision of the ecosystem.

Create governing ideals for your ecosystem—these are vision (what), mission (why) and core values/paradigm (how). The ideals you create are at the heart of the relationships and dynamics formed in your ecosystem. It is important to reiterate that *what* and *why* will make up the majority of your ecosystem's content with *how* being the cliffhanger for the next instalment.

Every product and item within your ecosystem will form dynamics as an effect of how it relates to every other aspect of your ecosystem. For instance, your first book will relate to every blog post you've written as part of your ecosystem. If you contradict yourself in either book or blog, you will create a dynamic that undermines your audience's trust in your overall ecosystem.

If you assert and reassert a cohesive and consistent paradigm throughout your ecosystem, you will amplify your message and form a really strong and lasting conversation with your audience. Thus, it is very important to monitor and evaluate the relationships within your ecosystem over time.

As you detect the cause of relationship building and diminishing dynamics, as well as the effect through time, you can adapt and leverage these to perfect the overarching range.

You can leverage conducive dynamics to create harmony in your overall range, these include audience engagement, transactions such as signups or sales and beneficial feedback.

Destructive dynamics will reinforce the issue when you allow them to continue. These can be lack of client retention, lack of sales or signups and harmful feedback (which often signifies the audience member is not a good fit for you).

Also, be aware delays in the overall system may occur—these require patience to get a true picture of what the results are. Sometimes an element of the system is destructive/conducive to the overall system, but is resulting in the polar opposite in quality—this may change over time on its own, but if you alter the offending aspect in some way, you cannot be immediately certain of the effect. Hence, the consistency of your monitoring process over time is essential.

Be aware that polarity is often a sign of success—if you are truly changing the world through your business, it will make waves, disrupt the status quo and cause the established power-controller to be vocal about their discomfort!

Transmedia

Creating a modern, effective ecosystem of content-related products requires various degrees of transmedia. While a book is a powerful place for you to start, contemporary consumers are not satisfied only with a printed book that offers one-way communication.

They desire a rich and tailored experience, which enables them to interact through a multi-sensory journey. So, once your initial creation process is underway, it is important to appreciate where your book sits within a greater transmedia ecosystem of content.

The use of multimedia has been available to us since the 1980s, but the world and the expectations of clients have changed. Not simply content to purchase what you think they want, they are hungry for something that immerses and engages them at a profound level.

When most hear the term *transmedia*, they think of digital, multimedia resources: usually a website with video and audio.

Transmedia is actually something different and very specific.

At the heart of a transmedia experience is the consumer and their environment. They are not going to a website or reading a book: they are engaging in an interaction that envelops them through their environment.

Thus, transmedia is sculpted in the audience's world by layering media that is interlaced and overlaps. When creating transmedia titles, we bring the content to the audience member, rather than them going somewhere to find it, i.e. online.

Here, content is delivered to the audience in their own context. It changes according to time of day or their location. The strategy will take into consideration the context of each audience member and delivers them media that reflects where they are, when and what is taking place in their surroundings.

So, we could sum up transmedia as an ecosystem-based approach of using

media as an immersive environment. Here you use various media forms to create a world and invite your reader to explore that world through different products and services.

Transmedia resources include:

- Images/Video/Diagrams
- Sound FX/Narration/Music
- Interaction/Action
- Environment/Olfactory/Gustatory
- Kinaesthetic/Print/Mobile/Touch
- Ecosystem/Overarching Strategy

However, more important than the individual resources, is how these relate to each other: how we interlace media to form a seamless journey. As the creator of such a journey, you need to be thinking about, planning and developing a range of products that considers who your audience is, what they want and where they are.

If your audience are mostly at home when they are interacting with you through your products, how can you make the experience more immersive in a place where highly engrained habits may distract them?

If they are in the office, how will you adapt this to take into consideration work commitments? What about audience comments and the various sensory input that your world will have to incorporate into the interaction?

So, appreciating what media form is best suited to delivering a particular piece of narrative is one aspect of your strategy. Understanding the variable context of that delivery is another. With an audience who want their content delivered in a fast, effective and interactive way—wherever they are—it is not simple a question of technology.

Technology is driven by content—if there is a sales, marketing or other business need that can be provided by specific content and that content needs enhanced technology, the tech will be manufactured. So, modern storysellers are content innovators, as well as content creators.

Technology born without content is destined to sit on a shelf waiting for content or simply fail altogether. Examples of this litter the augmented reality field, with tech companies seeking to blot out the world with content, rather than overlay it. Without the guidance of content that can be delivered by augmented reality, the devices have nothing to sustain them.

Your ecosystem of products will not only multiply your income, be the core of your business activities and provide extreme value to your audience—it will offer them ways of consuming content they had not even thought existed.

With a transmedia-based platform, you will be writing books, both printed and digital, recording video and audio, as well as designing the visual and experiential aspects of your products. More importantly, however, you will be sculpting how these are delivered; tailoring your presentations to the needs of your audience. By doing so they will keep returning to you, rather than your competitors.

As we develop new platforms in virtual and, more significantly, augmented reality, your content will literally overlay the physical world through your audience member's mobile devices. And if innovations in this field, such as Pokémon Go, have taught us anything, it is that new ways of delivering content bring up new challenges.

From people walking out in front of fast-moving traffic to the discovery of corpses in local woodlands, the media frenzy around these types of stories has only fuelled interest in the AR paradigm. However, as an author you will probably need to start small, but even on a low budget, you can still achieve a great deal using a transmedia platform.

The availability of media apps and design platforms is so wide now, any space you can use a device, becomes a makeshift studio. From filming and audio recording, music and sound effects, animation and presentations, even printing and physical product creation—if you know how to use the software, you can make it happen.

The vital piece of this endeavour is, of course, to focus on the quality of your audience's experience. The media must immerse them in your world, rather than

make it inaccessible. If you overwhelm your audience, the media elements will be for nought. Yet, when you sculpt each piece of media so it overlays your reader's world, they will appreciate the transmedia as an enhancement to their experience.

Each element of your transmedia strategy needs to be placed in a specific place and at a certain point of the narrative, because it makes sense at that point. It adds to the narrative, rather than dilutes it. This is particularly valuable in educational materials, where information overload can be negated by listening, rather than reading, watching a fun cartoon instead of a convoluted chapter of text.

Treat your media elements as rewards for your audience. Make them want to view each video or play every soundbite. You could even go as far as to employ the Skinner Method, where small rewards come thick and fast at first, with *reinforcement* becoming less frequent (in proportion) as the book goes on.

Match the feel and rhythm of media with the tone and pace of the book—be it light-hearted, tense or profound. And think about what accessing the media will mean logistically. Will your reader have to break their flow at a point where it is easy to forget their train of thought or as they are desperate to discover what happens next?

One of these will confuse, one will have them frantically grabbing their mobile device and interacting with you.

Most importantly, when devising your transmedia proposal for your book, look to your content ecosystem as integral to your world. Everything is connected. Your blogs and Twitter feed are not separate ventures to your book—they are all interrelated as part of your transmedia strategy.

To truly embrace the transmedia ethos, you need to envisage your audience completely encapsulated in the arena of your content. They want to be there and are thrilled by the experiences within. If, for some reason, they leave your world, they desperately want to be back there in a state of deep immersion.

Each media item is a nut, bolt or beam that supports the overall framework of your narrative: the architecture your readers meander through. As such, the strength of your world, your brand and your product range business are all derived from the weakest point of this structure. Make each and every aspect count towards the overall power of the experience.

Whether you are creating the media items yourself, outsourcing or partnering with a publisher, the vision and cohesion of that vision are crucial. You are delivering content to a specific reader in their specific environment. The media needs to be aware of this and reflect it in the presentation.

In this endeavour you demonstrate how well you know your audience, you give them reasons to trust you and you improve your brand in their eyes, minds and hearts.

The Gift Shop

The Walt Disney Company is a world leader in storyselling because when you take away the multiple layers of story, Disney World is nothing more than a shopping mall and their billion-dollar-revenue movies are merely ninety-minute adverts for various products, such as toys, media items and cake mix.

This pragmatic view of Disney may not necessarily be as inspiring as you would hope for your own business, but it does quantify the value of storyselling.

Yet, the real power of storyselling is best seen when you view Disney with all its potent story layers in place. For one of the most poignant memories I personally have of Disney is catching a glimpse of a terminally-ill child in the Magic Kingdom.

Strapped into a hefty wheelchair, he was both catheterised and being fed through a tube that was inserted into his nose. The sight of a young child experiencing such an ordeal could have been horribly painful to witness, yet it was joyfully haunting.

The little boy was the centre of attention for both Mickey and Minnie Mouse, as well as Donald Duck, Goofy and several exuberant cast members. I could see on his face that this overwhelming moment was far greater in effect and saturated in a deeper sense of enchantment than any other in his tragically short life.

In that brief fragment of time, everything that Disney is came together to demonstrate the true aim of storyselling: to develop a successful business, whilst benevolently impacting the lives of each advocate that partakes in the story.

For not only was the little boy changed in that instance, every single person in the park who saw his joy would have been haunted by it also.

So, we can view Disney as a money-making corporation, a saccharin-sweet pixie-dust factory or cookie-cutter media machine. But when it come to the advocacy experience, Disney has the power to bring wonder, happiness and enrichment to the lives of those who share the story.

As a business, Disney are the most successful and profitable media company in the world. They can use their influence to leverage major political and legislative decisions. They permeate the lives and minds of most people from childhood to grave, thus changing attitudes, beliefs and perspectives across cultural and social contrasts.

They do this by creating a perfect storm of creativity, branding, audience building, product proposition, marketing and sales, accounting and logistics, strategy and, finally, the ability to develop and evolve.

And, whilst we can marvel at how they achieve such a cohesive strategy, it is not until we experience the stories that Disney have created that we glimpse the nature of ecosystem and its effect upon us.

As a small- to medium-sized business, how do you use storyselling to construct anything near what Disney do?

Apart from time, labour and general creativity, you probably do not have access to billions of dollars to throw at creating an ecosystem!

Disney use a multitude of principles in the creation process alone, without even covering branding, audience and so on. It takes time to sculpt a book or online training product—stirring the various imagineering tools into the mix can become overwhelming. With different degrees of experience, even an established author can find effective storyselling impossible (which is why so many viral campaigns fail to gain traction).

The ability to multiply your time and effort through a media product range will not only leverage your resources in various ways, it will bring a whole other avenue of income—effectively developing a new business for you. The challenge, of course, is that this needs to be done under the time and financial constraints you are currently operating with.

However, in our transmedia world, there are ways of taking what Disney do so well and applying them to your product range with a fraction of the budget, time and other resources that may be limited in your business.

When you interweave a selection of carefully crafted media elements in a particular way, you develop an environment around your audience. Whilst there may be a vast contrast between environments, situations and context, you can still immerse them in your world through media.

When we reflect upon our ancestors, thousands of years ago in those terrifying forests with danger all around, we can appreciate why they mapped their knowledge of their surrounds onto folklore and spiritual beliefs. From sun gods and goat demons, alcoholic miracles and apocalyptic end times, they took what they knew and made it inspiring for their contemporaries.

In so many ways, despite our feelings of sophistication and growth from those darker ages, we are no different. We take what we know from the past two centuries and the era of our immediate ancestry, then we map this ideology into something greater than us.

Information, data, technology, digital evolution, AI—all distilled through the dogma of nineteenth- and twentieth-century attitudes. We saturate our advancements with the same attitudes that created world wars, paralysing propaganda and automated genocide.

When we appreciate how all these things were based on the stories our ancestors told themselves, we begin to understand how a set of different stories can completely change the world, now. And when those stories transcend a basic business message and create real value for others for our long-term future, we start to see our business mission as so much more than developing marketing tools or social media strategies. We seek to change the world.

Knowing that your message—everything you present through media to the world—in this lifetime will be your legacy, changes how you tell your stories. For you can tell a story of yourself, your business and your ethos for your clients now and next week—or you can inspire an audience for centuries—millennia—to come.

When we think of the phrase *once upon a time*, we envisage a place long ago and far, far away. However, *once upon a time* can introduce a story for the *right now*, next week or ten thousand years from now.

The Immersive Publishing Experience

AUTHORING YOUR OWN BOOK(S)
As you know by now, this isn't a regular, predictable, bland book. You don't want to read them and you certainly don't want to write one that is regular, predictable or bland...

If you are a business owner or expert wanting to create a book that transforms the lives and results of its readers... If you want help on the journey... Then Immersive Publishing may be the best route for you.

The Immersive Publishing author development period is an intensive, guided journey from first idea to complete first draft of your book. During this, depending on the nature of the project, you will:

- systemise your own unique IP (paradigm)
- clarify and deepen your understanding of your audience and how to communicate most effectively with them
- evolve your writing skills to more closely match the level of your business expertise
- ensure your IP is at the heart of your business
- create a coherent audience-building strategy for every aspect of your business

This is a personally guided process with Martyn Pentecost and Richard Hagen of mPowr Publishing and Immersive Publishing. You can find out much more and get on the waiting list at www.immersive.pub.

It is important to understand which kind of book is best suited for your readers and your business. The first project is usually a rapport book or disruptor book—established leaders may also be ready to work on their authority book.

A RAPPORT BOOK
You want to create something powerful and convincing as part of your general marketing and realationship-building strategy. A rapport book demonstrates your value and establishes trust in your ability to deliver results.

A DISRUPTOR BOOK

This is the starting point for those who are looking to establish your own leadership position in your field and create unique intellectual property. It challenges the established ways of seeing and doing things, opens up alternative perspectives and offers rich, strategic insghts that transform the results and lives of readers.

AN AUTHORITY BOOK

If a disruptor book is the *first* word in a new system or paradigm, then your authority book is the *last* word. This book emerges from years of testing, implementation and adaptation and becomes the go-to reference source for practitioners, trainers and students in the field.

BUILDING A PRODUCT ECOSYSTEM

Once an author has done the foundation work in writing their first brilliant book, the next step is often to start building the wider product ecosystem (advanced training programmes built on their system, online training courses, workbooks, manuals, audio programmes, etc.).

Having been actively involved in the foundation work, Martyn and Richard can be ongoing partners in developing the expansive product system. For more information visit www.immersive.pub

BRINGING STORYSELLING TO YOUR BUSINESS

Storyselling isn't simply about books, but about the story of your business, both internal and external.

Martyn and Richard consult on implementing and integrating a storyselling approach throughout a business to engage potential clients, existing customers and the company's employees. For more information visit www.immersive.pub.

Write Your Book, Grow Your Business
Richard Hagen
ISBN—978-1-907282-54-6
For consultants, trainers, entrepreneurs, speakers and business experts who want to write a book to grow your business. How to avoid the most dangerous pitfalls and set yourself up for maximum success before you start to write.

Other mPowr Titles

Speak Performance
Ges Ray
ISBN—978-1-907282-87-4
For those afraid of speaking in front of a small team, groups of strangers or large crowds. How to be a confident, compelling and convincing speaker.

When Fish Climb Trees
Mel Loizou
ISBN—978-1-907282-85-0
For those who are fed up of quick-fix solutions in the workplace and who want rich, productive relationships and results which flow from affirming values.

Legacy: You Get One Life... Make It Remarkable
Martyn Pentecost
ISBN—978-1-907282-48-5
For those who truly want to make a difference and achieve immortality. How to create your lasting legacy through relationships, creativity, family and your work or business.

X Change
Lucia Knight
ISBN—978-1-907282-90-4
For those who are ready to torch their work treadmill, retire their boss, dump the ingrates, torment the passive-aggressives, escape the toxic office, get their fierce on and design the career that lets them live, love and laugh after 40.

Your Money or Your Life
Steve Conley
ISBN—978-1-907282-77-5
For those who want to escape the debt traps that banks, financial institutions and society use to control us. How to develop a personal life plan that lets you take control of your own financial destiny whilst also allowing you to create the life you want to lead.

Your Slides Suck!
David Henson
ISBN—978-1-907282-78-2
For all speakers who need to show information visually. How to make engaging, empowering and effective PowerPoint presentations.